EXAM QUESTION PRACTICE PACK

OCR GCSE (9–1) RELIGIOUS STUDIES

HODDER
EDUCATION
AN HACHETTE UK COMPANY

Orders: please contact Hachette UK Distribution, Hely Hutchinson Centre, Milton Road, Didcot, Oxfordshire, OX11 7HH. Telephone: (44) 01235 827827. Email education@hachette.co.uk Lines are open from 9 a.m. to 5 p.m., Monday to Friday. You can also order through our website: www.hoddereducation.co.uk

ISBN: 978 1 5104 3358 8

© Hodder & Stoughton Ltd 2018

First published in 2018 by
Hodder Education,
An Hachette UK Company
Carmelite House
50 Victoria Embankment
London EC4Y 0DZ

www.hoddereducation.co.uk

Impression number 10 9 8 7 6 5 4 3

Year   2022

Cover image reproduced by permission of Fotolia/hongyphoto

Typeset by Aptara, India

Printed by Hobbs the Printers Ltd, Totton, Hampshire SO40 3WX

A catalogue record for this title is available from the British Library.

CONTENTS

Introduction

Exam questions

Paper 1: Beliefs and teachings and practices

Christianity

Islam

Paper 2: Religion, philosophy and ethics in the modern world

Christianity

Islam

Example responses and mark schemes

Paper 1: Beliefs and teachings and practices

Christianity

Islam

Paper 2: Religion, philosophy and ethics in the modern world

Christianity

Islam

OCR GCSE (9–1) Religious Studies Exam Question Practice

INTRODUCTION

This pack of exam-style questions, example responses and mark schemes is specially curated for the OCR GCSE (9–1) Religious Studies specification (J625). The pack is divided into two sections:

➤ **Exam questions.** A bank of questions similar to those found in OCR GCSE Religious Studies papers. You may wish to photocopy all or part of them for use with your class.

➤ **Example responses and mark schemes.** For each question, there are two student responses – a 'Student A' response that is typical of an answer receiving high marks, and a 'Student B' response that would receive fewer marks. Each response includes examiner-style commentary which describes why they receive the marks they do. The mark scheme for each question indicates how the responses can be graded, and can be used alongside each type of student answer or just with the question.

The mark schemes make reference to the two assessment objectives used in OCR GCSE (9–1) Religious Studies – AO1 and AO2 – full details of which can be found in the specification.

The pack is designed to help you to:

➤ encourage students to reflect on their responses and ensure they know how to succeed

➤ cultivate students' key skills and knowledge by regular assessment throughout the course or in the revision period before the exams

➤ incorporate question practice into your lesson plans in the final, vital stage of teaching a topic: putting theory into practice

➤ teach flexibly, choosing photocopiable pages as appropriate to share with students

➤ facilitate peer discussion of what is good or better about given answers, which allows greater insight into quality responses

➤ allow students to analyse responses without the bias that can come from looking at their own or their friends' work — and so get more from the task

EXAM QUESTIONS

Paper 1: Beliefs and teachings and practices

Christianity: beliefs and teachings

1   (a) Describe what is meant by the term incarnation.   (3 marks)

....

....

....

    (b) Describe what is meant by the Second Coming of Christ (Parousia).   (3 marks)

....

....

....

    (c) Outline **one** Christian belief about life after death.   (3 marks)

....

....

....

    (d) Explain why there are different Christian beliefs about salvation.   (6 marks)

....

....

....

....

....

....

(e) 'The Bible is never wrong.' Discuss this statement.

In your answer you should:

> analyse and evaluate the importance of points of view, referring to common and divergent views within Christianity

> refer to sources of wisdom and authority.

(15 marks)

....

....

....

....

....

....

....

....

....

....

....

....

....

....

....

Total: 30 marks

(Example student responses and mark scheme on p. 46).

2 (a) Describe what Christians mean when they talk about original sin.

(3 marks)

....

....

....

(b) Describe what Christians mean when they talk about the Messiah. (3 marks)

....

....

(c) Outline **one** Christian belief about agape. (3 marks)

....

....

....

(d) Explain why receiving the Eucharist is important to some Christians. (6 marks)

....

....

....

....

....

....

(e) 'It is wrong that God will judge people at the end of time.' Discuss this statement.
  In your answer you should:
  ▷ analyse and evaluate the importance of points of view, referring to common and
    divergent views within Christianity
  ▷ refer to sources of wisdom and authority. (15 marks)

....

....

....

....

....

....

....

....

....

....

....
....
....
....
....

Total: 30 marks

(Example student responses and mark scheme on p. 53).

Christianity: practices

3   **(a)** Name **three** places a Christian might visit on a pilgrimage.   **(3 marks)**

....
....
....

(b) What do Christians mean when they describe God as transcendent?   **(3 marks)**

....
....
....

(c) Describe **one** Christian belief about prayer.   **(3 marks)**

....
....
....

(d) Explain why evangelism is important to some Christians.   **(6 marks)**

....
....
....
....
....

(e) 'The best way to worship God is liturgically.' Discuss this statement.

In your answer you should:

➢ analyse and evaluate the importance of points of view, referring to common and divergent points of view within Christianity

➢ refer to sources of wisdom and authority.

(15 marks)

....

....

....

....

....

....

....

....

....

....

....

....

....

....

....

....

....

Total: 30 marks

(Example student responses and mark scheme on p. 61).

4   (a) Outline the purpose of the World Council of Churches.

(3 marks)

....

....

....

....

(b) Name **three** ecumenical communities. (3 marks)

....

....

....

(c) Outline **one** example of how the church is persecuted today. (3 marks)

....

....

....

(d) Explain how and why Christian churches support families in their communities. (6 marks)

....

....

....

....

....

....

....

(e) 'Persecution of the church is the biggest challenge facing Christians today.'
Discuss this statement.
In your answer you should:
  ➤ analyse and evaluate the importance of points of view, referring to common
     and divergent views within Christianity
  ➤ refer to sources of wisdom and authority. (15 marks)

....

....

....

....

....

....
....
....
....
....
....
....
....
....
....
....
....
....
....
....
....
....
....

Total: 30 marks

(Example student responses and mark scheme on p. 69).

Paper 1: Beliefs and teachings and practices

Islam: beliefs and teachings

1   (a) What is prophethood (risalah)?   (3 marks)

....

....

    (b) What do Muslims mean by predestination (al-Qad'r)?   (3 marks)

....

....

....

    (c) Outline the importance of the Day of Judgement for Muslims.   (3 marks)

....

....

....

    (d) Explain why there are differences between Shi'a and Sunni beliefs.   (6 marks)

....

....

....

....

....

    (e) 'It is not necessary for anyone to believe in angels (malaikah).' Discuss this statement.
        In your answer you should:
        ⊳ analyse and evaluate the importance of points of view, referring to common and
          divergent views within Islam
        ⊳ refer to sources of wisdom and authority.   (15 marks)

....

....

....

....

....

....

....

....

....

....

....

....

....

Total: 30 marks

(Example student responses and mark scheme on p. 77).

2   (a) Name **three** prophets who are important to Muslims.   **(3 marks)**

....

....

....

     (b) State what is meant by the term tawhid.   **(3 marks)**

....

....

....

     (c) State the importance of Allah's role as judge.   **(3 marks)**

....

....

....

(d) Explain why human freedom is significant to the Day of Judgement. **(6 marks)**

....

....

....

....

....

....

(e) 'The Qur'an was revealed so long ago it is no longer relevant.' Discuss this statement.
In your answer you should:
  ➢ analyse and evaluate the importance of points of view, referring to common and
    divergent points of view within Islam
  ➢ refer to sources of wisdom and authority. **(15 marks)**

....

....

....

....

....

....

....

....

....

....

....

....

....

....

Total: 30 marks

(Example student responses and mark scheme on p. 85).

Islam: practices

3 (a) Name **three** of the ten obligatory acts (furu al-din) for Shi'a Muslims. (3 marks)

....

....

....

(b) Describe **one** feature of how a Muslim prays. (3 marks)

....

....

....

(c) Describe **one** significant feature of Ashura. (3 marks)

....

....

....

(d) Explain the religious significance of munkar and maruf. (6 marks)

....

....

....

....

....

....

(e) 'The Hajj is the most important pillar of Islam.' Discuss this statement.
   In your answer you should:
   ▷ analyse and evaluate the importance of points of view, referring to common and divergent views within Islam
   ▷ refer to sources of wisdom and authority. (15 marks)

....

....

....

....

....

....

....

....

....

....

....

....

....

....

....

Total: 30 marks

(Example student responses and mark scheme on p. 91).

4   (a) State the purpose of tawalla.   (3 marks)

....

....

....

(b) State the meaning of zakah.   (3 marks)

....

....

....

(c) State the difference between du'a and salah prayers.   (3 marks)

....

....

....

(d) Explain the importance of Ramadan.   (6 marks)

....

....

....

....

....

....

(e) 'Doing good deeds is more important than prayer.' Discuss this statement.

In your answer you should:

> analyse and evaluate the importance of points of view, referring to common and divergent views within Islam

> refer to sources of wisdom and authority. **(15 marks)**

....

....

....

....

....

....

....

....

....

....

....

....

....

....

Total: 30 marks

(Example student responses and mark scheme on p. 99).

Paper 2: Religion, philosophy and ethics in the modern world

Christianity: relationships and families

1   (a) Give **three** reasons why a Christian couple want to get married.   (3 marks)

....

....

....

   (b) Describe Christian attitudes to same-sex marriages.   (6 marks)

....

....

....

....

....

....

   (c) Explain why Christians might look back to their wedding ceremony in times of difficulty in their marriage. You should refer to sources of wisdom and authority in your answer.   (6 marks)

....

....

....

....

....

....

....

(d) 'Divorce should never happen.' Discuss this statement.

In your answer, you should:

➤ draw on your learning from across your course of study, including reference to beliefs, teachings and practices within Christianity

➤ explain and evaluate the importance of points of view from the perspective of Christianity.

(15 marks)

....

....

....

....

....

....

....

....

....

....

....

....

....

....

....

....

Total: 30 marks

(Example student responses and mark scheme on p. 106).

2 **(a)** Describe **one** Christian teaching on equality. (3 marks)

....

....

....

(b) Describe different Christian teachings on the roles of men and women in a Christian family. **(6 marks)**

(c) Explain why there are different Christian attitudes to celibacy.
You should refer to sources of wisdom and authority in your answer. **(6 marks)**

(d) 'Wives should always obey their husbands.' Discuss this statement.
In your answer, you should:
- draw on your learning from across your course of study, including reference to beliefs, teachings and practices within Christianity
- explain and evaluate the importance of points of view from the perspective of Christianity. **(15 marks)**

....

....

....

....

....

....

Total: 30 marks

(Example student responses and mark scheme on p. 115).

Christianity: the existence of God, gods and the ultimate reality

3   (a) Give **three** reasons why Christians think God is good.   **(3 marks)**

....

....

....

(b) Outline the philosophical argument from cause (first cause) for the existence
of God.   **(6 marks)**

....

....

....

....

....

(c) Explain why miracles are important for some Christians. You should refer to
sources of wisdom and authority in your answer.   **(6 marks)**

....

....

....

(d) 'Religious experiences can never be proven to be true.' Discuss this statement.
In your answer, you should:
  ⪢ draw on your learning from across your course of study, including reference to beliefs, teachings and practices within Christianity
  ⪢ explain and evaluate the importance of points of view from the perspective of Christianity.

(15 marks)

Total: 30 marks

(Example student responses and mark scheme on p. 123).

4 (a) Describe **one** Christian belief about God's relationship with the world.   (3 marks)

....

....

....

   (b) Outline the moral argument for proving the existence of God.   (6 marks)

....

....

....

....

....

....

   (c) Explain why the anthropic principle is evidence for the existence of God for some
       Christians. You should refer to sources of wisdom and authority in your answer.   (6 marks)

....

....

....

....

....

....

   (d) 'No one can prove the existence of God.' Discuss this statement.
       In your answer, you should:
       ▷ draw on your learning from across your course of study, including reference
         to beliefs, teachings and practices within Christianity
       ▷ explain and evaluate the importance of points of view from the perspective
         of Christianity.   (15 marks)

....

....

....

....

....

....

....

....

....

....

....

....

....

....

Total: 30 marks

(Example student responses and mark scheme on p. 131).

Christianity: religion, peace and conflict

5   (a) Name **three** causes of terrorism.   (3 marks)

....

....

....

   (b) Outline different Christian attitudes to pacifism.   (6 marks)

....

....

....

....

....

....

(c) Explain why Christians have different beliefs about the concept of war. You should refer to sources of wisdom and authority in your answer.

(6 marks)

....

....

....

....

....

....

(d) 'Violence is always wrong.' Discuss this statement
In your answer, you should:
> draw on your learning from across your course of study, including reference to beliefs, teachings and practices within Christianity
> explain and evaluate the importance of points of view from the perspective of Christianity.

(15 marks)

....

....

....

....

....

....

....

....

....

....

....

....

....

....

Total: 30 marks

(Example student responses and mark scheme on p. 139).

6   **(a)** Describe **one** Christian teaching on forgiveness.   **(3 marks)**

....

....

....

(b) Outline different attitudes to the just war theory.   **(6 marks)**

....

....

....

....

....

....

....

(c) Explain the importance of Christian teachings on justice. You should refer to
sources of wisdom and authority in your answer.   **(6 marks)**

....

....

....

....

....

(d) 'It is not possible to forgive all the time.' Discuss this statement.
In your answer, you should:
> draw on your learning from across your course of study, including reference
to beliefs, teachings and practices within Christianity
> explain and evaluate the importance of points of view from the perspective
of Christianity.   **(15 marks)**

....

....

....

....

....

....

....

....

....

....

....

....

Total: 30 marks

(Example student responses and mark scheme on p. 147).

Christianity: dialogue between religious and non-religious beliefs and attitudes

7 (a) Give **three** ways in which religion plays a role in public life in the UK. **(3 marks)**

....

....

....

(b) Outline different Christian beliefs on exclusivism. In your response you must consider that religious traditions in Great Britain are diverse, but mainly Christian. **(6 marks)**

....

....

....

(c) Explain why Christians might disagree with secular marriages. You should refer to sources of wisdom and authority in your answer. **(6 marks)**

(d) 'Abortion is not a religious matter.' Discuss this statement.

In your answer, you should:

> draw on your learning from across your course of study, including reference to beliefs, teachings and practices within Christianity

> explain and evaluate the importance of points of view from the perspective of Christianity. **(15 marks)**

....

....

Total: 30 marks

(Example student responses and mark scheme on p. 155).

8   (a) Describe **one** reason why a secularist might be against faith schools.   **(3 marks)**

....

....

....

     (b) Describe the role of religion in public life in the UK.   **(6 marks)**

....

....

....

....

....

     (c) Explain why Christians are against forced marriages. You should refer to sources
          of wisdom and authority in your answer.   **(6 marks)**

....

....

....

....

....

....

(d) 'Religion is not wanted in a secular society'. Discuss this statement.

In your answer, you should:

> draw on your learning from across your course of study, including reference to beliefs, teachings and practices within Christianity

> explain and evaluate the importance of points of view from the perspective of Christianity.

(15 marks)

....

....

....

....

....

....

....

....

....

....

....

....

....

....

....

Total: 30 marks

(Example student responses and mark scheme on p. 163).

Paper 2: Religion, philosophy and ethics in the modern world

Islam: relationships and families

1 (a) State **one** Muslim belief about pre-marital sex.   (3 marks)

....

....

....

(b) Outline the role of the wife in a Muslim family.   (6 marks)

....

....

....

....

....

....

....

....

(c) Explain Muslim attitudes to civil partnerships. You should refer to sources of
wisdom and authority in your answer.   (6 marks)

....

....

....

....

....

....

....

....

(d) 'Everyone is different so equality cannot be achieved.' Discuss this statement.
In your answer, you should:

➢ draw on your learning from across your course of study, including reference to beliefs, teachings and practices within Islam

➢ explain and evaluate the importance of points of view from the perspective of Islam. **(15 marks)**

....
....
....
....
....
....
....
....
....
....
....
....
....
....
....

Total: 30 marks

(Example student responses and mark scheme on p. 171).

2 **(a)** State **one** Muslim teaching about contraception. **(3 marks)**

....
....
....

(b) Outline Muslim beliefs on the role of the family. **(6 marks)**

....

....

....

....

....

....

(c) Explain Muslim ideas about treating people differently on the basis of gender.
You should refer to sources of wisdom and authority in your answer. **(6 marks)**

....

....

....

....

....

....

(d) 'Muslims should never divorce.' Discuss this statement.
In your answer, you should:
  ➢ draw on your learning from across your course of study, including reference to beliefs, teachings and practices within Islam
  ➢ explain and evaluate the importance of points of view from the perspective of Islam. **(15 marks)**

....

....

....

....

....

....

....

....

....

....

....

....

....

Total: 30 marks

(Example student responses and mark scheme on p. 178).

Islam: the existence of God, gods and the ultimate reality

3 (a) Give **three** names of Allah which show His nature. (3 marks)

....

....

....

(b) Describe why Muslims believe Allah is good. (6 marks)

....

....

....

....

....

....

(c) Compare the different ways in which Muslims believe Allah might be experienced. You should refer to sources of wisdom and authority in your answer. (6 marks)

....

....

....

....

(d) 'If the world is designed it cannot have been done by Allah because there is so much evil and suffering.' Discuss this statement.

In your answer, you should:

➢ draw on your learning from across your course of study, including reference to beliefs, teachings and practices within Islam

➢ explain and evaluate the importance of points of view from the perspective of Islam.

(15 marks)

Total: 30 marks

(Example student responses and mark scheme on p. 185).

4 (a) State what is meant by the term fitrah.   (3 marks)

....

....

....

   (b) Describe Muslim beliefs about their relationship with Allah.   (6 marks)

....

....

....

....

....

....

   (c) Explain why the conscience is important. You should refer to sources of wisdom
       and authority in your answer.   (6 marks)

....

....

....

....

....

....

   (d) 'The world is Allah's creation so He should be responsible for it.' Discuss this statement.
       In your answer, you should:
       ▷ draw on your learning from across your course of study, including reference
         to beliefs, teachings and practices within Islam
       ▷ explain and evaluate the importance of points of view from the perspective
         of Islam.   (15 marks)

....

....

....

....

....

....

....

....

....

....

....

....

Total: 30 marks

(Example student responses and mark scheme on p. 193).

Islam: religion, peace and conflict

5 (a) Give **three** Muslim teachings about holy war. (3 marks)

....

....

....

   (b) Describe why a Muslim might work for peace. (6 marks)

....

....

....

....

....

(c) Explain why a Muslim might go to war. You should refer to sources of wisdom and authority in your answer. **(6 marks)**

....

....

....

....

....

....

(d) 'Justice is more important than peace.' Discuss this statement.

In your answer, you should:
> draw on your learning from across your course of study, including reference to beliefs, teachings and practices within Islam
> explain and evaluate the importance of points of view from the perspective of Islam. **(15 marks)**

....

....

....

....

....

....

....

....

....

....

....

....

....

....

Total: 30 marks

(Example student responses and mark scheme on p. 200).

6   (a) State the meaning of the term reconciliation.   (3 marks)

....

....

....

    (b) Describe different Muslim attitudes towards forgiveness.   (6 marks)

....

....

....

....

....

    (c) Explain Muslim attitudes towards violence. You should refer to sources of wisdom
        and authority in your answer.   (6 marks)

....

....

....

....

....

    (d) 'A Muslim cannot be a pacifist.' Discuss this statement.
        In your answer, you should:
        ➢ draw on your learning from across your course of study, including reference
          to beliefs, teachings and practices within Islam
        ➢ explain and evaluate the importance of points of view from the perspective
          of Islam.   (15 marks)

....

....

....

....

....

....

....

....

....

....

....

....

....

....

....

....

Total: 30 marks

(Example student responses and mark scheme on p. 208).

Islam: dialogue between religious and non-religious beliefs and attitudes

7 (a) Give **one** Muslim belief about proselytisation. (3 marks)

....

....

....

   (b) Describe different Muslim attitudes to inclusivism. In your response you must consider that religious traditions in Great Britain are diverse, but mainly Christian. (6 marks)

....

....

(c) Compare Muslim attitudes on genetic manipulation. You should refer to sources of wisdom and authority in your answer.

(6 marks)

(d) 'Faith schools should be abolished.' Discuss this statement.

In your answer, you should:

⫸ draw on your learning from across your course of study, including reference to beliefs, teachings and practices within Islam

⫸ explain and evaluate the importance of points of view from the perspective of Islam.

(15 marks)

Total: 30 marks

(Example student responses and mark scheme on p. 215).

8   **(a)** Describe the rise of humanism.   **(3 marks)**

   (b) Describe Muslim views on pluralism. In your response you must consider that religious traditions in Great Britain are diverse, but mainly Christian.   **(6 marks)**

   (c) Compare different Muslim attitudes on arranged marriages. You should refer to sources of wisdom and authority in your answer.   **(6 marks)**

(d) 'Allah created all life so euthanasia is always wrong.' Discuss this statement.
In your answer, you should:
➢ draw on your learning from across your course of study, including reference to beliefs, teachings and practices within Islam
➢ explain and evaluate the importance of points of view from the perspective of Islam.

(15 marks)

Total: 30 marks

(Example student responses and mark scheme on p. 223).

EXAMPLE RESPONSES AND MARK SCHEMES

Student responses

This section shows sample answers from two students. One set (Student A) is stronger, the other (Student B) is weaker. The answers are followed by examiner-style commentary (shown by the icon ⊜) that indicates where credit is due. In the weaker answers, it also points out areas for improvement, specific problems and common errors. In some instances, 'Muhammad' is followed by '(pbuh)'. This stands for '(peace be upon him)'.

Paper 1

Christianity: beliefs and teachings

Question 1
Student A

(a) The term incarnation literally means 'in flesh'. The incarnation refers to the time when God became flesh in Jesus Christ. John's prologue tells us that 'the word became flesh and dwelt among us'. Meaning that God was born on earth.

⊜ **The first mark is awarded for an accurate definition of the term. The second mark is awarded for an explanation of how the term relates to Christian theology, and the third term is for scriptural evidence to support Christian beliefs in incarnation.**

(b) The Second Coming of Christ – of Parousia – refers to the time when Christ will return to earth, as prophesied by the two men in white who told the disciples after the ascension of Jesus that 'he will come back in the same way you have seen him go into heaven'. According to the Nicene Creed, Christians believe that at the Second Coming, the living and the dead shall be judged.

⊜ **The first mark is awarded for an accurate understanding of the Second Coming of Christ. The second mark is awarded for scriptural evidence for this belief, and the third mark is awarded for explaining what will happen – according to the Nicene Creed – on this day.**

(c) Catholics believe in purgatory. This is a place between heaven and hell which everyone must go to make sure that their soul is purified before they can enter heaven. This is because the Bible says: 'Nothing impure will ever enter heaven, nor will anyone who does what is shameful or deceitful.'

⊜ **The student gives one belief by making a statement about what purgatory is and why people must go there and gives a reason for this belief. This is a statement (what purgatory is – a place) with development (purification of the soul) and supporting quote, so 3 marks are awarded.**

(d) Salvation is the belief in the deliverance from sin and its consequences (hell). Christians believe that the relationship between God and humans was broken because of the original sin, but that this relationship has been repaired through the sacrifice of Christ. There are different Christian beliefs about salvation because there are different interpretations of the Bible due to different translations and different teachings from the different churches. Literal or fundamentalist Christians believe that every word in the Bible is true – it is inerrant – whereas modernist or liberal Christians believe that the Bible can be interpreted to fit in with today's society because it was written by different people over many centuries. So, some believe that Jesus's death on the cross gives salvation to everyone if they believe in Christ because Jesus taught 'whoever believes in the son shall have eternal life'. Although some – for example, Roman Catholics – believe that salvation occurs through doing good things such as charitable acts and following the example of the parable of the sheep and goats. However, St Paul taught that it is not good works but through the grace of God that people are saved. This contrasts with the early Jewish Christians who believed that they should follow the Jewish laws of the Torah, such as sacrifices in the temple, in order to be saved.

It is really a matter of which denomination the Christian is as to what they believe about salvation, but if God is considered to be all-loving and has already sacrificed himself as his son (the incarnation) – 'For God loved the world so much He gave his only son,' John 3:16 – surely it is a combination of belief, good works and grace.

(e) **The student demonstrates good knowledge and understanding with respect to why there are different beliefs about salvation. They give specific details of different views and offer some explanation as to why those views are held. They attempt analysis.**

(e) Fundamentalists would argue that the statement is correct. They believe every word is true and is inerrant. They hold this view because St Paul in his second letter to Timothy wrote that 'all scripture is god-breathed and is useful for teaching and training in righteousness'. They believe that God inspired the different writers of the Bible and therefore the Bible is the true word of God and every commandment within the Bible is correct. For example, someone who has this view would understand the Genesis creation stories to be completely true. Therefore, when Genesis 1 says that the world was made in 7 days, these were 7 24hr days. As a result of this, there is no room for evolution. Genesis 1 says that humans were made 'in God's image'. However, some people might question this creationist view by saying that a literal reading of Genesis doesn't make sense, for example, God makes light and dark on day 1 but doesn't make sun and moon until day 4, so how is this possible? A creationist might say that God being omniscient means God can do the possible and impossible. Also, if God makes the laws of nature, he can therefore change them at his will. Problem solved?

(e) **The student responds well to the stimulus and maintains focus on the trigger word 'wrong'. With the support of quotes and references to the content of the Bible, they outline different views on how the Bible should be interpreted.**

However, many Christians would not see this response as acceptable, because the Bible was put together by the early Christian church in the fourth century and was written by different writers over many centuries. Liberal Christians believe that the Bible, although containing spiritual truths, is not the literal truth but is portraying the views of the times in which the writer was inspired by God. In relation to the Genesis creation stories, liberal Christians will still see the stories in Genesis as 'right' because they can look at the theological truths in these stories. For example, in Genesis 2 'God formed the man from the dust of the ground and breathed into his nostrils the breath of life.' The theological truth from this quote is telling us that man is special among all other aspects of creation. A liberal Christian can believe in evolution and the Big Bang theory as God's way of bringing about his creation. Therefore, even though the Bible isn't literally true, it doesn't make it wrong or pointless. In response to this an atheist might ask whether we need to tag God onto these theories? Is the simplest solution to the inconsistencies in interpretations just that the Bible is wrong? That God doesn't exist? There is no man behind the curtain?

🄴 **An alternative Christian viewpoint is given on whether or not the Bible cannot be wrong. This answer builds on the interpretations of the Genesis creation stories. It also begins to make evaluative comments on this viewpoint that are further developed in the next section.**

People who are not believers in Christianity would argue that the Bible is just a collection of stories made up to try and convince people that there is a deity and an after-life in order to give them hope and a purpose in life. Non-believers will point to contradictions in the Bible to suggest that it is wrong. For example, in the Genesis accounts there are different interpretations on the role of women. Genesis 1 states both male and female were made 'in the image of God' whereas Genesis 2 describes that Eve was created as a companion for Adam out of his rib, perhaps indicating she was not as important as him.

They might point to the fact that Jesus treated men and women equally, for example Jesus addressed women directly while in public – like the Samaritan woman at the well – which was unusual for the time. Where there are such conflicting views, which ones should be followed? An atheist might suggest that the entirety of the Bible should be scrapped as a result.

🄴 **The student considers the statement from a non-believer's point of view. They present conflicting ideas from to Bible to illustrate the point that is being made and make a case for disagreeing with the statement.**

In conclusion, even if you do not believe in what the Bible says, it is difficult not to agree that most societies are based around the final six of the Ten Commandments, for example 'you shall not steal, kill, etc…' So surely there are some parts of the Bible which can be seen as 'right' because many people and societies base their lives on them. Therefore, the statement 'the Bible cannot be wrong' is true to an extent.

🄴 **The student rounds off with a judgement on the issue within the stimulus and a balanced conclusion to the discussion.**

Question 1
Student B

(a) Incarnation is when God becomes human in Jesus. Jesus is God in human form. Jesus is one part of the trinity of God.

🄴 **The first mark is awarded for the first sentence. The second sentence is not worthy of credit as it just repeats what was said in the first sentence. The third sentence gains a second mark because it shows an awareness that Jesus is God.**

(b) Christians will understand that the Second Coming of Christ is a future event when Jesus will come back to earth in judgement.

🄴 **2 marks are awarded. A mark is given for a future event and the second for saying that Jesus will come in judgement. The student does not give evidence to back up their views on the Second Coming or judgement.**

(c) Christians believe in heaven and hell. They will go to heaven where God is if they have been good and will go to hell where the devil is if they have sinned.

(e) **Unfortunately the student has not read the question correctly and gives two beliefs, not one, about life after death. The response is not developed so only earns 1 mark.**

(d) Salvation is when someone has been forgiven for their sins because they have said they believe in Christ. There are lots of different views about salvation because there are lots of different Christian churches who believe in different things. This is because some believe that every word in the Bible is true while others believe that the Bible holds spiritual truths, not factual truths. A born-again Christian is someone who has said sorry for their sins and who has turned to Christ in order to be saved. Jesus taught that in order for people to see the kingdom of God they had to be reborn again. Some believe you must have faith to be saved while others believe it is by being good and doing good things, such as donating to charity.

(e) **The student acknowledges and explains why there are different views on salvation but does not go into specific details. The definition of salvation needs to be developed in order to show a deep understanding of the concept (i.e. why salvation is needed). The student gives no examples or quotes in support.**

(e) For some Christians, for example fundamentalists, to suggest that the Bible could be wrong would be blasphemous. They believe every word is true and cannot be wrong. St Paul, in one of his Timothy letters, wrote that 'all scripture is god-breathed and is useful for teaching, rebuking, correcting and training in righteousness'. So they believe that God inspired the different writers of the Bible and therefore the Bible should be followed word for word. In relation to the miracles in the Bible, these Christians believe that Jesus walked on water, fed 5,000 people with 5 loaves and 2 fishes and calmed a storm by word alone. They say that God is omnipotent so it is possible for Jesus to do all these things.

However, because the Bible was put together so many years ago and was written by different writers over many centuries, some believe that the Bible, although containing spiritual truths, is portraying the views of the times in which the writer was inspired by God. For instance, more modern Christians, liberalists, consider that the Bible can be updated to fit in the views and values of modern society. In relation to the miracles of Jesus they might not believe that Jesus actually fed 5,000 people with 5 loaves and 2 fishes, but the moral of the story is to share the little we have with those in need.

(e) **The student responds well to the question and with the support of quotes and references to the content of the Bible, outlines different views on how the Bible should be interpreted. However, they don't consider the potential challenges to criticism or counter-criticisms.**

Because there appear to be outdated views in the Bible, according to some believers, it causes confusion among Christians and can lead to arguments such as whether there should be women priests or how homosexuals should be treated. This confusion sounds silly if a believer believes that God has issued commands on how to live a righteous life. Surely he would not say that someone can do something in one century but then does not have to do it in the next century? Either God issued a commandment which was correct for all time or he did not. There would be no point in ordering people to do something if it was not correct.

(e) **The student offers a comment/analysis on the problem of stating that the Bible can be reinterpreted to fit in with modern times.**

Liberal Christians, however, would state that the Bible can be reinterpreted because humankind and times have changed: there have been technological and scientific advances which were not even thought of in the times of Jesus. And they would state that a loving God would understand how things have changed and accept that commandments made in the past are not relevant today. However, fundamentalists would argue that what God ordered in the past is as relevant today as it was then, for example the sixth commandment.

(e) **The student wanders off the point and although they are attempting to support the analysis of the eternal word, they are not addressing the specifics of the stimulus.**

Mark scheme

1 (a) Marks are awarded for a correct definition which is developed and/or has examples. Marks may also be awarded for any combination of statements. The student **might** suggest:
   - Jesus is not just a good human being whose example is worth following; for Christians he is God made man – God incarnate.
   - The incarnation refers to the time when God became flesh in Jesus Christ.
   - John's prologue tells us that 'the word became flesh and dwelt among us', meaning that God was born on earth.
   - Because Jesus is God in human flesh it means that he is not affected by the original sin that all human beings are born with.
   - When God becomes man in Jesus we have the perfect example of how God wants everyone to live.

Hints and tips

Try to give a clear, developed response and try to include some biblical evidence to illustrate your understanding of the term.

(b) Marks are awarded for correct beliefs which are developed and/or have examples. The student **might** suggest:
   - Definition of Parousia, eschatological belief, Second Coming: general resurrection of the dead, judgement of the dead and living, full establishment of the kingdom of God on earth.
   - Reference to the rapture: pre/mid/post-tribulation (rule of the anti-Christ), millennium, rapture, tribulation, armageddon, 1 Thessalonians 4:17, 2 Thessalonians: 1–7.
   - Biblical support: Matthew 25:31–46, Mark 13:26–27, Mark 13:32, Luke 12:2–5, John 14:3, Acts 1:11, Hebrews 9:27, Revelation 21:27.
   - Nicene Creed.

Hints and tips

Try to give a clear, developed response and try to include biblical support for the views you present.

(c) Marks are awarded for correct beliefs which are developed and/or have examples. The student **might** outline beliefs about:
   - the Catholic belief in purgatory
   - heaven – what it is like, when does a person go there, Jesus's description of heaven: 'my father's house' or 'paradise'
   - hell – what it is like, biblical support describing 'gnashing teeth', who goes there, Satan

Hints and tips

➤ Read the question carefully. If it asks for **one** belief/teaching/idea then give only one – do not try to hedge your bets by giving lots of ideas. Only the first response will be marked.

➤ Make sure your response is clear, not muddled. You are asked to make a statement and then you can either develop it or explain it and support it with a specific example or a quote.

(d) This response is given **two** separate marks, both of which are determined by levels of response. Only **one** response is written but two different sets of **skills** are assessed by the examiner. The first mark is given for knowledge and understanding (AO1) and the second mark is awarded for the student's analysis and evaluation of the question (AO2). If the student simply writes down all they know about a specific topic, then the marks will be limited to the maximum marks for AO1. The examiner is assessing how the student uses their knowledge and understanding to relate to the specifics of the question/stimulus.

Knowledge and understanding AO1

Level	Description
1	A **weak** demonstration of knowledge and understanding which is given 1 mark. This might include a brief idea about what salvation is and why it is an important concept.
2	A **limited** demonstration of knowledge and understanding which is given 2 marks. This might include some relevant information on different Christian ideas on salvation and why it is important to them. This may be one point with slight development.
3	An **adequate** but **underdeveloped** demonstration of knowledge and understanding which is given 3 marks. The student will have shown knowledge and understanding of different beliefs of what salvation is and why it is important, but the explanations as to why will not be detailed.
4	A **good** demonstration of knowledge and understanding which is given 4 marks. The student will have given detailed, relevant information on what salvation is and why different denominations consider it to be important. Such information **might** include: – salvation – restoring the relationship between God and humankind – atonement – God in Christ suffering on the cross – original sin and free will – liberal or fundamentalist interpretations of the Bible – St Paul – predestination – biblical support: John 3:36, Romans 3:28, Romans 8:38–39, Romans 10:9–10, Hebrews 7:25, Revelation 22:17, Ephesians 2:8–9, 1 Corinthians 15:22.

Analysis and evaluation AO2

Level	Description
1	**Some** demonstration of analysis has been shown but it may be implicit or even unsuccessful = 1 mark. Some attempt to reflect the significance of the issue on different Christian groups.
2	A **good** response – the student has shown successful analysis and evaluation of the issue = 2 marks. The student **might**: – comment on the problem of different interpretations – comment on the need for salvation and its relevance in the modern world – analyse and comment on the problem of free will or predestination or any of the other concepts.

Hints and tips

➤ Read the question carefully and support your answers with teachings or examples.

➤ You are being asked to show a deep understanding of why Christians hold their beliefs.

(e) This response is given **two** separate marks, both of which are determined by levels of response. Only **one** response is written but two different sets of **skills** are assessed by the examiner. The first mark is given for knowledge and understanding (AO1) and the second mark is awarded for the student's analysis and evaluation of the question (AO2). If the student simply writes down all they know about a specific topic, then the marks will be limited to the maximum marks for AO1. The examiner is assessing how the student uses their knowledge and understanding to relate to the specifics of the question/stimulus.

Knowledge and understanding AO1

Level	Description
1	A **limited/weak** demonstration of knowledge and understanding which is given 1 mark. This might include some general information and understanding about the Bible and the different interpretations, the ideas may be listed and lacking in detail.
2	An **adequate** but **underdeveloped** demonstration of knowledge and understanding which is given 2 marks. This might include some relevant information on the Bible and how the different denominations might interpret it.
3	A **good** demonstration of knowledge and understanding which is given 3 marks. The student will have given detailed, relevant information on the different interpretations of the Bible supported with quotes. Such information **might** include: – fundamental, literal, or conservative interpretations of the Bible – that it is seen as inerrant, infallible – examples from the Bible of consistency or inconsistency – societal views or views from the other religion you have studied.

Analysis and evaluation AO2

Level	Description
1	A **weak** attempt to respond to the stimulus with a simplistic/descriptive account with no or very little attempt to offer a judgement on the significance of the issues raised (1–3 marks). The student may have suggested one view either for or against the stimulus but has not made a specific conclusion or judgement. In other words, the information is communicated in a basic way and there is no evidence of a **discussion** taking place.
2	A **limited** attempt – the student has made some attempt to respond to the stimulus and has shown different ideas on why the Bible is interpreted differently by the denominations, but the judgement/conclusion is limited. **Or** one specific interpretation may have been discussed with an attempt at a conclusion (4–6 marks). In other words, there is a line of reasoning/**discussion** which has some relevance to the stimulus.
3	An **adequate** but **underdeveloped** attempt to discuss the stimulus showing different viewpoints on interpretations of the Bible, which are supported with reference to sources of wisdom and authority, and the student has made some comments on them. In other words, there is a discussion of the stimulus supported with evidence of comparison and criticism along with a judgement/conclusion (7–9 marks). A line of reasoning has been presented and **discussed** which is mostly relevant.

| 4 | A **good** attempt which has shown a structured discussion while comparing and criticising/commenting on the different ideas of how the Bible is interpreted and how these interpretations have significance in the lives of believers (10–12 marks). The student has offered a well-developed and sustained **discussion** which is coherent, relevant and well structured. The student **might**:
– analyse and comment on the difficulties of so many different interpretations of the Bible and/or different viewpoints from the many denominations
– analyse and comment on the impact of the Bible in the lives of modern Christians as compared with those in other periods of time
– comment on and analyse God's word as being inerrant and infallible and/or the possible inconsistencies in the Bible
– compare and contrast the Bible with other sources of authority or other religion/s |

Hints and tips

➤ Read the stimulus carefully and identify its significance in your response, making sure you stick to the wording in the stimulus and do not divert into a concept that you would prefer to discuss.

➤ Demonstrate that you understand that there are common beliefs but also contradictory beliefs within Christianity. You will need to compare and contrast these different beliefs.

➤ Support your statements/ideas/information with reference to sources of wisdom and authority, e.g. biblical and the different church teachings.

➤ Remember that you do not have to express a personal view – if you want to, you can, but make sure you justify your point of view with evidence and argument.

➤ Remember too that your response should be a **discussion** – try to present viewpoints for both sides as if you were having a conversation. Do not just list all the ideas for the stimulus in one paragraph and then all the ideas against in another paragraph.

➤ You are allowed to compare and contrast the Christianity ideas with the other religion you have studied.

Question 2

Student A

(a) Christians believe that original sin was when Eve took the fruit from the tree which God had forbidden her to do. It is the first time humans disobeyed God and as a result the perfect relationship between humankind and God was broken.

🄴 **The student achieves 3 marks for the three separate points within this response: 'Eve taking the forbidden fruit' gets the first mark, 'first time of disobedience' is a development of the action so gets the second mark, and the third mark is given to 'the breaking of the relationship'.**

(b) The term Messiah means 'anointed one'. Anointing someone is a religious act which shows that someone has been specially chosen by God to perform a special purpose. So the Messiah refers to the belief that Jesus was seen as the saviour of humankind chosen by God.

🄴 **The student explains the term which achieves the first mark. This is developed to explain the significance of anointing, gaining the second mark, and then developed further to show that Jesus is the Messiah, which achieves the third mark.**

(c) Agape refers to Christian love, which is not the same as ordinary love but has a much deeper meaning, embracing unconditional love. This is when a person loves someone else no matter who they are or what they look like or even what they do without expecting anything in return.

(e) **The student gives one belief by stating that agape is 'Christian love' for the first mark. This is then developed to show that it is completely different to other kinds of love and that it is 'unconditional', which gets the second mark. The third mark is given to the explanation of what 'unconditional' means.**

(d) For Roman Catholics, receiving the Eucharist is important because when a priest repeats the words Jesus said at the last supper, 'this is my body … this is my blood', the bread and wine change substance. The bread and wine look the same as before the prayer of consecration, but they have been substantially changed. Through transubstantiation, the Eucharist is now the body and blood of Christ (real presence). For a Catholic to receive the Eucharist, they are following the commandment that Jesus gave at the Last Supper, 'do this in memory of me'. By receiving the bread and wine, Catholics are making Jesus physically and spiritually present in their lives.

This contrasts with the view of most Anglicans that the bread and wine make Jesus spiritually present at that part of the service but not physically present in the Eucharist. The Anglican idea is that Jesus's death was a single event in time, never to be repeated again, and yet effective throughout all time. By partaking in the Eucharist an Anglican remembers the sacrifice of Jesus on the cross, 'For God so loved the world that He gave his one and only Son, that whoever believes in him shall not perish but have eternal life.' John 3:16. Anglicans acknowledge that Jesus's death on the cross was the atonement necessary for the reconciliation of man's relationship with God. As such, the Eucharist is extremely important in reminding Anglicans that they can get to heaven because of Jesus's death and subsequent resurrection.

However, the Eucharist isn't important for all Christians because some Christian denominations don't even partake in Eucharistic celebrations. For example, the Quakers do not have any requirement to celebrate the Eucharist. Their primary focus of worship is not centred on the altar; a greater emphasis is on the word of God in the Bible and in trying to understand the messages contained therein and how it relates to their daily lives.

(e) **Different Christian views are offered on the importance of the Eucharist. There is a clear understanding of the differences, backed up with scriptural evidence for these views. In the final section, the student attempts to evaluate the statement by suggesting that the Eucharist is not important to some Christians.**

(e) This statement in a way refers to the problem of evil which questions how an omnibenevolent, omniscient and omnipotent God will allow evil to exist in his creation. Since God wanted humans to love him of their own free will and not as robots, this means there has to be a choice between good and evil. It was humans who first allowed sin to enter the world: Eve taking the fruit from the forbidden tree. She made a choice to disobey God's command and jeopardise the relationship. The Messiah, God's son – the incarnation of God in human form – atoned for that sin, which Christians believe to be present in every human being, and so re-established the relationship and opened up the door to heaven for good souls. However, the choice to follow God is still there and since Christians believe humans are God's creations, 'I knew you in the womb', and so is the world (Genesis), therefore they would disagree with the statement because they believe everyone is created with a purpose, which is known to God, to follow him and fulfil his expectations. Thus, if people have chosen not to follow him and do evil acts, then of course they should be judged.

e **The student opens the response by linking the problem of evil to the stimulus. They do not then launch into the various responses to the problem but focus on free will/choice to follow God or not and argue that the gift of free will gives God the right to judge.**

Someone who did not believe in God would not have cause to respond to the statement other than perhaps agree to the view that if people do evil acts, they should be judged/punished during their lives. Anyone would state that it would be very unfair if a mass murderer was allowed to roam the streets and perhaps murder again. So judgement in this respect is accepted, although the judgement is by the courts of the country a person lives in and not a deity at the end of the world, when secularists would just believe that the world will explode or something and that will be it. But what about the Christian who believes in Calvin's ideas on predestination, which is the idea that God has already decided who shall be saved: the Book of Revelation says only 144,000 will be saved. Surely this means that it is wrong for God to judge people on their sins if he has already decided who will enter heaven and who will not. It seems very unfair that an omnibenevolent God would arrange for this to happen. But if God is omniscient, he must have known Eve would be tempted by the serpent (Genesis 3) and bring sin and death into the world. So was it right that he banished both her and Adam from Eden when he put in a rule which he knew would be broken? After all, what is wrong with trying to be 'like God' – surely Adam and Eve were made in his image?

Also, there were many prophecies about the coming of the Messiah in the Old Testament and Jesus even said when he was praying in the garden of Gethsemane, 'it was for this very reason I came to this hour'. So since there are scriptural references to support predestination, it could be argued that it is wrong for God to judge.

e **The student discusses a secular view and also predestination to show agreement with the statement.**

Returning to the secular view that judgement is essential to ensure justice and promote a society which obeys rules, and to ensure that peace and equality are good values held by everyone, surely it could be said that this is what God is trying to promote: a good world in which peace and harmony exist. Therefore it is not wrong for him to judge. His teachings/commands in the Bible are rules to ensure that this happens. The parables of Jesus promote compassion and Christian love, such as the good Samaritan, the parable of the sheep and the goats and the parable of the rich man and Lazarus. The latter two refer to judgement when the sinner will be in torment because they have not shown love and compassion to their fellow human beings. Sometimes humans do not have the willpower to be good all the time, they can be apathetic and lazy and as a result will take the easy way out. If someone is being beaten up, sometimes it may be more prudent to run away than to wade in and get hurt yourself, although that is what agape is all about. So perhaps there has to be the stick and the carrot to ensure that people behave in the correct way. But then again, if people know about the threat of punishment, are they actually performing good deeds through free will or out of fear? Does someone decide not to murder another person just because there is the threat of life imprisonment or is there something else which stops them? Although the statement appeared to be clear cut when first read, and it seemed as though all Christians would argue that of course God has the right to judge, there is perhaps the need to reflect on why God created humans in the first place with the capacity to be so evil, such as people like Adolf Hitler. The free will argument does not address all the problems of whether God has a right to judge because if we have free will, why should we be punished or judged for making a free decision to disobey?

e **The student analyses the statement and some of the arguments within this essay and comes to a balanced judgement.**

Question 2
Student B

(a) Original sin is the teaching by St Augustine which states that everyone is sinful and wants to disobey God.

(e) **The student achieves 2 marks for the two separate points within this response: 'teaching by St Augustine' gains the first mark and 'everyone being sinful and wanting to disobey' gains the second. Further development or an explanation such as the 'state of the original sin is present through the act of Adam and Eve' would have gained the third mark.**

(b) The term Messiah means 'anointed one' and usually refers to the act of anointing a king with oil to show he is special, for example King Saul. Due to the original sin and humankind's relationship with God being broken, God became incarnated as Jesus to atone for all the sins and thus repair the relationship.

(e) **The opening statement might have been credited but is more specific to a Judaism response than a Christian one. Also, because the attempt at development appears to be a separate idea/point, it will not be credited. It needs to be linked back to the idea of the Messiah and being chosen/made special by God. No marks are awarded.**

(c) Agape is Christian love which follows the commandment to 'love thy neighbour as thyself'.

(e) **The student states that it is Christian love (first mark) supported by the commandment (second mark).**

(d) Methodists celebrate the Eucharist but not as much as other denominations. They call it the 'Service of the Table', or more generally 'communion'. They practise open communion, which anyone is welcome to partake and receive the wine and wafer. This is important to them because it is essentially about equality.

Orthodox Christians also celebrate the Eucharist and they call it the 'Divine Liturgy'. In their communion service they share the bread and wine with non-orthodox believers as a symbol of wider Christian fellowship. This again expresses the idea of equality.

Not all Christians think the Eucharist is important. Some think doing good deeds is more important.

(e) **The student demonstrates some knowledge and understanding of different Christians views on the Eucharist. They try to offer a judgement at the end but it is underdeveloped. There is no reference to scriptural evidence to back up the views on these Christian groups. They mention the idea of equality in the Methodist and Orthodox beliefs but do not explain why equality might be an important Christian idea.**

(e) Christians believe that at the end of time Jesus and God will return to earth to judge whether believers should go to heaven or hell. In fact, some Christians believe that even good people who are not Christians but who have led a Christian-like life (being kind, etc.) can also go to heaven. So if people, whatever their religion, have been good, they should not be bothered at all that they are going to be judged by God at the end of time. It is only the evil people who need to be worried and perhaps argue that God has no right to judge.

(e) **The student shows some understanding of the significance of the statement.**

Humanists have no problem with the statement because they seek to live a good life in a material world without religious beliefs about the last judgement. However, they would encourage others to lead moral lives because they consider every human to have inherent worth – that every life is valuable and important. Therefore, after a person dies there is a form of judgement made because people will base their memories on what the deceased did in their lifetime. If they did horrendous, evil acts, then their memory will be tainted by criticisms and hate. So although it is not a deity which judges them, their actions will be judged nevertheless.

ℯ **This is a valid argument but it does not really address whether it is wrong to be judged.**

The parable of the rich man and Lazarus tells how God will punish those who do not look after the poor. There are many teachings within the Bible about concern for the poor and this is what Jesus showed by example when he was on earth. He taught the poor, he fed the poor (feeding of the 5,000) and he praised the poor: 'Blessed are the poor'. So if God created humans in his image, surely he has the right to judge because he has told them what to do and if they do not do it he has a right to be angry and punish them. A parent punishes their children if they disobey the rules, so therefore God should be able to do this to his children.

ℯ **The student argues that God has a right to judge people because they were made in his image and he has given them instructions on how to act. This is compared to parental judgement.**

However, there are times when a person may have to do an evil act out of desperation, such as stealing in order to feed a family. Abortion is considered sometimes to be the lesser of two evils, so does God have the right to judge these people? After all, it is his world which he created and he has allowed the existence of evil and suffering, and if he is not prepared to stop it and help everyone, then does he have the right to judge?

ℯ **The student makes another valid point that sometimes it could appear as though there is no choice between an evil act and a good one. This response has a lot of potential but the ideas need to be developed more and linked more directly into the statement, creating more opportunities for analysis. The student needs to make more reference to sources of wisdom and authority.**

Mark scheme

2 (a) The student is asked to describe the meaning of original sin. So the student **might** refer to:
 – the first sin by Adam and Eve
 – breaking the special relationship between God and humans
 – St Augustine's teachings
 – the belief that original sin explains the presence of so much evil in God's good created world

Hints and tips

Try to give a clear, developed response which has three separate points which are related through development, examples or explanations.

(b) Marks are awarded for a correct meaning of the term which is developed with explanations and/or examples or even reference to specific quotes. The student **might** suggest:
 – that Messiah means 'anointed one', with development to show what that entails
 – reference to Jesus being the anticipated saviour
 – atonement/repairing of the broken relationship
 – anointing of Jesus – Mark 14:3–9 – and its significance
 – Psalm 2:2, Luke 9:20.

Hints and tips

Try to give a clear, developed response which has three points that are related through development, examples or explanations.

(c) Marks are awarded for correct beliefs which are developed and/or have examples. The student **might** refer to:
- Christian love, unconditional love, sacrificial love
- its application to Jesus on the cross
- the second greatest commandment: Matthew 22:37–38.

Hints and tips

➤ Read the question carefully. If it asks for **one** belief/teaching/idea then give only one – do not try to hedge your bets by giving lots of ideas. Only the first response will be marked.

➤ Make sure your response is clear, not muddled. You are asked to make a statement and then you can either develop it or explain it and support it with a specific example or a quote.

(d) This response is given **two** separate marks, both of which are determined by levels of response. Only **one** response is written but two different sets of **skills** are assessed by the examiner. The first mark is given for knowledge and understanding (AO1) and the second mark is awarded for the student's analysis and evaluation of the question (AO2). If the student simply writes down all they know about a specific topic, then the marks will be limited to the maximum marks for AO1. The examiner is assessing how the student uses their knowledge and understanding to relate to the specifics of the question/stimulus.

Knowledge and understanding AO1

Level	Description
1	A **weak** demonstration of knowledge and understanding which is given 1 mark. This might include a brief idea about what the Eucharist is.
2	A **limited** demonstration of knowledge and understanding which is given 2 marks. This might include some relevant information on different Christian ideas on the Eucharist. This may be one point with slight development.
3	An **adequate** but **underdeveloped** demonstration of knowledge and understanding which is given 3 marks. The student will have shown knowledge and understanding of different beliefs on the Eucharist, but the explanations will not be detailed.
4	A **good** demonstration of knowledge and understanding which is given 4 marks. The student will have given detailed, relevant information on the Eucharist from different denominational viewpoints. Such information **might** include: – Reference its origins at the last supper. – The main differences associated with the bread and wine during the Eucharist between different denominations within Christianity. – Catholic ideas of transubstantiation (the transformation of the bread and wine into the body and blood of Christ). – Anglican ideas that Jesus's death was a single event in time, never to be repeated again, and yet effective throughout all time. – Orthodox ideas of the Eucharist as the Divine Liturgy. The fact that the bread can be shared with non-orthodox believers as a symbol of wider Christian fellowship. – Methodist ideas about the Eucharist might be expressed. It is known as the 'Service of the Table', but more generally as communion. The fact that they practise open communion, which anyone is welcome to partake and receive the wine and wafer.

Analysis and evaluation AO2

Level	Description
1	**Some** demonstration of analysis has been shown but it may be implicit or even unsuccessful = 1 mark. Some attempt to reflect the significance of the issue on different Christian groups.
2	A **good** response – the student has made successful analysis and evaluation of the issue = 2 marks. The student **might** comment on: – the issues surrounding different denominational views – the idea that good deeds are more important than rites and rituals – the idea of faith in the Bible and how it applies to the lives of believers is more important than receiving the Eucharist

Hints and tips

➤ Read the question carefully and support your answers with teachings or examples.

➤ Include different denominational views where you can.

➤ You are being asked to show a deep understanding of why Christians hold their beliefs.

(e) This response is given **two** separate marks, both of which are determined by levels of response. Only **one** response is written but two different sets of **skills** are assessed by the examiner. The first mark is given for knowledge and understanding (AO1) and the second mark is awarded for the student's analysis and evaluation of the question (AO2). If the student simply writes down all they know about a specific topic, then the marks will be limited to the maximum marks for AO1. The examiner is assessing how the student uses their knowledge and understanding to relate to the specifics of the question/stimulus.

Knowledge and understanding AO1

Level	Description
1	A **limited/weak** demonstration of knowledge and understanding which is given 1 mark. This might include some general information and understanding about whether it is wrong for God to judge at the end of time, the ideas may be listed and lacking in detail.
2	An **adequate** but **underdeveloped** demonstration of knowledge and understanding which is given 2 marks. This might include some relevant ideas about whether it is wrong for God to judge people at the end of time.
3	A **good** demonstration of knowledge and understanding which is given 3 marks. The student will have given detailed, relevant information on whether it is wrong for God to judge people at the end of time. Such information **might** include: – information on the last judgement – an understanding of predestination – reference to the problem of evil, free will theodicy – linking them to the stimulus – societal views or views from the other religion you have studied – sources of wisdom and authority: Genesis 1:27, Genesis 3, John 12:27, Romans 8:29–30, Revelation 7:4, sermon on the Mount, decalogue, parables: the good Samaritan, rich man and Lazarus, sheep and the goats

Analysis and evaluation AO2

Level	Description
1	A **weak** attempt to respond to the stimulus with a simplistic/descriptive account with no or very little attempt to offer a judgement on the significance of the issues raised (1–3 marks). The student may have suggested one view either for or against the stimulus but has not made a specific conclusion or judgement. In other words, the information is communicated in a basic way and there is no evidence of a **discussion** taking place.
2	A **limited** attempt – the student has made some attempt to respond to the stimulus and has shown different ideas on whether it is wrong for God to judge people at the end of time but the judgement/conclusion is limited. **Or** one specific interpretation may have been discussed with an attempt at a conclusion (4–6 marks). In other words, there is a line of reasoning/**discussion** which has some relevance to the stimulus.
3	An **adequate** but **underdeveloped** attempt to discuss the stimulus showing different viewpoints on whether it is wrong for God to judge people at the end of time, supported with reference to sources of wisdom and authority, and the student has made some comments on them. In other words, there is a discussion of the stimulus supported with evidence of comparison and criticism, along with a judgement/conclusion (7–9 marks). A line of reasoning has been presented and **discussed** which is mostly relevant.
4	A **good** attempt which has shown a structured discussion while comparing and criticising/commenting on the different ideas of whether or not it is wrong for God to judge people at the end of time (10–12 marks). The student has offered a well-developed and sustained **discussion** which is coherent, relevant and well structured. The student **might** analyse and comment on: – whether God's gift of free will entitles him to be a judge – the idea that punishment is a threat which negates the idea of free choice – the fact that no one can be good all the time – the incompatibility of free will and predestination

Hints and tips

➤ Read the stimulus carefully and identify its significance in your response, making sure you stick to the wording in the stimulus and do not divert into a concept that you would prefer to discuss.

➤ Demonstrate that you understand that there are common beliefs but also contradictory beliefs within Christianity. You will need to compare and contrast these different beliefs.

➤ Support your statements/ideas/information with reference to sources of wisdom and authority, e.g. biblical and the different church teachings.

➤ Remember that you do not have to express a personal view – if you want to, you can, but make sure you justify your point of view with evidence and argument.

➤ Remember too that your response should be a discussion – try to present viewpoints for both sides as if you were having a conversation. Do not just list all the ideas for the stimulus in one paragraph and then all the ideas against in another paragraph.

➤ You are allowed to compare and contrast the Christianity ideas with the other religion you have studied.

Christianity: practices

Question 3

Student A

(a) Christians might visit:
1 Rome where the Pope is.
2 Lourdes for miracles.
3 Bethlehem where Jesus was born.

ⓔ **Three correct places are given so this response is awarded 3 marks. The student does not need to explain why they are special as the command word is 'name'.**

(b) The word transcendent means existing outside time and space and above all created things. Christians believe that God is transcendent because according to the Nicene Creed, he was the creator of heaven and earth, of all that is seen and unseen. Therefore God is outside of time and space to create time and space.

ⓔ **The first mark is given for the definition, 'Existing outside time and space and above all created things', the second mark is awarded for links to a source of wisdom and authority, and the third mark for explaining how that source links to the question.**

(c) Christians will see prayer as a conversation between God and his believers (God listens and the believers listen). This conversation helps the individual or congregation to get closer to God and in this way discover God's purpose for our lives, which then encourages us to share our faith by living good Christian lives.

ⓔ **The first mark is given to the idea of getting closer to God, the second mark is given to the idea of discovering God's purpose and then there is further development which receives the third mark.**

(d) Evangelism is when Christians tell people about their faith in Jesus and his gift of salvation. They show through their example what it is to be a Christian and so influence people to become Christians themselves. They believe in evangelism because they are following Christ's last commandment to his disciples before he ascended into heaven 'to go forth and make disciples of all nations'. In essence Jesus was an evangelist. God came to earth in human form to reveal his wishes for humankind. Jesus showed that the message was not just for a few people when he talked to the Samaritan woman at the well, which showed that he was not excluding anyone. Because of their belief in their duty to evangelise people, many Christian organisations today both preach the good news and persuade others through the example of showing Christian love, agape, to become Christians. CAFOD and Christian Aid travel the world to help those in poverty and people suffering from oppression and natural disasters. They are following Jesus's own words when he preached in the synagogue in Nazareth saying he had come to 'proclaim the good news to the poor' and to 'set the oppressed free'. Therefore, for a Christian, evangelism is considered to be important because it is not just telling people about Jesus but showing them what it is all about – pictures or actions are better than just words.

ⓔ **The student demonstrates good knowledge and understanding about Christian beliefs about evangelism. They make reference to biblical authority and offer analysis in the conclusion.**

(e) There are various ways in which a Christian can worship God. Whether or not liturgical worship is the best way is open to scrutiny, since many Christian denominations do not worship God in this manner. However, a Roman Catholic might agree with the statement because a main part of liturgical worship is the celebration of the sacrament of the Eucharist. For a Catholic the Eucharist is of incredible importance because when they partake in it they believe that they are following Jesus's commandment to 'do this in memory of me'. At the last supper Jesus told his disciple that the bread and wine were his body and blood. Catholics believe that at the Mass, the priest – through transubstantiation – makes the 'real presence' of Christ dwell among them. When a Catholic receives the Eucharist, they believe that they physically receive Christ in their lives. They believe that by taking the Eucharist they are physically and spiritually strengthened. Therefore, because receiving the Eucharist was commanded by Christ it is important to worship God liturgically.

(e) **The student responds to the stimulus and offers a conclusion agreeing with the stimulus. They show knowledge of a specific denominational viewpoint and back their ideas up with reference to scripture. They also show how the practice of the Eucharist has an impact on the life of a believer.**

However, it could be argued that worshipping God isn't just about attending public liturgical services. Private worship helps a Christian build up a discipline which gives them strength to cope in times of trouble. For example, when Jesus was anguished before his crucifixion he went to the garden of Gethsemane and prayed privately to God to seek strength. Private prayer encourages a routine where a Christian takes time out to honour God. Through private prayer Christians can find peace and a sense of communication with God. A group of Christians who would disagree with this statement would be Baptists. The Baptist church – and other free churches – teach that God is directly accessible by all believers. They do not believe that priests are necessary to intercede between humans and God in any way, unlike the beliefs of Roman Catholics who believe the priest can intercede at the sacrament of Eucharist and reconciliation. The free church emphasis is on the personal and accessible nature of God. This relationship they believe is shown in Jesus's teaching, for example when Jesus teaches the disciples to pray using the phrase 'Abba' to speak to God. Abba means 'daddy/father' and shows this close personal relationship. Therefore, private prayer is the best way to worship God because praying privately to God has been shown to strengthen a person's belief in God, and help a believer understand God's plan for us, as evidenced with Jesus in the Garden of Gethsemane. When Jesus prayed to God he asked that God take away the 'cup of suffering from him', but by the end of his time praying, Jesus came to the understanding 'thy will be done' showing that he now understood that what God had planned for him was the right course of action.

(e) **The student demonstrates good knowledge and understanding of an alternative form of worship and relates it to the stimulus. This section also contains a specific denominational response and sources of wisdom and authority**

It could also be argued that the best way to worship God is in an informal fashion. This type of worship is exemplified by Quaker meetings. They do not have the rigid step-by-step approach of Catholics, Anglicans or Orthodox Christians, that may become boring and predictable. Neither do they have the spectacle of charismatic worship, e.g. being slain in the spirit or speaking in tongues. Informal worship involves worshippers sitting in silence and reflecting on scripture. Extempore prayer is also encouraged but in a more considered way than might take place in charismatic worship. It could be argued that this type of worship is a middle ground between the overly rigid liturgical worship and the no-holds barred charismatic worship often found in the evangelical and Pentecostal denominations. The big difference with this is that the prayer isn't in private, but with other believers which the Bible tells us is important.

In Matthew's Gospel it says, 'where two or more are gathered in my name, I am there.' This quote emphasises the need for Christians to pray communally with other believers, and as such is more important than private worship.

ⓔ **The student discusses Quaker worship and the impact this has upon the individual. They compare and contrast this view with other forms of worship.**

In conclusion, it could be argued that there is no one 'best' way to worship God. The main thing for all Christians is that they worship God in their own way. In whatever way a Christian chooses to worship God, they all keep in mind the first commandment which is 'I am the Lord your God, you shall have no other but me.' All forms of worship keep this commandment at the forefront of what they do.

ⓔ **The student rounds off with a judgement on the issue within the stimulus and a balanced conclusion to the discussion.**

Question 3
Student B

(a) 1 Jerusalem.
   2 The Holy Lands.
   3 Santiago de Compostela.

ⓔ **Only 2 marks are given to this response because the first two are similar – Jerusalem is a site in the Holy Lands.**

(b) The word transcendent means that God is close and able to know us. A Baptist Christian might believe this.

ⓔ **The student confuses the terms 'transcendent' and 'immanent', so no marks are awarded. It is important not to make this mistake in the exam. The specification requires you to learn the meaning of many key terms and you should ensure you don't get mixed up on the specific meanings of terms.**

(c) Christians believe that there are different types of prayer, such as praising God, asking for his help for ourselves or others, or confessing our sins.

ⓔ **The student focuses on prayer, giving different types (all of which only amount to 1 mark). They do not address the full significance of the question, so no further marks can be awarded.**

(d) Christians believe that it is their job to tell everyone about Jesus and get them to become Christians themselves. This is called evangelism. In the past there were missionaries who went out to different countries, such as Eric Liddell, who won a gold medal in the 1924 Olympics, who went to China, or David Livingstone in Africa. In 2015 the Archbishop of Canterbury said that making new disciples was one of the priorities for a modern Christian. The Salvation Army's main purpose is to save souls and help others. They do this by going out onto the streets to help the homeless and preach the gospel of Christ. Paul O'Grady showed the work of the Salvation Army in a series by the BBC. In one episode it showed him handing out sandwiches to the homeless while other members washed their feet. The Gideons spread the word by putting Bibles in hotel rooms and giving out New Testaments to school children.

(e) The student gives a description of evangelism instead of an explanation of why it is important to some christians. They list examples of people who were/are evangelists along with organisations and their work. The student does not support any statements with reference to biblical teachings other than the Archbishop of Canterbury's statement and they make no attempt at analysis.

(e) Someone might agree with this statement because liturgical worship is very formal in organisation. As such the congregation responds to the person leading the service, reading set words from a service sheet or book. This is a good way to worship God because it allows the individual to partake in a communal activity with fellow believers. An important part of liturgical services is the Lord's Prayer. It is important for Christians to say this prayer because Jesus told them to. It is also important because in the Lord's prayer, Christians will ask for forgiveness, they will show adoration towards God, and they will petition God. Therefore the statement is correct.

(e) The student responds to the stimulus in a simplistic way but demonstrates some understanding of the issue within the statement.

However, some might argue that because the Holy Spirit is present during charismatic worship that this form of worship actually connects more closely with God. This type of worship is also heartfelt and is more meaningful to the worshipper rather than the repetitive, impersonal nature of liturgical worship. Praying in the spirit is important because of the day of Pentecost. However, some non-Christians might look at Pentecostal services and believe that what is happening is in fact a product of mass delusion. People trick themselves into believing that they are being 'slain in the spirit' because they have a sense of expectation that something will happen.

(e) The student shows some knowledge of charismatic worship, although this is limited. They make a satisfactory attempt to evaluate the impact of this type of worship on the individual but the use of biblical evidence is not explained to show the significance of the day of Pentecost and its relevance to charismatic worship.

Alternatively, some might argue that worshipping God in the privacy of your own home is more important than either of the other ways. This is because Jesus was known to pray to God by himself. For example, in the Garden of Gethsemane, Jesus prayed to God for guidance and strength. Therefore, Christians should worship God in the same way that Jesus did. Although, Jesus did tell people to pray in groups of two or more, so just praying on your own might not be the best.

(e) The student attempts to show the significance and impact of private prayer on an individual but in a very simplistic way. Again, there is an attempt to use a source of wisdom and authority but the explanation of this is limited.

In conclusion, liturgical worship is about worshipping God collectively in a formal way. Charismatic worship is worshipping God in an informal/unstructured way and private prayer is something you can do at home when you have time to. I do not think there is a 'best' way to worship God.

(e) The conclusion does not add to anything which has been said already. Although the student demonstrates that they recognise there is diversity in Christian beliefs regarding worship, they offer no real analysis and no reference to sources of wisdom and authority. In the conclusion do not just repeat what you have said earlier.

Mark scheme

3 (a) The student is asked to 'name' three places, so 1 mark is awarded for each correct place up to a maximum of three. The student could suggest:
  - Walsingham
  - Lourdes
  - Rome
  - Canterbury
  - St David's (Wales)
  - Santiago de Compostela
  - Holy Lands: Bethlehem, Sea of Galilee, Jerusalem, Nazareth
  - any other relevant/valid pilgrimage site.

Hints and tips

The command word is 'name' so three correct place names are sufficient.

(b) Marks are awarded for a correct definition that is developed and/or has examples. Marks may also be awarded for any combination of statements. The student **might** suggest:
  - that the word transcendent means beyond or above the range of normal or physical human existence
  - that God exists outside of our time and space
  - that God is eternal and not created
  - God is transcendent because, according to the Nicene Creed, he was the creator of heaven and earth, of all that is seen and unseen

Hints and tips

Try to give a clear, developed response.

(c) Marks are awarded for a correct description which is developed or has examples. The student **might**:
  - refer to the example and teachings of Jesus on prayer
  - refer to one of the different types of prayer – adoration, contrition, thanksgiving and supplication
  - refer to personal, private, public and corporate worship, prayers in school assemblies or council meetings

Hints and tips

Make sure you read the question carefully and include all aspects within the question. The question only asks for *one* Christian belief about prayer. Ensure that one reason is given and developed.

(d) This response is given **two** separate marks, both of which are determined by levels of response. Only **one** response is written but two different sets of **skills** are assessed by the examiner. The first mark is given for knowledge and understanding (AO1) and the second mark is awarded for the student's analysis and evaluation of the question (AO2). If the student simply writes down all they know about a specific topic, then the marks will be limited to the maximum marks for AO1. The examiner is assessing how the student uses their knowledge and understanding to relate to the specifics of the question/stimulus.

Knowledge and understanding AO1

Level	Description
1	A **weak** demonstration of knowledge and understanding which is given 1 mark. This might include a brief description of what evangelism is. Points are only listed and contain factual errors.
2	A **limited** demonstration of knowledge and understanding which is given 2 marks. This might include some relevant information on different Christian beliefs on evangelism, perhaps supported with an example, however this is limited in development.
3	An **adequate** but **underdeveloped** demonstration of knowledge and understanding which is given 3 marks. The student will have shown knowledge and understanding of different beliefs about evangelism with some examples, but their explanations will not be detailed.
4	A **good** demonstration of knowledge and understanding which is given 4 marks. The student will have given detailed, relevant information on what evangelism is. Such information might include: – a definition of evangelism, perhaps supported by reference to biblical authority – examples of evangelists: Eric Liddell, David Livingstone, Gladys Aylward, David Wilkerson, Nikki Cruz – examples of specific Christian organisations: CAFOD, Christian Aid, Gideons, the World Council of Churches, Salvation Army or any other relevant organisation – reference to the Archbishop of Canterbury's message in 2015

Analysis and evaluation AO2

Level	Description
1	**Some** demonstration of analysis has been shown but it may be implicit or even unsuccessful. Some attempt to reflect the significance of the issue on different Christian groups = 1 mark.
2	A **good** response – the student has shown successful analysis and evaluation of the issue = 2 marks. The student **might**: – evaluate the importance of the belief in the duty of evangelism – evaluate and analyse why evangelism might not be an important duty or why it might cause conflict – evaluate and analyse that other aspects of the faith are more important

Hints and tips

➤ Read the question carefully and support your answers with teachings or examples.

➤ You are being asked to show a deep understanding of why Christians hold their beliefs.

(e) This response is given **two** separate marks, both of which are determined by levels of response. Only **one** response is written but two different sets of **skills** are assessed by the examiner. The first mark is given for knowledge and understanding (AO1) and the second mark is awarded for the student's analysis and evaluation of the question (AO2). If the student simply writes down all they know about a specific topic, then the marks will be limited to the maximum marks for AO1. The examiner is assessing how the student uses their knowledge and understanding to relate to the specifics of the question/stimulus.

Knowledge and understanding AO1

Level	Description
1	A **limited/weak** demonstration of knowledge and understanding which is given 1 mark. This might include some general information and understanding about Christian worship, the ideas may be listed and lacking in detail.
2	An **adequate** but **underdeveloped** demonstration of knowledge and understanding which is given 2 marks. This might include some relevant information on different types of Christian worship and biblical evidence to support different types of worship.
3	A **good** demonstration of knowledge and understanding which is given 3 marks. The student will have given detailed, relevant information on different Christian views and will have made reference to the stimulus trigger words 'the best way'. Such information might include: – Jesus praying in the Garden of Gethsemane – Baptists who believe that God is directly accessible to all people – The use of prayer aids in private worship to focus worship – An understanding of liturgical, informal and charismatic worship – Reference to the sacraments as part of liturgical worship – Quaker worship (informal) – Reference to denominational service prayer books (Catholic Missal) – John 4:24, Romans 8:14

Analysis and evaluation AO2

Level	Description
1	A **weak** attempt to respond to the stimulus with a simplistic/descriptive account of liturgical worship with little or no attempt to offer a judgement on the significance of the issues raised (1–3 marks). The student may have suggested one view either for or against the stimulus but has not made a specific conclusion or judgement. In other words, the information is communicated in a basic way and there is no evidence of a **discussion** taking place.
2	A **limited** attempt – the student has made some effort to respond to the stimulus and has shown various ideas on why there are different beliefs within different denominations but the judgement/conclusion is limited. **Or** one specific interpretation may have been discussed with an attempt at a conclusion (4–6 marks). In other words, there is a line of reasoning/**discussion** which has some relevance to the stimulus.
3	An **adequate** but **underdeveloped** attempt to **discuss** the stimulus showing different viewpoints on the various ways Christians can worship God, which are supported with reference to sources of wisdom and authority, and the student has made some comments on them. In other words, there is a discussion of the stimulus supported with evidence of comparison and criticism along with a judgement/conclusion (7–9 marks). A line of reasoning has been presented and **discussed** which is mostly relevant.

4	A **good** attempt which has shown a structured discussion while comparing and criticising/commenting on the various aspects/beliefs of the different ways in which a Christian can worship God and how these interpretations have significance in the lives of believers (10–12 marks). The student has offered a well-developed and sustained **discussion** which is coherent, relevant and well structured. The student **might**: – analyse and compare different Christian viewpoints/beliefs about the importance of different forms of worship – compare and contrast whether or not different forms of worship are more significant on the lives of believers – analyse the view that there may not be one specific way to worship God

Hints and tips

➤ Read the stimulus carefully and identify its significance in your response, making sure you stick to the wording in the stimulus and do not divert into a concept that you would prefer to discuss.

➤ Demonstrate that you understand that there are common beliefs but also contradictory beliefs within Christianity. You will need to compare and contrast these different beliefs.

➤ Support your statements/ideas/information with reference to sources of wisdom and authority, e.g. biblical passages and the different church teachings.

➤ Remember that you do not have to express a personal view – if you want to, you can, but make sure you justify your point of view with evidence and argument.

➤ Remember too that your response should be a **discussion** – try to present viewpoints for both sides as if you were having a conversation. Do not just list all the ideas for the stimulus in one paragraph and then all the ideas against in another paragraph.

➤ You are allowed to compare and contrast the Christianity ideas with the other religion you have studied.

     OCR GCSE (9–1) Religious Studies Exam Question Practice

Question 4
Student A

(a) The World Council of Churches is an ecumenical movement which joins together many different denominations and churches within the Christian faith in order to promote cooperation and unity between them in accordance with Jesus's teaching 'that they may all be one'.

(e) **This is a three-point question for 3 marks. The first mark is given to the overall understanding of the World Council of Churches and the idea of ecumenism, 'joining together of the different churches', the second mark is given to the purpose 'promote cooperation', and the third mark goes to the supporting quote, John 17:21. The student does not have to write out/remember the whole verse but can quote just enough to show they have fully understood.**

(b) 1 Taizé

2 Iona

3 Corrymeela

(e) **3 marks are awarded for three correct examples.**

(c) In 2015 in Mosul (Iraq) the Christian community was told by the invading ISIS troops that they had to convert to Islam, pay an expensive religious tax or be executed. As a result, thousands of them fled and probably will never return.

(e) **The first mark is given to the example of Mosul, while the second mark is given to the description of the ISIS demands. There is further development about the impact of the demands, which receives the third mark.**

(d) Christian churches can support families in their communities in many ways. One of these is the support of local food banks which collect non-perishable foods such as long-life milk or tinned food and these are then distributed to families in need who are struggling. Christians will do this because they are following the parable of the sheep and the goats: 'For when I was hungry … when I was thirsty'. This parable sets the foundation for Christian love, agape, and is one on which Mother Teresa and Oscar Romero based their actions. What is done for the poor is done for Christ.

Another way Christians support families is through the work of the street pastors – they are helping the vulnerable who are out on the streets, usually teenagers. They listen to them and care for them, even if it is just to make sure that they get home to their families safely. This again is supported by sources of wisdom such as Jeremiah: 'and I will give you pastors of my own heart'. Jesus could be described as a street pastor because he toured around the countryside helping people in need and telling them about God's love, which endorses the work of the street pastors.

A final way in which the church supports the family is through visiting the sick to give them comfort. If someone is ill then they cannot contribute to family life. This is again one of the actions within the parable of the sheep and the goats which shows that by doing this, a Christian is doing it for Christ, but it is also the directive of James who said if anyone is sick they must 'call the elders of the church to pray over them'. All these are important actions and sum up what it means to be a Christian to live a life helping others which is fulfilling God's wishes.

(e) **The student demonstrates good knowledge (the how) and understanding (the why) of how churches support families in their communities. They use three examples and these are explicitly connected to families and not to people in general. This is important because** it would be too easy to suggest ways of helping people in need. The student describes the examples and then supports them with references to sources of wisdom. They offer analysis/comment about all the examples and give a judgement at the end of the response.

(e) It is a sad fact that Christians have been persecuted from the time of Christ and it has still not stopped. Incidents in Somalia, India, Syria, etc. sometimes do not even make headline news, which perhaps is a symbol of our times that being persecuted for your faith is a common thing and does not warrant much attention. People are appalled but somewhat immune to pictures in the media of ISIS beheading people who will not convert to their radical views, and images of people fleeing their homes to avoid execution. But is this the biggest challenge facing the church in our modern world? The list of challenges is frightening: poverty, war, racism, child abuse, people renouncing their faith, dwindling numbers in certain congregations, not to mention the fact that the church itself is divided into numerous denominations, each professing to be the true church, and so the list stretches on. While every challenge needs to be tackled, does it mean that they should be ranked into the most important and least important? God must be holding his head in his hands so to speak at the inhumanity which exists in his creation.

(e) **The student responds to the stimulus and questions whether it is possible to rank the challenges which exist and so indicates that they have recognised the implications of the stimulus.**

It could be argued that there are so many challenges facing the modern church today because the church cannot agree within itself as to how to tackle the problems. St Paul urged that 'there should be no divisions among you', yet many of the denominations argue about what it means to be a Christian. There are differences in worship between Catholics and Protestants, Quakers and the Salvation Army, who all believe they have the 'truth'. But each of these churches does what it can to alleviate poverty and promote peace and reconciliation. The ecumenical movement attempts to promote cooperation and discourse between the different factions so that they can work together (Churches Together Movement) to bring the message of God's love to those who have either rejected him or who have not heard his message. So surely this attempt to reconcile differences, or at least understand them so that they can work together, is fulfilling the message in the parable of the sheep and the goats and so their differences are not a challenge. As a result, they can focus on the persecution of the church. However, not all of the different denominations will agree to work together, because some denominations have an exclusivist view and will believe that their specific denomination is the only correct denomination and that all other Christian groups are wrong. So perhaps division in the church is a bigger challenge than persecution.

(e) **The student discusses the divisions within the church and the work of the ecumenical movement in order to evaluate whether the divisions are more of a concern than the persecution. There is reference to sources of wisdom and authority, key terms (exclusivist) and denominational understanding.**

Is it really a challenge that Christians are being persecuted for their faith? This may sound harsh, but it could in fact be a test from God as Job was tested in the Old Testament. Jesus taught that the persecuted should be blessed in the Beatitudes. The incidents of persecution throughout the world are numerous. Yet China, where there was extreme persecution when Chairman Mao ruled an atheist country, is now cited as one of the world's fastest-growing Christian communities. It has been said that by 2030 the Christian community there will overtake that in the USA. So it could be said that persecution has its benefits or rewards because even though persecution exists, it does not stop people becoming Christians. Jesus taught that following him would be difficult (Gospel of St Luke). The early church was persecuted: many of the apostles and St Paul were martyrs, and early Christians were thrown to the lions by the Romans. The myth of Peter fleeing persecution from Rome and seeing a vision of Christ who said he was going to be crucified again made Peter turn back to face the persecution indicates that although it is horrible to be persecuted and you can lose your life, standing up to the persecutors is the true strength of someone's faith. It serves as an example and allows non-believers to realise the significance of what believing in Christ means. It could be argued that if Christians had not been persecuted in the early beginnings of the religion then people may not have been encouraged and converted by those who stood up for their faith and who were willing to die for what they believed. If this is a true argument, then it could be claimed that persecution of the church is not a bad thing but is in fact helping to re-establish the word of Christ on earth. Tertullian famously said; 'the blood of the martyrs is the seed of the church', therefore persecution was in fact the main reason that Christianity became the dominant religion it is today.

ⓔ The student discusses the implications of persecution and considers whether or not people being prepared to die for their faith is a convincing example to others of the truth of Christianity.

Obviously the persecution of the church is a challenge to many Christians and organisations such as the Barnabas Fund and Open Doors work hard to alleviate this challenge. However, not everyone in the world is a Christian; all the different faiths believe that their religion is the true one and so it is doubtful that persecution can ever be stopped. In the past Christians were persecutors themselves; the slave trade was when Christians believed they were doing the African people a favour by kidnapping them and taking them to America. The crusade against the Cathars was because Christians believieved that they were heretics. So while it can be said that persecution is a terrible thing, it can be argued that it is wrong to say it is the biggest challenge facing Christians today, because Christians should be working together to overcome all the problems, not just one particular one, in order to be ready for the Parousia and so be able to face God and say, 'I did my best'.

ⓔ The student rounds off with a judgement on the issue within the stimulus and a balanced conclusion to the discussion.

Question 4
Student B

(a) The purpose of the World Council of Churches is to bring together all the different churches so that they can have an increased understanding of each other.

ⓔ Only 2 marks are given for this response: the first for 'bring together' and the second for 'increased understanding'. Further development is needed to achieve the third mark, such as an explanation of why they need to be brought together or the idea of working together to promote peace.

(b) 1 Churches Together
   2 Iona
   3 Pax Christi

ⓔ Only 2 marks are achieved because the third example, although working for peace, is just a Catholic organisation, not a member of the ecumenical movement.

(c) Christians are persecuted in Odisha in India. They are also persecuted in North Korea because they are tortured or imprisoned and even executed because they believe God is a higher authority than the ruler Kim Jong-un.

(e) **The student only receives only 1 mark for this response – for the first example of Odisha. The second example, although valid, cannot be credited because the question asked for one example only. The student needs to develop the Odisha example by detailing how Christians are persecuted.**

(d) Churches often help families in need through supporting the work of local charities in their area, running youth clubs to keep teenagers off the streets, running mother-and-child groups or visiting the lonely to make sure they are okay. Sunday schools are held in conjunction with Sunday worship to teach the young about Jesus. This is done in accordance with Jesus telling his disciples to let the little children come to me.

Christians might volunteer to help in local charity shops or by going out at night to feed the homeless with soup. All of these actions show agape, which is loving anyone no matter who they are without expecting anything in return. Paul O'Grady promoted the work of the Salvation Army and the homeless by going on a soup run and giving out sandwiches and talking to the homeless so that they did not feel so lonely and neglected. All the things the church does to help the poor is summed up by Pope Francis, who said the church is the living body of Christ. So all this work is important if a person wants to go to heaven.

(e) **The student lists various examples but does not tie these into the command word 'families' – the examples could apply to anyone in need. They make an attempt to evaluate the importance at the end of the response but again it is more about helping the poor.**

(e) There are many challenges a Christian has to deal with in today's world. Technology means that the news of natural disasters and man-made atrocities is heralded around the world in a matter of minutes. To be a Christian is just not a matter of going to church once a week and praying and reading the Bible, it is all about leading a life which follows the teachings and example set by Jesus when he was on earth. It is all about Christian love, which is unconditional and means treating everyone how you would like to be treated – the golden rule. So Christians need to devote their daily lives to helping with all the challenges the world faces. It is true that Christians are persecuted for their faith in many parts of the world and so Christians will pray for them and campaign for their release if they have been falsely imprisoned. But the statement is saying that the persecution of Christians is the biggest challenge to be tackled – is this true?

(e) **The student responds by saying there are many challenges in the world which need to be addressed and attempts to show some understanding of the stimulus.**

There are many countries in the world where Christians are persecuted. In some they are forbidden to have a Bible and in other countries they can be forcibly imprisoned or beaten up. Although many Christians believe that everyone is entitled to follow their own faith and follow an inclusivist view, they think that this should allow them to worship freely wherever they want in the world.

(e) **The student offers some thoughts on Christian persecution but the response is quite simplistic and there are no specific examples or links to the stimulus.**

Worshipping God is not a challenge but it is what a Christian needs to focus on. However, as said earlier, worship is not just going to church, singing and praying, it is showing God that he is adored and respected and that his commands are so important they must be followed. The Ten Commandments are not just about how to show respect to God but also how a person can show respect to other people. Jesus added two other commandments which encapsulate the Ten Commandments and these are to 'love thy Lord God with all thy heart' and 'to love thy neighbour as thyself'. Jesus specifically said the first one was the most important. So facing the challenges of persecution is important, but can it be said that it is more of a challenge than loving God or could it be said that loving God means that a Christian is in fact dealing with the challenges of persecution and all the rest of the challenges in the world?

ⓔ **The student attempts to analyse and comment on the stimulus by suggesting that worshipping God is what a true Christian should focus on and whether this means that Christians should be dealing with all the challenges in the world.**

Mark scheme

4 (a) Marks are awarded for correct ideas about the purpose of the World Council of Churches which are developed and/or have examples. The student **might** suggest:
 - the bringing/joining together the different movements within the Christian religion
 - the purposes of cooperation and unity, working together to help the poor and promote peace, promote understanding, reconciliation
 - scriptural support: John 17:21, Ephesians 4:3–6
 - possible reference to the movement beginning after the First World War, the First Council of Nicea in 325CE being the first ecumenical meeting of Christians, and the Churches Together Movement.

Hints and tips

Try to give a developed response with three clear points that are relevant to the question.

 (b) 1 mark is awarded for each correct community up to a maximum of 3 marks. The student **might** suggest:
 - Taizé
 - Iona
 - Corrymeela
 - Churches Together
 - Christian feminist network

Hints and tips

Give three distinct examples.

 (c) Marks are awarded for a correct example with development/explanation. The student **might** refer to:
 - Mosul, Iraq, 2015 – Christians fleeing from execution or forced conversion by the invading ISIS troops.
 - North Korea – Christians imprisoned, tortured or killed because they believe God is the highest authority.

– Somalia – instant execution if a Christian is discovered.
– Odisha, India, 2007 – argument over a Christmas arch which Hindus said was disrespectful to their Durga Puja festival resulting in continuing violence.
– Vietnam, 2016 – Christian beaten for refusing to deny the faith.
– France, 2016 – 86-year-old French priest, Father Jacques Hamel, murdered while taking mass.

Hints and tips

Make sure you read the question carefully and follow the command word 'one'.

(d) This response is given **two** separate marks, both of which are determined by levels of response. Only **one** response is written but two different sets of **skills** are assessed by the examiner. The first mark is given for knowledge and understanding (AO1) and the second mark is awarded for the student's analysis and evaluation of the question (AO2). If the student simply writes down all they know about a specific topic, then the marks will be limited to the maximum marks for AO1. The examiner is assessing how the student uses their knowledge and understanding to relate to the specifics of the question/stimulus.

Knowledge and understanding AO1

Level	Description
1	A **weak** demonstration of knowledge and understanding which is given 1 mark. This might include a list of examples of the church helping people.
2	A **limited** demonstration of knowledge and understanding which is given 2 marks. This might include some relevant information on how the church helps families, but in a simplistic way. This may be one point with slight development.
3	An **adequate** but **underdeveloped** demonstration of knowledge and understanding which is given 3 marks. The student will have shown knowledge and understanding of how the church helps families, by giving information on two or more specific examples with explanations that could have been developed.
4	A **good** demonstration of knowledge and understanding which is given 4 marks. The student will have given detailed relevant information on how churches support families, backed up by scriptural authority or sources of wisdom. Such information **might** include: – examples of how: food banks, Sunday schools, youth clubs, mother-and-child groups, visiting the elderly and the sick, street pastors, support through the sacraments (baptism, marriage), funeral services, etc … – scriptural support: agape, parable of the sheep and the goats (Matthew 25:31–46), Mark 10:14, John 13:34–35, Acts 2:42–47, 1 John 3:17, James 5:13–15, Jeremiah 3:15, Pope Francis: 'the church is the living body of Christ'

Analysis and evaluation AO2

Level	Description
1	**Some** demonstration of analysis – the why – has been shown but it may be implicit or even unsuccessful = 1 mark.
2	A **good** response – the student has shown successful analysis and evaluation of the issue = 2 marks. The student **might**: – analyse/evaluate each specific example – comment on and compare the importance of all the examples together

Hints and tips

➤ Read the question carefully and follow the command words: 'how' is different to 'why' and you need to explain both.

➤ Relate the examples you use to 'families'.

➤ You are being asked to show a deep understanding of why Christians hold their beliefs.

(e) This response is given **two** separate marks, both of which are determined by levels of response. Only **one** response is written but two different sets of **skills** are assessed by the examiner. The first mark is given for knowledge and understanding (AO1) and the second mark is awarded for the student's analysis and evaluation of the question (AO2). If the student simply writes down all they know about a specific topic, then the marks will be limited to the maximum marks for AO1. The examiner is assessing how the student uses their knowledge and understanding to relate to the specifics of the question/stimulus.

Knowledge and understanding AO1

Level	Description
1	A **limited/weak** demonstration of knowledge and understanding which is given 1 mark. This might include some general information about modern persecution and about whether or not persecution of Christians is the biggest challenge to Christianity, by suggesting alternative challenges. The ideas may be listed and lacking in detail.
2	An **adequate** but **underdeveloped** demonstration of knowledge and understanding which is given 2 marks. This might include some relevant information on different views about whether or not persecution of Christians is the biggest challenge facing Christians today.
3	A **good** demonstration of knowledge and understanding which is given 3 marks. The student will have given detailed, relevant information on different Christian views about whether or not persecution of Christians is biggest challenge facing Christians today. Such information **might** include: – specific examples of Christian persecution today (see part (c) above) and in the past: Romans throwing Christians to the lions, martyrdom of the apostles, persecution of St Paul (2 Corinthians 4:8–12) – examples of Christian organisations: Barnabas Fund, Open Doors – examples of other problems: poverty, racism, environment, refugees, Pope Francis saying that 'we are at war' – biblical support: Beatitudes, Mark 12:29–31, Luke 14:25–35, 1 Corinthians 1:10.

Analysis and evaluation AO2

Level	Description
1	A **weak** attempt to respond to the stimulus with a simplistic/descriptive account of persecution with no or very little attempt to offer a judgement on the significance of the issues raised (1–3 marks). The student may have suggested one view either for or against the stimulus but has not made a specific conclusion or judgement. In other words, the information is communicated in a basic way and there is no evidence of a **discussion** taking place.
2	A **limited** attempt – the student has made some attempt to respond to the stimulus and has shown different ideas on whether or not persecution is the biggest challenge facing Christians today, but the judgement/conclusion is limited. **Or** one specific interpretation may have been discussed with an attempt at a conclusion (4–6 marks). In other words, there is a line of reasoning/**discussion** which has some relevance to the stimulus.
3	An **adequate** but **underdeveloped** attempt to **discuss** the stimulus showing different viewpoints about whether or not persecution is the biggest challenge facing Christians today, which are supported with reference to sources of wisdom and authority, and the student has made some comments on them. In other words, there is a discussion of the stimulus supported with evidence of comparison and criticism along with a judgement/conclusion (7–9 marks). A line of reasoning has been presented and **discussed** which is mostly relevant.
4	A **good** attempt which has shown a structured discussion while comparing and criticising/commenting on whether or not persecution is the biggest challenge facing Christians today (10–12 marks). The student has offered a well-developed and sustained **discussion** which is coherent, relevant and well structured. The student **might**: – analyse and compare persecution with another challenge, e.g. poverty – compare and contrast whether or not persecution is actually a challenge or is a test from God – analyse and make a judgement on the concept of worship

Hints and tips

➤ Read the stimulus carefully and identify its significance in your response, making sure you stick to the wording in the stimulus and do not divert into a concept that you would prefer to discuss.

➤ Because the stimulus is asking you whether or not persecution is the biggest challenge facing Christians today, you need to assess the phrase 'biggest challenge' with comparisons. But be careful not to divert into long, detailed arguments about lots of challenges. Keep it simple and focus on one or two if you want to follow that line of response. This is only one way in which you could tackle the stimulus – there are other ways.

➤ Demonstrate that you understand there are common beliefs but also contradictory beliefs within Christianity. You will need to compare and contrast these different beliefs.

➤ Support statements/ideas/information with reference to sources of wisdom and authority, e.g. biblical passages and the different church teachings.

➤ Remember that you do not have to express a personal view – if you want to, you can, but make sure you justify your point of view with evidence and argument.

➤ Remember that too that your response should be a **discussion** – try to present viewpoints for both sides as if you were having a conversation. Do not just list all the ideas for the stimulus in one paragraph and then all the ideas against in another paragraph.

➤ You are allowed to compare and contrast the Christianity ideas with the other religion you have studied.

Paper 1: Beliefs and teachings and practices

Student responses

This section shows sample answers from two students. One set (Student A) is stronger, the other (Student B) is weaker. The answers are followed by examiner-style commentary (shown by the icon ⓔ) that indicates where credit is due. In the weaker answers, it also points out areas for improvement, specific problems and common errors.

Islam: beliefs and teachings

Question 1
Student A

(a) Prophethood is the way Allah communicates with humankind. Allah has chosen people to be his prophets since the beginning of creation because humans need to be guided about their purpose and how to live a virtuous life because human knowledge is limited.

ⓔ **The student explains that prophethood is a channel of communication (first mark). They then develop this by explaining the purpose of prophethood – to be a guide (second mark) – and the reason why this guidance is needed (third mark).**

(b) Belief in predestination is the sixth and last article of Islam. It is the belief that everything good or bad, all moments of happiness or sorrow, pleasure or pain, come from Allah. Although humans are given the gift of free will by Allah, it is Allah who is omniscient and knows everything in the past, present and future, so he is the one who knows the best course of action.

ⓔ **The student states that the belief in predestination is the sixth article, which earns the first mark. Explanation of the pillar 'everything comes from Allah' is credited with the second mark, and the third mark is given for further development of the explanation that 'Allah knows best'.**

(c) Belief in Yawmuddin is the fifth article of faith for Muslims. It is when they are judged on their deeds in life as to whether they will go to paradise (al-Jannah) or to hell (Jahannam). It is important to Muslims because the Qur'an teaches that when it arrives it will be too late for people to repent.

ⓔ **The student states that Yawmuddin is the fifth article of faith, which is an implicit statement of why it is important (first mark). This is developed by a description of what happens (second mark) and the third mark is given to the explicit reason of why it is important.**

(d) Sunni Muslims are the largest group: about 90% of the world's Muslims are Sunnis. They regard themselves as the orthodox branch and another name for them is 'People of the Tradition'. There has been a divide between the two groups for many centuries, but they agree on many fundamental beliefs and practices and share the same Holy Book, the Qur'an. However, there are differences in teachings, rituals and political organisation. One of the reasons for the political differences originates from the dilemma of who would succeed the Prophet Muhammad (pbuh). The group who later became the Sunnis wanted Abu Bakr to lead them, but the group who later became the Shi'as claimed that Muhammad (pbuh) had announced at the end of his last pilgrimage that his son-in-law Ali should be his successor. As a result, the Shi'as have different Hadith collections from those used by many Sunnis and this leads to different interpretations of practices such as prayer, fasting and pilgrimage.

There are also differences in the prayer rituals. Shi'a Muslims pray three times a day as they join two salahs (midday and afternoon plus the evening and night-time) together. This is because the Qur'an only directly speaks of three prayer times: dawn, midday and evening. However, Sunni Muslims pray five times a day. Another difference is how Muslims view the Imam. Shi'a Muslims believe that the Imam is sinless by nature and that he is infallible because his authority comes directly from God – the Imam is seen as being divinely appointed: 'O believers, obey Allah…and those in authority among you' (Surah 4). Therefore they may sometimes go on pilgrimages to their tombs and shrines. However, Some Sunnis disagree with this and argue that such pilgrimages may be heretical and that leadership of the community should be based on merit and not birthright. Therefore, although both groups follow Allah and have the Qur'an as their major revelation from Allah, there are differences because of a different political bias and as a result there can be conflict between the two groups.

(e) **The student demonstrates good knowledge and understanding of why there are differences between the Sunnis and the Shi'as. At times it appears to be a historical narrative but there are links to the Qur'an to explain the differences and the student attempts analysis.**

(e) All devout Muslims would disagree with this statement because the Qur'an teaches that they exist and for Sunnis it is important to believe in angels as the second article of faith. It was the Angel Jibril who revealed Allah's wishes to Muhammad (pbuh) which were later written down in the Qur'an. Surah 96 teaches that Allah 'taught Man, that which he knew not'. There are many mentions in the Qur'an about angels and there are so many that only Allah knows the true number. However, a non-believer would agree with the statement because they see angels as fictional characters or myths from legends. A Christian, however, would agree with Muslims that angels exist because within the Bible there are mentions of angels, such as when the Angel Gabriel said to Mary 'Greetings, you are highly favoured' to tell her she would give birth to Jesus. Also some modern theologians have explained the annunciation as a metaphor for a more earthly kind of messenger. As a result, it might be stated that many religious people believe in angels whereas non-religious people do not.

(e) **The student opens the response by announcing that Muslims believe in angels and then compares this belief with a non-believer and Christian beliefs. They suggest that the belief is important and distinct to religious people.**

It could be said that although Muslims believe in angels, this is not essential within their overall system of beliefs. Muhammad (pbuh) gave the messages to people and Allah created the Qur'an to pass on. Angels were the middle messengers who did not have a direct role to play in encouraging the people to believe. A Muslim might first believe in Allah and then in Muhammad (pbuh), as His Prophet, as both are mentioned in the statement of faith, but angels are not. Angels are important as the ones who passed on the Qur'an and without them, Muhammad (pbuh) might not have received the message at all, so they can be seen as essential in that sense. However, when Muslims are explaining their religion to others, and encouraging them to join Islam, it could be said that it is not essential to explain their belief in angels and some might question why they should believe in beings they cannot see, whereas the message in the form of a book, the Qur'an, they can see and read.

Others might argue that if such things as angels existed then why do so many people suffer so much, why do they become homeless, why do dreadful things happen to them? Isn't it more important to make sense of suffering in the world and take steps to help others, than believing in beings you cannot see? A Muslim would answer this by saying that it is because life is a test. The Qur'an teaches: 'And surely we shall test you…' The reason that life is a test is that there are two recording angels: 'And indeed, there are over you scribes, generous and recording. They know what you do'.

The angel on the right side records all the good deeds while the angel on the left records all the bad deeds. This is because when a Muslim dies, the Angel Izra'il separates the soul from the body. And then on the Day of Judgement the Angel Israfil blows the trumpet and Allah judges each person by their deeds: 'And to every soul will be paid in full (the fruit) of its deeds, and Allah knoweth best of all that they do.' If Muslims did not feel that angels were recording their deeds and watching over them then they might think they could hide their bad deeds and become less moral in their actions. There would be no reward for helping others in need. Therefore, belief in angels could be seen as essential to keep the faithful on the straight and narrow.

e **The student follows their line of argument that angels might not be essential in explaining the main beliefs of Islam, and that non-Muslims might find it difficult to understand belief in beings they cannot see.**

In conclusion, someone could say that it is not essential for Muslims to believe in angels because they have not seen one or maybe they are going through a very bad time in their life and since there is no such thing as a divine being there are no such things. The major religions in the world have various and sometimes different ideas of angels – Christianity sees Satan as a fallen angel who disobeyed God, but Muslims refute this because angels were created from light (hadith) and without free will, they are immortal and have no physical needs, so Shaytan could not be a fallen angel. But for a Muslim the statement that it is not necessary to believe in angels could throw into doubt the authenticity of the Qur'an and therefore the role of these messengers is a core article of faith.

e **The student concludes with the judgement that one of the central beliefs for a Muslim is in angels but that within the various religions there are different theological concepts. A non-believer would not believe in a divine creation anyway.**

Question 1
Student B

(a) The purpose of prophethood is to reveal the will of Allah. Muhammad (pbuh) is the last of the 25 prophets mentioned in the Qur'an.

e **1 mark is awarded for the purpose of prophethood given in the first sentence. However, the second sentence is a new point – it gives Muhammad (pbuh) as an example of a prophet and the question was asking about prophethood.**

(b) Muslims often say 'In Sha'a Allah', meaning 'if Allah wills it'. This means Allah knows and decrees what will happen at any time.

e **Although this is a correct response it does not have enough development to achieve the full 3 marks. The first mark is given for the explanation of 'In Sha'a Allah' and the second mark is given for the idea that Allah knows what will happen at any time. Further development is required for the third mark – the student could have referred to free will or used a quote from the Qur'an in support.**

(c) Muslims believe that the Day of Judgement is important because justice is an important value in Islam and on this day justice will be seen to be done because Allah will send those who commit wrongdoings to hell.

e **The student explains that the importance of the day is justice being seen to be done (first mark) and this is developed with the explanation of Allah sending sinners to hell (second mark). Further development or a quote from the Qur'an is needed for the third mark.**

(d) There is a lot of discord between the Shi'a and Sunni beliefs. The Sunnis often describe Shi'as as heretics who should be killed. The Sunnis are the major group while Shi'as are in the minority. The Shi'as have a different Hadith because they think the sayings and teachings associated with the Prophet Muhammad's (pbuh) family are more important. But the Sunnis believe all the sayings from any of Muhammad's (pbuh) companions have equal validity. The Hajj, the fifth pillar of Islam, is considered to be a compulsory obligation for all Muslims and the rituals which have to be done are laid out in the Qur'an (Surah 2): 'complete the Hajj in the service of Allah'. But Shi'a Muslims also believe there are other holy places of pilgrimage such as the shrines of their Imams. However, Sunni Muslims disagree with this because they view it as a form of shirk to worship anyone but Allah and to pray to anyone but Allah for help because the Qur'an teaches 'set not up with God another god, or thou wilt sit condemned and forsaken'.

(e) **The student explains in detail, supported with quotes from the Qur'an, two differences between the practices of Sunnis and Shi'as. However, there is no attempt to analyse or evaluate.**

(e) Muslims believe it is necessary to believe in angels because there are many references to them in the Qur'an. Some of the angels are even given names, such as Mika'il, the guardian of heaven, who is also responsible for the wind and the rain, and Jibril, who is Allah's messenger. The Prophet Muhammad (pbuh) described him as having 600 wings. A non-believer would criticise this as superstitious and having no proof in science.

(e) **The student opens the response with a denial of the statement through Muslim beliefs and then counter-argues by giving a non-believer's view.**

Muslims believe that angels were Allah's first creation and that he created them from nur (divine light). They have no free will and are immortal, with no physical needs. Their role is to glorify Allah: 'They glorify Him night and day: they do not halt.' There are also two recording angels who write the good and bad deeds a Muslim does throughout their life and then on judgement day the records will be judged by Allah. There is also the belief that the angels Nakir and Munkar will question the soul of a Muslim while they waits in the grave for judgement day. They will ask three questions and if the Muslim answers them correctly, the time waiting for resurrection on judgement day will be nice, but if they do not answer correctly then their souls will be punished until judgement. Therefore Muslims believe in angels.

(e) **The student gives a descriptive account of the Muslim belief in the role of angels. There is no discussion or attempt to link the account to the statement except the 'tag on' in the final sentence. There is no analysis.**

Other religions believe in angels. Indeed, Judaism has some belief in angels, similar to Muslims. Jews believe in the Angel Gabriel who interpreted the vision for Daniel. In the book of Enoch, Gabriel is seen as an avenging angel who incites sinners into war. Muslims believe in the Angel Jibril who is Allah's messenger and who revealed the words of the Qur'an to the Prophet Muhammad (pbuh) when he was meditating in the cave. Christians also believe in the Angel Gabriel who announced both the birth of John the Baptist to Zacharias and Jesus's birth to Mary. Muslims also believe this about Jibril.

(e) **The student attempts to compare religious belief in angels between the three Abrahamic religions and so there is implicit analysis.**

Secular people would argue that angels are just a figment of imagination. Some Muslims might say that they should be doing good deeds to please Allah, not because angels are checking up on them. They do not worship the angels in themselves so it is not necessary to believe in them. They could also say that they have never seen angels so why should they think it is necessary to believe in them? Atheists also say that science does not prove angels at all so it is superstitious to believe in angels.

ⓔ **The student shows a secular point of view and returns to the statement. They attempt to address the specifics of the statement, and there is some good knowledge and understanding, but the response is not discursive (it does not discuss) and there is little comment or analysis.**

Mark scheme

1 **(a)** Marks are awarded for a statement plus further development of that statement with either examples or references to sources of wisdom and authority to support it. Students **might** refer to:
   - the purpose of prophethood – to be a channel of communication between Allah and humans
   - the bringer of a holy book
   - providers of perfect examples for humankind
   - a status given to an ordinary human being as a messenger protected by Allah
   - features of the prophets: respected in the community, supported by miracles, state clearly that the message revealed is from Allah and for the benefit of humankind

Hints and tips

➤ Read the question carefully – it is asking what prophethood is, not who the prophets were.

➤ Do not try to hedge your bets by giving lots of ideas. Only the first response will be marked.

➤ Make sure you are clear, not muddled. You are asked to make a statement and then you can either develop it or explain it and support it with a specific example or a quote.

(b) Marks are awarded for a statement plus further development of that statement with either examples or references to sources of wisdom and authority to support it. Students **might** refer to:
   - the definition of predestination from a Muslim point of view
   - support from the Qur'an: 'truly, nothing is hidden from God, in the earth or in the heavens'
   - al-Qad'r being the sixth article of faith
   - how predestination relates to free will

Hints and tips

➤ Try to give a clear, developed response which is not contradictory.

(c) Marks are awarded for a statement plus further development of that statement with either examples or references to sources of wisdom and authority to support it. Students **might** refer to:

– Muslims knowing what will happen on the Day of Judgement but that it is not possible to describe the afterlife because it belongs to a totally different dimension
– free will means a judgement is needed at some point
– it is a necessary condition for the period of eternal afterlife to begin
– it allows Allah to meet out justice
– supporting quotes from the Qur'an
– it is an article of faith
– it is the time when angels read records of deeds

Hints and tips

➤ Read the question carefully. It is not asking what happens on the Day of Judgement but **why** it is important. So make sure you address the proper focus.

(d) This response is given **two** separate marks, both of which are determined by levels of response. Only **one** response is written but two different sets of **skills** are assessed by the examiner. The first mark is given for knowledge and understanding (AO1) and the second mark is awarded for the student's analysis and evaluation of the question (AO2). If the student simply writes down all they know about a specific topic, then the marks will be limited to the maximum marks for AO1. The examiner is assessing how the student uses their knowledge and understanding to relate to the specifics of the question/stimulus.

Knowledge and understanding AO1

Level	Description
1	A **weak** demonstration of knowledge and understanding which is given 1 mark. This might include simplistic ideas on the differences between the Sunnis and the Shi'as but they have not been explained in detail or supported with reference to sacred writings.
2	A **limited** demonstration of knowledge and understanding which is given 2 marks. This might include some relevant ideas on the differences between the Sunnis and the Shi'as which have been supported with reference to sacred writings.
3	An **adequate** but **underdeveloped** demonstration of knowledge and understanding which is given 3 marks. The student will have shown knowledge and understanding of various ideas on the differences between the Sunnis and the Shi'as which have been supported with reference to sacred writings but the explanations will not be detailed enough to reach the next level.
4	A **good** demonstration of knowledge and understanding which is given 4 marks. The student will have given detailed, relevant information on the differences between Sunnis and Shi'as which are explained in detail. Such information **might** include: – political differences: the issue of the successor to the Prophet (pbuh) – differences in practices: pilgrimages, shrines, prayer, reverence of the Imam – reference to the Qur'an, e.g. Surah 2:196 (Hajj), 24:58 (which mentions the dawn and night prayer), Surah 2:238 (which mentions the middle prayer), 4:59, 17:22, 39:65 (shirk) and the Hadith – possible political differences and the position martyrs

Analysis and evaluation AO2

Level	Description
1	**Some** demonstration of analysis has been shown but it may be implicit or even unsuccessful = 1 mark. The student may have made an implicit comment on the reasons for the differences.
2	A **good** response – the student has made successful analysis and evaluation of the issue = 2 marks. The student **might** have: – compared and commented on the reasons for the differences – suggested that they still have major similarities in beliefs – reasoned that the differences have more of an impact in certain countries, e.g. Iraq and Iran being the only two countries to have a majority of Shi'a Muslims – commented on the Hajj being organised by the ruling Sunni Muslims

Hints and tips

➤ Read the question carefully and support your answer with teachings or examples.

➤ Include some analysis and evaluation.

➤ You are being asked to show a deep understanding of why Muslims hold their beliefs.

(e) This response is given **two** separate marks, both of which are determined by levels of response. Only **one** response is written but two different sets of **skills** are assessed by the examiner. The first mark is given for knowledge and understanding (AO1) and the second mark is awarded for the student's analysis and evaluation of the question (AO2). If the student simply writes down all they know about a specific topic, then the marks will be limited to the maximum marks for AO1. The examiner is assessing how the student uses their knowledge and understanding to relate to the specifics of the question/stimulus.

Knowledge and understanding AO1

Level	Description
1	A **limited/weak** demonstration of knowledge and understanding which is given 1 mark. This might include some general information and understanding about a Muslim's belief in angels, the ideas may be listed or simplistic and/or lacking in detail.
2	An **adequate** but **underdeveloped** demonstration of knowledge and understanding which is given 2 marks. This might include some knowledge and understanding about a Muslim's belief in angels.
3	A **good** demonstration of knowledge and understanding which is given 3 marks. The student will have given detailed, relevant information on a Muslim's belief in angels, supported with quotes. Such information **might** include: – belief in angels being the Sunnis' second article of faith – knowledge and understanding of the role of the different angels: Jibril, Izra'il, Mika'il, Israfil, the two recording angels, Nakir and Munkar – the belief that Allah created them from nur but with no free will, immortal and no physical needs – support from the Qur'an: 2:155, 16:49, 21:20, Surah 29, 35:1, 32:11, 39:20, 74:31, 82:10–12, 96:1–5 – support from the Hadith: Sahih Muslim Book 42 Hadith 7134.

Analysis and evaluation AO2

Level	Description
1	A **weak** attempt to respond to the stimulus with a simplistic/descriptive account with no or very little attempt to offer a judgement on the significance of the issues raised (1–3 marks). The student may have suggested one view either for or against the stimulus but has not made a specific conclusion or judgement. In other words, the information is communicated in a basic way and there is no evidence of a **discussion** taking place.
2	A **limited** attempt – the student has made some attempt to respond to the stimulus and has shown different ideas on a Muslim's belief in angels, but the judgement/conclusion is limited. **Or** one specific interpretation may have been discussed with an attempt at a conclusion (4–6 marks). In other words, there is a line of reasoning/**discussion** which has some relevance to the stimulus.
3	An **adequate** but **underdeveloped** attempt to discuss the stimulus showing different viewpoints on a Muslim's belief in angels, which are supported with reference to sources of wisdom and authority, and the student has made some comments on them. In other words, there is a discussion of the stimulus supported with evidence of comparison and criticism along with a judgement/conclusion (7–9 marks). A line of reasoning has been presented and **discussed** which is mostly relevant.
4	A **good** attempt which has shown a structured discussion while comparing/contrasting and criticising/commenting on the different ideas on a Muslim's belief in angels (10–12 marks). The student has offered a well-developed and sustained **discussion** which is coherent, relevant and well structured. The student **might** suggest: – comparison with other Islamic beliefs and how important the belief is within the overall beliefs framework – comparison with non-believers, other religions and whether it is essential to believe in angels to have religious faith – analysis on the fact that it is a core belief and for Sunnis it is the second article of faith

Hints and tips

➤ Read the stimulus carefully and identify its significance in your response, making sure you stick to the wording in the stimulus and do not divert into a concept that you would prefer to discuss.

➤ Refer to different beliefs and teachings and evaluate the importance of these differences.

➤ Remember that your response should be a **discussion** – try to present viewpoints for both sides as if you were having a conversation. Do not just list all the ideas for the stimulus in one paragraph and then all the ideas against in another paragraph.

➤ Remember that you do not have to express a personal view – if you want to, you can, but make sure you justify your point of view with evidence and argument.

➤ Support your statements/ideas/information with reference to sources of wisdom and authority, e.g. teachings from the Qur'an or Hadith.

➤ Do not fall into the trap of saying 'An atheist does not believe in Allah and therefore would not agree with the religious point of view'. You are not adding to the argument/discussion at all.

Question 2
Student A

(a) 1 Muhammad (pbuh)
   2 Adam
   3 Musa/Moses

ⓔ **The student gives three correct responses and so achieves full marks.**

(b) Tawhid means the oneness of Allah, meaning that he is indivisible and is the one God of all time. This teaching is set out in Surah 112: 'Say: He is Allah, the One and Only…'

ⓔ **The first mark is given to 'oneness', the explanation of 'indivisible' receives the second mark and the further development that Allah is the one and only God receives the third mark. Although the supporting reference to the Qur'an is correct, it is not required.**

(c) Allah as judge is very important to Muslims because only he will be their judge to see whether they have lived their lives in submission to his will and have followed the teachings in the Qur'an.

ⓔ **The first mark is given to the statement that only Allah will be judge. This is then developed, 'submission to his will', and further developed, 'teachings in the Qur'an', which are credited with 2 further marks.**

(d) Sunni Muslims believe in predestination, which is that Allah knows everything which will happen. They believe Allah has a master plan for the world which only he knows but that he gives and requires people to use free will when faced with moral choices. However, Allah already knows what choices they will make. This raises a problem of Allah's benevolence because it seems wrong for Allah to send people to hell at the last judgement when he already knows in advance that they will make bad choices. It seems rather unfair. Shi'a Muslims believe in partial free will. They believe Allah can change things if he so desires because the Qur'an teaches that he changed the period of worship for Moses from 30 to 40 nights. The Ash'ari school of thought puts forward another middle way because it teaches that humans have the ability to acquire how to act and through their free will make a choice. But these attempts to try and get round the unfairness of free will and predestination seem to be rather confusing. Also the Qur'an teaches that Allah created the angels with no free will (Surah 16:49–50), so why did he not make humans the same? Muslims accept that life is a test and that anything bad or good which happens to them is through the will of Allah. But they would not like to be a robot with no sense of choice. So perhaps it can be argued that on judgement day whether or not Allah knew about the good and bad deeds in advance, they can look to themselves and say it was my choice.

ⓔ **The student demonstrates good knowledge and understanding of the significance of free will and judgement by explaining how the belief in predestination can lead to questions about Allah's benevolence. They attempt analysis.**

(e) A Muslim would disagree with this statement because they believe the Qur'an is unchanging and unchangeable. It is seen as the direct revelation of Allah's sacred word to the Prophet Muhammad (pbuh) and is the last and most complete book of guidance for people of all times. Yet the Qur'an was in existence long before the Angel Jibril told Muhammad (pbuh) to 'recite in the name of your Lord'. When Adam was made a khalifa of Allah's creation he was given guidance on how to act. These values and instructions were also revealed to the prophets, including Jesus. In Surah 5, Allah says he gave 'Jesus, the son of Mary' the gospel. However, Muslims believe that Allah's instructions became distorted and as such no were no longer the true word.

So in this sense a Muslim would agree that the distorted words were no longer relevant but would not accept the same statement about the Qur'an.

ⓔ **The student opens the discussion by stating that the Qur'an is the true eternal word of Allah and is thus always relevant, but also states that previous instructions from Allah became distorted. This sums up the implications within the statement.**

Christians might point out that since the reformation, the Bible has been translated and interpreted to make it more relevant and more easily understandable to Christians today. It could be said that Muslims have not yet gone through a period of reformation during which religious text might be questioned. There are many new moral issues which did not exist at the time the Qur'an was revealed, such as genetic engineering. However, Surah 4 teaches that 'I will command them so they will slit the ears of cattle … (and) change the creation of Allah'. This has been done by Japanese scientists to make clones. So perhaps the Qur'an is entirely relevant. Some Muslims believe the Qur'an is partly relevant but needs to be reinterpreted to answer new questions, by finding general guidance or parallels from within the original text.

ⓔ **The student compares arguments that both the Bible and the Qur'an are not relevant and proposes counter-arguments for both.**

Many people may say that because the Qur'an is written and memorised in Arabic that this makes it difficult for modern people to read and understand it unless it is translated into their own language. However, once it has been translated, the Qur'an is just that – a translation or interpretation. So although the words can be understood and as such be relevant to everyday living, such as caring for the poor (zakat), they have been changed from one language to another and as such a discrepancy or misuse of a common word can alter the relevancy. The Sunnah and the Hadith are accounts of Islamic law based on the examples of Muhammad's (pbuh) sayings and actions. However, they do not cover all areas of behaviour and can sometimes be seen as being contradictory, so they are only used in conjunction with the Qur'an. So while the Qur'an stands on its own, the other two sources of wisdom do not. Therefore it can be argued that the Qur'an is relevant in today's modern world because Allah is eternal and so is his revealed sacred word. Maybe the reason why people believe an 'old' book cannot be relevant in today's society is because they do not want to listen to the words, they would rather find a book which fits in with their own materialistic and selfish beliefs.

ⓔ **The student addresses the view that translations of the Qur'an can misinterpret Allah's unchanging word but it still does not make the Qur'an irrelevant. A pertinent observation concludes the response.**

Question 2
Student B

(a) 1 Ibrahim
2 Dawud

ⓔ **The student gives only two responses but both are correct and so they achieve 2 marks.**

(b) Tawhid means the oneness of Allah, which means that Allah is the one true God, there are no others.

(e) **Although this is a correct response it does not have enough development to achieve the full 3 marks. The first mark is given to the explanation of the term tawhid, 'oneness', and the second mark goes to the explanation 'one true God'. The apparent further development 'no others' is not saying anything new, it is just repeating the previous explanation and therefore is not credited. Further development is required for the third mark – the student could refer to Allah being indivisible or that oneness is central to Allah's nature, or use a quote from the Qur'an in support.**

(c) When Allah judges all the people on earth at the last judgement he will take into account not only the actions people have done but also the intentions behind the actions.

(e) **The student does not address the question, which asks about the importance of Allah's role as judge, they just describe what will happen at the last judgement. No marks can be awarded.**

(d) The Day of Judgement is important to all Muslims because they believe this is when they will be standing in front of Allah to answer for all the bad and good deeds they have committed during their lifetime. They believe they have made a choice about those actions because Allah has given them the gift of free will. Yet what is this free will worth? Muslims also believe in predestination, which means Allah has already decided what can happen and that nothing can change. Everything that happens is the will of Allah. So is it fair that Allah already knows what a person will decide to do and if he cannot change those actions, does this mean he is not all-powerful?

(e) **The student explains the importance of free will on judgement day and has queried the omnipotence of Allah because of the belief in predestination. They show analysis in the final sentence, but the response is underdeveloped and needs more details/explanation and analysis.**

(e) Muslims believe the Qur'an is the sacred word of Allah which gives guidance to all people in the past, present and future. Therefore to them it is not irrelevant. However, when the Qur'an was revealed in its entirety to Muhammad (pbuh) over 23 years, times were very different. People travelled around on camels, today people have cars and there is space travel. Medical advances mean heart transplants or even face transplants, people who have difficulty in having a baby can have one through IVF. So can it be said that the Qur'an is really relevant today – can it give guidance on modern-day problems? Muslims might argue that life is a test by Allah and so scientists are trying to replace Allah in coming up with all these new inventions, which are the act of shirk. So in a way, just because the Qur'an does not teach about 'iPhones' and 'Pokémon' games, it does not mean it is not relevant because these things are just modern materialistic values and wants, they are not teachings on what we need to find peace and harmony.

(e) **The student demonstrates some understanding of the significance of the statement and shows reasons for and against the idea of relevance.**

The fundamental teachings in the Qur'an are belief in Allah, prayer and good deeds. Surah 49 teaches that 'all believers are brothers together'. This is reflected in the ummah, which is the community of Muslims throughout the world. All these teachings were relevant in the past, and are in the present, and will be in the future. They are essential if we are to live in peace. Therefore the Qur'an is relevant in today's world because the teachings in it really matter.

(e) **The student indicates that the teachings which really matter for a good moral life are within the Qur'an and therefore this makes the Qur'an still relevant today. Although this is a valid discussion, it needs more depth and analysis of the points made, along with more references to sources of wisdom and authority.**

Mark scheme

2 (a) 1 mark is awarded for each correct response up to a maximum of three. Students **might** refer to:
- Adam
- Ibrahim (Abraham)
- Isma'il
- Musa (Moses)
- Dawud (David)
- Isa (Jesus)
- Muhammad.

Hints and tips

➤ Do not try to hedge your bets by giving lots of ideas. Only the first three responses will be marked and if they are wrong it will not matter if the following examples are correct.

(b) Marks are awarded for a statement plus further development of that statement with either examples of references to sources of wisdom and authority to support it. Students **might** refer to:
- the oneness of Allah, indivisible, central to the nature of Allah (reflects such things as omniscience, omnipotence)
- that tawhid reflects the monotheistic nature of Islam
- that tawhid shows that Allah only is worthy of worship – no other gods, one true God
- support of Surah 112, Shahadah

Hints and tips

➤ Try to give a clear, developed response which is not contradictory.

(c) Marks are awarded for a statement plus further development of that statement with either examples or references to sources of wisdom and authority to support it. Students **might** refer to:
- Allah is the only judge, judgement on obedience and submission to Allah's commands
- 'the judge' and 'the Just Decider' names of Allah
- life is a test; the result of judgement is eternal life in heaven or hell, so Allah has the most important decision to make for a person's future
- since Allah is just and merciful and he judges intentions as well as the actions, he will take this into account if a bad deed is done for a good reason

Hints and tips

➤ Read the question carefully. It is not asking what happens on the Day of Judgement but **why** the role of Allah as judge is important, so make sure you address the proper focus.

(d) This response is given **two** separate marks, both of which are determined by levels of response. Only **one** response is written but two different sets of **skills** are assessed by the examiner. The first mark is given for knowledge and understanding (AO1) and the second mark is awarded for the student's analysis and evaluation of the question (AO2). If the student simply writes down all they know about a specific topic, then the marks will be limited to the maximum marks for AO1. The examiner is assessing how the student uses their knowledge and understanding to relate to the specifics of the question/stimulus.

Knowledge and understanding AO1

Level	Description
1	A **weak** demonstration of knowledge and understanding which is given 1 mark. This might include simplistic ideas about the significance of free will to the Day of Judgement but they have not been explained in detail or supported with reference to sources of wisdom and authority.
2	A **limited** demonstration of knowledge and understanding which is given 2 marks. This might include some relevant ideas about the significance of free will to the Day of Judgement which have been supported with reference to sources of wisdom and authority.
3	An **adequate** but **underdeveloped** demonstration of knowledge and understanding which is given 3 marks. The student will have shown knowledge and understanding of different ideas about the significance of free will to the Day of Judgement which have been supported with reference to sources of wisdom and authority, but the explanations as to the significance will not be detailed enough to reach the next level.
4	A **good** demonstration of knowledge and understanding which is given 4 marks. The student will have given detailed, relevant information about the significance of free will to the Day of Judgement which is explained in detail. Such information **might** include: – humans have the gift of free will so they are not robots, angels do not – predestination (al-Qad'r) – Sunni and Shi'a interpretations, Ash'ari school of thought – reference to the Qur'an: Surah 2:34, Surah 13:11, Surah 13:39, Surah 16:49–50, Surah 76:30

Analysis and evaluation AO2

Level	Description
1	**Some** demonstration of analysis has been shown but it may be implicit or even unsuccessful = 1 mark. The student may have made an implicit comment on the reasons for the differences.
2	A **good** response – the student has shown successful analysis and evaluation of the issue = 2 marks. The student **might** have: – commented on how the belief in predestination causes problems – compared and commented on the different ways of explaining Allah's benevolence in regard to predestination – reasoned that free will/choice is important or not

Hints and tips

➤ Read the question carefully and support your answers with teachings or examples.

➤ Remember that the trigger/command word in this question is 'significance'.

➤ Include some analysis and evaluation.

➤ You are being asked to show a deep understanding of why Muslims hold their beliefs.

(e) This response is given **two** separate marks, both of which are determined by levels of response. Only **one** response is written but two different sets of **skills** are assessed by the examiner. The first mark is given for knowledge and understanding (AO1) and the second mark is awarded for the student's analysis and evaluation of the question (AO2). If the student simply writes down all they know about a specific topic, then the marks will be limited to the maximum marks for AO1. The examiner is assessing how the student uses their knowledge and understanding to relate to the specifics of the question/stimulus.

Knowledge and understanding AO1

Level	Description
1	A **limited/weak** demonstration of knowledge and understanding which is given 1 mark. This might include some general information and understanding about whether or not the Qur'an is still relevant today, the ideas may be listed or simplistic and/or lacking in detail.
2	An **adequate** but **underdeveloped** demonstration of knowledge and understanding which is given 2 marks. This might include some knowledge and understanding about whether or not the Qur'an is still relevant today.
3	A **good** demonstration of knowledge and understanding which is given 3 marks. The student will have given detailed, relevant information about whether or not the Qur'an is still relevant today, supported with quotes. Such information **might** include: – information about the composition of the Qur'an: sacred, revealed word of Allah, unchanging and unchangeable, last and most complete book of guidance, eternal and essence of Allah – information about today's modern world and how the Qur'an might or might not be relevant – support of: Surah 4:119, Surah 4:163, Surah 5:46, Surah 49:10, Surah 96

Analysis and evaluation AO2

Level	Description
1	A **weak** attempt to respond to the stimulus with a simplistic/descriptive account with no or very little attempt to offer a judgement on the significance of the issues raised (1–3 marks). The student may have suggested one view either for or against the stimulus but has not made a specific conclusion or judgement. In other words, the information is communicated in a basic way and there is no evidence of a **discussion** taking place.
2	A **limited** attempt – the student has made some attempt to respond to the stimulus and has shown different ideas about whether or not the Qur'an is still relevant today, but the judgement/conclusion is limited. **Or** one specific interpretation may have been discussed with an attempt at a conclusion (4–6 marks). In other words, there is a line of reasoning/**discussion** which has some relevance to the stimulus.
3	An **adequate** but **underdeveloped** attempt to discuss the stimulus showing different viewpoints about whether or not the Qur'an is still relevant today, which are supported with reference to sources of wisdom and authority, and the student has made some comments on them. In other words, there is a discussion of the stimulus supported with evidence of comparison and criticism along with a judgement/conclusion (7–9 marks). A line of reasoning has been presented and **discussed** which is mostly relevant.
4	A **good** attempt which has shown a structured discussion while comparing/contrasting and criticising/commenting on the different ideas about whether or not the Qur'an is still relevant today (10–12 marks). The student has offered a well-developed and sustained **discussion** which is coherent, relevant and well structured. The student **might** suggest: – a comparison between different sacred writing of another religion/other religions – analysis and judgement on today's values, which are materialistic and selfish compared with the values taught in the Qur'an – analysis that within the Qur'an there are references to what is happening in today's world, e.g. genetic modification

Hints and tips

➤ Read the stimulus carefully and identify its significance in your response, making sure you stick to the wording in the stimulus and do not divert into a concept that you would prefer to discuss.

➤ Refer to different beliefs and teachings and evaluate the importance of these differences.

➤ Remember that your response should be a **discussion** – try to present viewpoints for both sides as if you were having a conversation. Do not just list all the ideas for the stimulus in one paragraph and then all the ideas against in another paragraph.

➤ Remember that you do not have to express a personal view – if you want to, you can, but make sure you justify your point of view with evidence and argument.

➤ Support your statements/ideas/information with reference to sources of wisdom and authority, e.g. teachings from the Qur'an or Hadith.

➤ Do not fall into the trap of saying 'An atheist does not believe in Allah and therefore would not agree with the religious point of view'. You are not adding to the argument/discussion at all.

Islam: practices

Question 3
Student A

(a) 1 Salat
2 Khums
3 Tawalla

ⓔ **Three correct acts have been named – 3 marks awarded.**

(b) One of the major features of prayer for a Muslim is the preparation and the act of wudu. The ritual of washing the hands, mouth, nose, etc. is symbolic of washing themselves both physically and spiritually because the Qur'an teaches 'Allah loves those who turn to him and who care for cleanliness'.

ⓔ **The student responds by describing wudu as a feature of prayer (the first mark). The second mark is given to the idea of both physical and spiritual cleansing while the third mark is given to the supporting quote from the Qur'an.**

(c) The day of Ashura is a day of fasting for Sunni Muslims because it is when they remember two historical events, which are Nuh (Noah) leaving the Ark and when Musa (Moses) was saved from the Egyptians.

ⓔ **The student states that Ashura is a time when fasting occurs for Sunni Muslims to gain the first mark. The second mark is given to the idea that it remembers historical events and the third mark goes to the examples.**

(d) The word 'munkar' means evil or doing what is wrong. The word 'maruf' means good or striving to do good and as a result overcome evil. These actions are significant because they are part of the greater jihad, which is a Muslim's personal struggle in trying to become perfect or good enough to please Allah and, as a result, their soul being allowed to go to jannah on judgement day. The Qur'an teaches Muslims to 'do great jihad with the help of the Qur'an', meaning that Muslims need to fight against evil and do good by abiding by the teachings in the Qur'an rather than resorting to physical action. Munkar and maruf are also a collective act, not just a personal struggle, because the Qur'an teaches that 'you order what is right and forbid what is wrong and believe in Allah'. This is significant because it refers to the religious collective duty of the Muslim community, the ummah, to make sure that good deeds are done and bad deeds are stopped in order that a just and fair Muslim society can be established. This is significant because it will ensure that the ummah becomes the best representation of a good community for all societies. It could be argued that by extending the concepts of munkar and maruf to be included in a collective act rather than just a personal response, this has established Shari'ah law, which to non-Muslims can appear to be very harsh, such as public floggings and executions by stoning. A Shi'a Muslim might respond by saying that Amr-bil-Maroof and Nahi Anil are two of their articles of faith and as such the religious significance is very important.

(e) **The student demonstrates good knowledge and understanding of the concepts of munkar and maruf and links the response to the specifics of the question by indicating the religious significance of the concepts. They show analysis at the end of the response.**

(e) The Hajj is the fifth pillar of Islam and a compulsory obligation for all Muslims but the shahadah is the first of the five pillars, on which all the other pillars and the whole faith rests. Allah is the starting points of their beliefs. The idea of tawhid, the oneness and unity of Allah, is central to all Muslims and it was a significant part of the message of Prophet Muhammad (pbuh). The shahadah is their creed, it is the focus or cornerstone from which all their beliefs and practices come from: 'There is no god but Allah.' However, it can also be said that the other pillars are important too because why else would they have been specifically spelled out by Muhammad (pbuh) as an injunction for Muslims to follow? Muhammad (pbuh) is regarded as a perfect example and following his teachings are seen as essential because he was the seal of the prophets, the last messenger from Allah for all Muslims to follow.

(e) **The student opens the response by indicating that all the five pillars are important but has suggested that the shahadah is the cornerstone, the basis on which the religion stands.**

The five pillars are five duties which are equally essential in ensuring a Muslim lives a good life as decreed by Allah. So it might seem as if declaring tawhid, prayer, fasting, charity and the Hajj are all equally important. All the pillars encourage discipline and they all have the purpose of enhancing the spiritual development of a Muslim while at the same time encouraging the idea of equity. Yet there are arguments which could claim that the Hajj is the most important because within the purposes, rituals and practices all the other four pillars are contained.

(e) **The student focuses on the five pillars and their importance. They do not divert into explaining what happens in all of them but concentrate on the outcomes of practising the pillars. The final sentence returns to the statement.**

The Hajj is made in accordance with instructions from the Qur'an: 'Fulfil the Pilgrimage and the Visitation unto God.' It is for the main purpose of glorifying Allah, proclaiming his name and reminding the pilgrim of his constant presence. During the Hajj, pilgrims will fast, pray, perform various rituals such as throwing pebbles at the three stone pillars representing Iblis's failed attempts to tempt Isma'il, and performing charity by sacrificing an animal and distributing the meat to the poor. Although it could be argued that the fasting is not the same as the fasting prescribed in the pillars for Ramadan, and the charity donated is not the same as the prescribed zakah, 2.5% of annual income, the concept of fasting and charity to bring the pilgrims closer to an understanding of people worse off than themselves is present in the practices.

(e) **The student develops the idea of the Hajj being the most important pillar by suggesting that the rituals and practices of the Hajj incorporate all of the other pillars.**

The Hajj develops faith and trust in Allah. During the hardships pilgrims have the joy of being closer to Allah and also get the chance to find out what life may have been like in the times of Muhammad (pbuh). After they return home they may find their commitment to Islam is deeper. They will have experienced the unity and diversity of the ummah, unity from the wearing of the ihram, and diversity from coming into contact with Muslims from all corners of the world. Malcolm X returned from his Hajj with a changed perception of the interaction between black and white people. Before he went he was adamant that white people were devils, but then on the Hajj he met with white-skinned Muslims. The Hajj is a profound experience and as such could be deemed to be the most important pillar, but it is one of the pillars and not everyone can go on the Hajj, so perhaps while it can be said it is very important, it might be easier to suggest that all the pillars are as important as each other.

(e) **The student focuses on the spiritual development of the pilgrim and uses the example of Malcolm X. After a discussion which looks at all the five pillars, the student comes to a balanced conclusion.**

Question 3
Student B

(a) Three of the obligatory acts are pilgrimage, praying five times a day and tabarra.

(e) **The student gives only two correct acts because the response about prayer is specific to the Sunni Muslims and not the Shi'a. If the student had just stated prayer, this would have been a correct response. 2 marks awarded.**

(b) The rak'ahs, which involves putting the head on the floor, hands behind the ears, bowing, standing upright, sitting on the floor with hands on the knees, turning the head to the left and right.

(e) **Although this looks like a complete answer it is not because the descriptions of the different movements are basic and so count all as 1 mark. In order to gain full marks, the student would need to demonstrate understanding that the rak'ahs are movements in each prayer sequence and then show the religious significance of one specific movement.**

(c) Shi'a Muslims commemorate the martyrdom of Hussein, a grandson of the Prophet Muhammad (pbuh). Sunni Muslims remember events taught in the Qur'an.

(e) **The student achieves 2 marks for this response. The first mark is given to the idea of commemoration of the martyrdom, while the second mark is given to the development/ explanation of who Hussein was. Since the next statement is a completely new point about Sunni Muslims, it will not achieve a mark because the question was asking for one feature. In order to gain the further third point the student might have described how the Shi'a commemorate the martyrdom, such as with plays or processions.**

(d) Munkar means evil or vices which a Muslim should not have or do. These actions, such as lying, drinking alcohol or committing adultery, are haram and are therefore forbidden. Maruf/maroof/ma'ruf is seen as good actions such as salah, fasting, and going on the pilgrimage, the Hajj, which the Qur'an specifically teaches that all Muslims should do in Surah 2. These are all part of the great jihad, which is the inward struggle that every Muslim has to make sure they do not stray away from what Allah wants and as such they avoid evil actions and vices. This is so that on judgement day their souls will be judged to be good and they can go to jannah. This is of religious significance because the word 'Islam' means submission.

It is submission to the will of Allah, to follow his wishes, and to avoid munkar and do maruf because no one knows when the Angel Israfil will blow his trumpet sounding the arrival of judgement day.

ⓔ The student shows knowledge and understanding of the concepts of munkar and maruf and links the response to the specifics of the question, the religious significance. However, there is no attempt to analyse or evaluate.

(e) The Hajj is the fifth pillar of Islam and its purpose is to commemorate the name of Allah. It is all about glorifying Allah, not for the glory of the person undergoing the pilgrimage. Pilgrims are expected to set out hoping to seek Allah's forgiveness for things they have done wrong in the past and to try and atone for those sins. It is important for a Muslim's spiritual development and to emphasise that every Muslim must submit to the will of Allah. It is considered to be a compulsory obligation for all Muslims: the Qur'an teaches 'Proclaim among men the Pilgrimage'. However, it is recognised that sometimes someone cannot go because of financial or health problems. Because of the cost, if a Muslim does not live near or in Saudi Arabia, sometimes a community will collect enough money to send just one person. Although there are some scholars who believe that this is a wrong interpretation of the scriptures. Those who cannot, for genuine reasons, make the journey might declare that it is their niyyah (intention) and then the duty is considered to have been fulfilled. If a person dies before they have gone on the Hajj, even if they meant to go, it is considered to be sinful. So as such it would seem that the Hajj is the most important pillar.

ⓔ The student gives various reasons as to why the Hajj is considered to be an important part of the Islamic faith.

However, while the various teachings stress its importance, can we really say that the Hajj is the most important pillar? The Hadith teaches that in the last sermon of the Prophet Muhammad (pbuh), he encouraged followers to 'worship Allah and offer salah, observe sawm in the month of Ramadan and pay zakah'. The shahadah is the declaration of faith – it is the first pillar and the other pillars are founded on that. All the pillars support the faith. Prayer is essential in the glorification and submission to Allah. Sunni Muslims pray five times a day while Shi'a Muslims only three, but prayer is considered to be vital to their spiritual growth. The Qur'an teaches: 'So (give) glory to Allah, when ye reach eventide and when ye rise in the morning.' Muslims stand in the presence of Allah which is why the ritual washing (wudu) is performed before prayer and is so essential. Zakah is the purification of wealth. Muslims regard wealth as a gift from Allah for the benefit of all humanity and therefore it is an obligation for them to donate, but they can also give voluntary contributions called sadaqah. Sawm, fasting during Ramadan, is also important because it involves self-discipline while also reminding the worshipper of the plight of others. Jihad, which means 'striving' or trying to be the best possible person you can be, is also important because it is a requirement in the life of a Muslim to fulfil the will of Allah and gain his favour. So all of these are important because they were all set down in the Qur'an, which was Allah's special revelation to humankind to live their lives in the way he wants. Therefore it could be said that the Hajj is not the most important but is just as important as all the other ones.

ⓔ The student explains the purpose and importance of the other pillars and jihad and attempts to come to a conclusion. However, this is a response which is not discussed. One paragraph shows all the points of view the student wants to make about why the Hajj is the most important pillar and the second paragraph focuses on the other pillars.

Mark scheme

3 (a) 1 mark is awarded for each correct response up to a maximum of three. The student **might** suggest:
   – salat (prayer)
   – sawm (fasting)
   – zakah (purification of wealth – paying a charity tax to benefit the poor)
   – khums (annual taxation of one fifth of savings to be given to the religious leaders)
   – hajj (pilgrimage)
   – jihad (struggle)
   – amr-bil-maroof (commanding what is good)
   – nahi ani munkar (forbid what is evil)
   – tawalla (expressing love towards Allah)
   – tabarra (expressing dissociation from evil)

Hints and tips

Remember that this question is just asking for knowledge so be precise and do not waste time on lengthy explanations – you will not achieve any more marks.

(b) Marks are awarded for a statement plus further development of that statement with either examples or references to sources of wisdom and authority to support it. Students **might** refer to:
   – any of the features of prayer (salat) such as adhan, wudu, details of the actions within the rak'ahs, Jumu'ah prayer – with reference to the religious significance of such acts
   – use of prayer beads, hats/ veils, du'a (personal) prayers
   – recitation of the Qur'an in Arabic during prayers always including Surah Fatiah (Surah 1) with possible supporting quotes from the Qur'an: Surah 1, 4:103, 11:114, 62:10
   – the practice of the Prophet Muhammad
   – the practices of the Sunnis (five times a day) and the Shi'a (three times)

Hints and tips

Try to give a clear, developed response with three points which relate to each other, not three separate ideas.

(c) Marks are awarded for a statement plus further development of that statement with either examples or references to support it sources of wisdom and authority. Students **might** refer to:
   – the Sunni actions at this time including: fasting, historical events, Nuh and Moses
   – the Shi'a rituals: martyrdom of Hussein, plays, mourning rituals, processions in which males may self-flagellate in memory of the suffering and death of Hussein

Hints and tips

Try to give a clear, developed response with three points which relate to each other, not three separate ideas.

(d) This response is given **two** separate marks, both of which are determined by levels of response. Only **one** response is written but two different sets of **skills** are assessed by the examiner. The first mark is given for knowledge and understanding (AO1) and the second mark is awarded for the student's analysis and evaluation of the question (AO2). If the student simply writes down all they know about a specific topic, then the marks will be limited to the maximum marks for AO1. The examiner is assessing how the student uses their knowledge and understanding to relate to the specifics of the question/stimulus.

Knowledge and understanding AO1

Level	Description
1	A **weak** demonstration of knowledge and understanding which is given 1 mark. This might include simplistic ideas on the religious significance of the concepts of munkar and maruf but they have not been explained in detail or supported with reference to sacred writings.
2	A **limited** demonstration of knowledge and understanding which is given 2 marks. This might include some knowledge of the religious significance of the concepts of munkar and maruf which has been supported with reference to sacred writings.
3	An **adequate** but **underdeveloped** demonstration of knowledge and understanding which is given 3 marks. The student will have shown knowledge and understanding of the religious significance of the concepts of munkar and maruf which have been supported with reference to sacred writings, but the explanations will not be detailed enough to reach the next level.
4	A **good** demonstration of knowledge and understanding which is given 4 marks. The student will have given detailed, relevant information on the religious significance of the concepts of munkar and maruf which are explained in detail. Such information **might** include: – explanations of the terms munkar and maruf/ma'ruf/maroof – a link to the religious significance: submission to the will of Allah, instructed by the Qur'an, judgement day – articles of faith of the Shi'a – references to the Qur'an: Surah 3:110, 25:52

Analysis and evaluation AO2

Level	Description
1	**Some** demonstration of analysis has been shown but it may be implicit or even unsuccessful = 1 mark. The student may have made an implicit comment on the religious significance of the concepts.
2	A **good** response – the student has shown successful analysis and evaluation of the religious significance of the concepts = 2 marks. The student **might** have: – made explicit comparison of the fact that the Shi'a have the concepts within their articles of faith whereas the Sunni do not – linked the collective greater jihad to Shari'ah law – linked the concepts to predestination

Hints and tips

➤ Read the question carefully and address both aspects, munkar and maruf.

➤ Support your answers with teachings or examples.

➤ Include some analysis and evaluation.

➤ You are being asked to show a deep understanding of why Muslims hold their beliefs.

(e) This response is given **two** separate marks, both of which are determined by levels of response. Only **one** response is written but two different sets of **skills** are assessed by the examiner. The first mark is given for knowledge and understanding (AO1) and the second mark is awarded for the student's analysis and evaluation of the question (AO2). If the student simply writes down all they know about a specific topic, then the marks will be limited to the maximum marks for AO1. The examiner is assessing how the student uses their knowledge and understanding to relate to the specifics of the question/stimulus.

Knowledge and understanding AO1

Level	Description
1	A **limited/weak** demonstration of knowledge and understanding which is given 1 mark. This might include some general information and understanding about the Hajj and its importance as one of the pillars of Islam, the ideas may be listed or simplistic and/or lacking in detail.
2	An **adequate** but **underdeveloped** demonstration of knowledge and understanding which is given 2 marks. This might include some knowledge and understanding of the importance of the Hajj as one of the pillars of Islam.
3	A **good** demonstration of knowledge and understanding which is given 3 marks. The student will have given detailed, relevant information on the importance of the Hajj as one of the pillars of Islam, supported with quotes. Such information **might** include: – the Hajj: reference to the purpose of its rituals and spiritual development – information on the other pillars – shahadah, salah, zakah and sawm – with reference to their purpose and spiritual development – the concept of tawhid – examples of Muhammad, Malcolm X or any other valid examples – support from the Qur'an, Hadith

Analysis and evaluation AO2

Level	Description
1	A **weak** attempt to respond to the stimulus with a simplistic/descriptive account with no or very little attempt to offer a judgement on the significance of the issues raised (1–3 marks). The student may have suggested one view either for or against the stimulus but has not made a specific conclusion or judgement. In other words, the information is communicated in a basic way and there is no evidence of a **discussion** taking place.
2	A **limited** attempt – the student has made some attempt to respond to the stimulus and has shown different ideas on whether or not the Hajj is the most important pillar, but the judgement/conclusion is limited. **Or** one specific interpretation may have been discussed with an attempt at a conclusion (4–6 marks). In other words, there is a line of reasoning/**discussion** which has some relevance to the stimulus.
3	An **adequate** but **underdeveloped** attempt to discuss the stimulus showing different viewpoints on the importance of the Hajj, which are supported with reference to sources of wisdom and authority, and the student has made some comments on them. In other words, there is a discussion of the stimulus supported with evidence of comparison and criticism along with a judgement/conclusion (7–9 marks). A line of reasoning has been presented and **discussed** which is mostly relevant.
4	A **good** attempt which has shown a structured discussion while comparing/contrasting and criticising/commenting on the different ideas of whether the Hajj could be considered to be the most important pillar (10–12 marks). The student has offered a well-developed and sustained **discussion** which is coherent, relevant and well structured. The student **might** suggest: – after the comparisons and contrasts, that all pillars are equally important or that one of them (not just the Hajj) is more important – that the articles of faith or the Usul al-Din are more important – that it is blasphemous/shirk to consider this since by trying to determine which is more important than the other, it is a way of trying to be Allah

Hints and tips

➤ Read the stimulus carefully and identify its significance in your response, making sure you stick to the wording in the stimulus and do not divert into a concept that you would prefer to discuss.

➤ Refer to different beliefs and teachings and evaluate the importance of these differences.

➤ Remember that your response should be a **discussion** – try to present viewpoints for both sides as if you were having a conversation. Do not just list all the ideas for the stimulus in one paragraph and then all the ideas against in another paragraph.

➤ Remember that you do not have to express a personal view – if you want to, you can, but make sure you justify your point of view with evidence and argument.

➤ Support your statements/ideas/information with reference to sources of wisdom and authority, e.g. teachings from the Qur'an or Hadith.

➤ Do not fall into the trap of saying 'An atheist does not believe in Allah and therefore would not agree with the religious point of view'. You are not adding to the argument/discussion at all.

Question 4

Student A

(a) Tawalla is about showing love towards good, meaning that in order to show their love for Allah, a Muslim will work hard to do good deeds, such as being supporters of truth and justice with the purpose of being allowed to go to heaven (jannah) on judgement day.

(e) **Although this response has to be read back to front there are three points which can be credited. The purpose of 'being able to go to jannah' gain the first mark, the meaning of tawalla gains the second mark and the further development of what it entails gains the third mark.**

(b) Zakah is a duty for all Muslims because it is the third pillar of Islam and, as such, it is regarded as a type of worship because it is not just a one-off act but is an annual requirement to purify one's wealth in acknowledgement that wealth is a gift from Allah.

(e) **The first mark is given for the word 'duty'. The development of duty, 'the third pillar', receives the second mark and the third mark is given for the further development of qualifying the term 'worship' which is 'annual requirement'.**

(c) The difference between du'a and salah prayers is that du'a are private prayers when a Muslim asks for individual guidance from Allah for a particular personal problem, whereas salah prayers refers to the obligatory five-times-a-day prayers which are the second pillar of Islam.

(e) **The first mark is given for du'a being personal private prayers, the second mark is for the development which explains that the prayer is asking for guidance, and the third mark goes to the description of salah prayer.**

(d) Ramadan is important because it is the ninth month of the Islamic year which celebrates the time when the Qur'an was revealed, as told in Surah 2. It is when all Muslims fast (sawm), they go without food, drink and sex from dawn to dusk for the whole of the month of Ramadan in order to focus on personal reflection and prayer. They will also avoid evil acts such as swearing. Fasting is the fourth pillar of Islam for the Sunnis and one of the obligatory ten acts which Shi'a Muslims follow. Therefore it is a duty for all Muslims to do unless they are exempt, such as pregnant women and young children, showing how important Ramadan is. In countries where many people do not fast, Muslims might see it as a test of faith for which they might gain extra reward for their increased efforts. It is also important because Allah commanded sawm to take place and because Muhammad (pbuh) set the example by doing so himself. Its importance is shown through an attitude of repentance. Muslims will ask Allah to forgive their sins while at the same time thanking Allah for all the gifts he sends. This shows that even though sins are done, Allah is still compassionate and good. Fasting during Ramadan is an act of worship, one which demonstrates a Muslim's complete submission to Allah. It shows their complete obedience (muttaqi). Fasting also reminds them of people who do not have the luxury of eating every day and so it raises their awareness of the people's misfortune and this feeling of empathy will encourage Muslims to do something about their plight. This is important because it underlines the significance of the third pillar, which is zakah.

(e) **The student demonstrates good knowledge and understanding of the importance of Ramadan. They avoid the trap of simply stating or describing what happens during Ramadan and focus on the key word 'importance'. They show analysis in the comments on the importance.**

(e) Prayer, salah, is one of the five pillars of Islam. During prayer the shahadah, the first pillar and the statement of belief in Allah, is said, so some might argue that prayer is the most important. It was made an obligation when Muhammad (pbuh) ascended into heaven. But then again the Qur'an is always teaching 'do good to others'. Doing good deeds is not specifically stated as one of the pillars, but zakah is, which is the third pillar, which refers to the annual tax donation of 2.5% be given to the poor. This is one specific good deed; of course, there are many others. The Qur'an teaches that all Muslims should 'establish prayer and give zakah' because Allah sees all. Yet it should be mentioned that sadaqah, although voluntary is also considered to be a duty although it is not one of the five pillars. Therefore it seems as though it is wrong to try and establish which of the two actions is the more important. If a Muslim is a small child or is ill, they may not be able to do many good deeds but can concentrate on prayer, whereas a healthy adult can do both. Therefore, it would be wrong to say that the healthy adult is better than the small child.

(e) **The student opens the discussion by demonstrating the importance of both prayer and doing good deeds and so shows an understanding of the implications of the statement.**

Within the Hadith there are teachings which could be said to point to different answers. When the Prophet Muhammad (pbuh) was asked about the most virtuous deed, he is said to have said 'prayer' three times but on the fourth 'jihad'. But the Hadith also contains the account of Allah telling people on the day of resurrection that they had not given Allah food, drink or visited him when he was sick because if they had bothered to visit someone who was ill they 'would have found Me (Allah) by him'. This suggests that doing good deeds is important. Although this might seem confusing, both teachings could be said to have the same theme. 'Jihad' refers to the inner struggle a Muslim has against sin. So there could be days on which a believer could be tempted away from doing good deeds but if they resort to prayer Allah would help them. So doing good deeds might need the input of prayer since the Qur'an teaches that 'prayer keeps one from the great sins and evil deeds' and as a consequence both are as important as each other.

(e) **The student shows understanding of the apparent contradictory teachings within the Hadith while linking them to the statement.**

All Muslims are aware that on the Day of Judgement their deeds, both bad and good, which have been recorded by the two angels (Surah 45) will have to be accounted for. They know that if they are judged favourably, 'whoever does righteous', they will be rewarded in paradise. Allah judges both the intention (niyyah) and the deed. Doing good deeds is not just about doing charitable works but it is also about being righteous, loving good (tawalla) and avoiding evil – not just actions but also thoughts. It is difficult to be good all the time and therefore prayer will petition Allah for his guidance. The Qur'an teaches that 'they who have believed and done righteous deeds – those are the best'. With belief comes prayer, with prayer comes Allah's guidance, with Allah's guidance comes good deeds. So everything is connected and there is no ranking of importance.

(e) **The student discusses the purpose of doing good deeds and concludes that all the duties promoted by Islam are as important as each other.**

Question 4
Student B

(a) The purpose of tawalla is to please Allah because Allah is pleased with those of 'his servants who believe and do righteous deeds'.

(e) **The first mark is given for the purpose 'to please Allah' and the second is given for the supporting quote from the Qur'an. Further development is needed in order to gain the third mark, such as examples of actions or an explanation as to why they want to please Allah.**

(b) Zakah is the giving of 2.5% of one's wealth to the poor every year. Its purpose is about acknowledging that wealth comes from Allah, promoting self-discipline and freeing oneself from the love of money.

(e) **The first mark is given for the description of the action of zakah. However, the next sentence is a new point in that it is describing the purpose of zakah and not the meaning, so will not be credited.**

(c) Du'a prayers are supplication prayers and salah prayers refer to the obligatory five prayers a day.

(e) **The first mark is given for the description of du'a prayer and the second mark is given for the description of salah prayer – the difference is implicit. However, either du'a or salah prayers need further development in order to achieve the third mark.**

(d) Ramadan is the name for the ninth month in the Islamic calendar and it is when all Muslims have to fast during daylight hours because it was commanded by Allah in the Qur'an so that they will 'become mindful of God'. During Ramadan there are three types of worship: sawm, zakah (often paid during Ramadan) and salah. All these three are important because they are not only three of the five pillars of Islam but they are a demonstration of obedience to Allah's guidance on how to show love for good (tawalla). They will study the Qur'an during Ramadan. This is important because the Night of Power, when the Qur'an was first revealed to Muhammad (pbuh) is celebrated on the 27th of the month. At the end of Ramadan is the Eid-ul-Fitr festival.

(e) **The student shows some knowledge and understanding of why Ramadan is important, but the response needs more depth by including sources of wisdom to support it and analysis which demonstrates the full understanding of the importance of Ramadan.**

(e) The Hadith teaches that on the Day of Judgement the first matter that the Muslim will be brought to account for is prayer. 'If it is sound, then the rest of his deeds will be sound.' This would suggest that prayer is more important than good deeds, especially since for Sunni Muslims prayer is a duty five times a day, instituted when Muhammad (pbuh) ascended into heaven to speak to Allah. Shi'a Muslims pray three times a day but it is still a duty. However, good deeds are also important to Muslims because they will also be judged on them on the Day of Judgement.

(e) **The student attempts to show that both prayer and doing good deeds are important, but although the first part of the response on prayer is clear, it looks as if the 'doing good deeds' has been put in simply to try to achieve balance. It needs to be developed in depth to give an argument as to why good deeds may or may not be as important as prayer.**

Salah is done at prescribed times with the purpose of unifying Muslims across the world. It keeps them humble and reminds them of their duties to Allah. However, because of the differences of interpretation between Sunnis and Shi'as regarding the prescribed number of times prayer should be held, then perhaps it could be argued that prayer is not as important as good deeds. Allah created everyone and this world is his creation, therefore good deeds is not just about helping the poor but making sure that peace and justice are established throughout the world. The Qur'an teaches 'do good to others'. In doing these things a Muslim is worshipping Allah, perhaps not by prayer, but through the actions they carry out. So it could be argued that prayer and doing good deeds are both worship and duties to Allah and are therefore just as important as each other.

e **The student has a valid argument but it is underdeveloped. They need to provide more support from sources of wisdom and more ideas which could be compared and analysed.**

Mark scheme

4 (a) Marks are awarded for a statement plus further development of that statement with either examples or references to sources of wisdom and authority to support it. Students **might** refer to:
   – the meaning of tawalla – expressing love towards good which involves loving the friends of Allah, righteous people, supporters of truth and justice
   – possible contrast with tabarra – distancing yourself from evil
   – purpose: pleasing Allah, going to jannah, fulfilling the teachings in the Qur'an, duty/ obligation, love for Allah is the foundation of Islamic belief
   – Qur'an quotes: Surah 2:165, Surah 42:23

Hints and tips

Remember this question is just asking for knowledge, so be precise and do not waste time on lengthy explanations – you will not achieve any more marks.

   (b) Marks are awarded for a statement plus further development of that statement with either examples or references to sources of wisdom and authority to support it. Students **might** refer to:
   – the third pillar of Islam, duty/obligation, worship of Allah, annual requirement
   – 2.5% of wealth to the poor, purification, acknowledgement that wealth is a gift from Allah
   – contrast with sadaqah
   – the Qur'an: Surah 2:215, Surah 17:26–29, Surah 21:73

Hints and tips

Try to give a clear, developed response with three points which relate to each other, not three separate ideas.

(c) Marks are awarded for a statement plus further development of that statement with either examples or references to sources of wisdom and authority to support it. Students **might** refer to:
  - a description of both types of prayer, suggesting the difference
  - du'a – personal/private/supplication seeking Allah's guidance, best times, how to proceed/correct etiquette, Surah 40:60
  - salah – second pillar, five times a day obligatory, Surah 2:3–5, 43, 45

Hints and tips

Try to give a clear, developed response with three points which relate to each other, not three separate ideas.

(d) This response is given **two** separate marks, both of which are determined by levels of response. Only **one** response is written but two different sets of **skills** are assessed by the examiner. The first mark is given for knowledge and understanding (AO1) and the second mark is awarded for the student's analysis and evaluation of the question (AO2). If the student simply writes down all they know about a specific topic, then the marks will be limited to the maximum marks for AO1. The examiner is assessing how the student uses their knowledge and understanding to relate to the specifics of the question/stimulus.

Knowledge and understanding AO1

Level	Description
1	A **weak** demonstration of knowledge and understanding which is given 1 mark. This might include simplistic ideas on the religious importance of Ramadan but they have not been explained in detail or supported with reference to sacred writings.
2	A **limited** demonstration of knowledge and understanding which is given 2 marks. This might include some relevant ideas on the religious importance of Ramadan which have been supported with reference to sacred writings.
3	An **adequate** but **underdeveloped** demonstration of knowledge and understanding which is given 3 marks. The student will have shown knowledge and understanding of the religious importance of Ramadan, supported with reference to sacred writings, but the explanations will not be detailed enough to reach the next level.
4	A **good** demonstration of knowledge and understanding which is given 4 marks. The student will have given detailed, relevant information on the religious importance of Ramadan which is explained in detail. Such information **might** include: – an explanation that Ramadan is the name of the ninth month, its connection to sawm, the fourth pillar of Islam (Sunni)/one of the ten acts (Shi'a), three types of worship: sawm, zakah, salah – importance: attitude of repentance, commanded by Allah, example of Muhammad, submission/complete obedience (muttaqi), taqwa (developing awareness of God's presence), Night of Power – references to the Qur'an: Surah 2:183, Surah 2:185, Surah 97:3, Hadith Bikhara Vol. 1. Book 2:34

Analysis and evaluation AO2

Level	Description
1	**Some** demonstration of analysis has been shown but it may be implicit or even unsuccessful = 1 mark. The student may have made an implicit comment on the religious significance of the concepts.
2	A **good** response – the student has shown successful analysis and evaluation of the religious significance of the concepts = 2 marks. The student **might**: – compare the importance of Ramadan to the other obligations – analyse and comment on the difficulties – analyse and comment on how sawm during Ramadan is also a type of worship.

Hints and tips

➤ Read the question carefully and address all aspects. This question is asking you to explain the importance of Ramadan, it is **not** asking you to describe what happens.

➤ Support your answers with teachings or examples.

➤ Include some analysis and evaluation.

➤ You are being asked to show a deep understanding of why Muslims hold their beliefs.

(e) This response is given **two** separate marks, both of which are determined by levels of response. Only **one** response is written but two different sets of **skills** are assessed by the examiner. The first mark is given for knowledge and understanding (AO1) and the second mark is awarded for the student's analysis and evaluation of the question (AO2). If the student simply writes down all they know about a specific topic, then the marks will be limited to the maximum marks for AO1. The examiner is assessing how the student uses their knowledge and understanding to relate to the specifics of the question/stimulus.

Knowledge and understanding AO1

Level	Description
1	A **limited/weak** demonstration of knowledge and understanding which is given 1 mark. This might include some general information and understanding about which is more important, prayers or good deeds, the ideas may be listed or simplistic and/or lacking in detail.
2	An **adequate** but **underdeveloped** demonstration of knowledge and understanding which is given 2 marks. This might include some knowledge and understanding about which is more important, prayers or good deeds.
3	A **good** demonstration of knowledge and understanding which is given 3 marks. The student will have given detailed, relevant information about which is more important, prayers or good deeds, supported with quotes. Such information **might** include: – the importance and purpose of prayer contrasted with the importance and purpose of doing good deeds – the Day of Judgement – the five pillars – sources of authority: Qur'an: Surah 2:110, Surah 2:195, Surah 16:97, Surah 29:45, Surah 45:29, Hadith Sahih, Hadith Sahih Muslim 2569, Hadith Hasan

Analysis and evaluation AO2

Level	Description
1	A **weak** attempt to respond to the stimulus with a simplistic/descriptive account with no or very little attempt to offer a judgement on the significance of the issues raised (1–3 marks). The student may have suggested one view either for or against the stimulus but has not made a specific conclusion or judgement. In other words, the information is communicated in a basic way and there is no evidence of a **discussion** taking place.
2	A **limited** attempt – the student has made some attempt to respond to the stimulus and has shown different ideas about which is more important, prayers or good deeds, but the judgement/conclusion is limited. **Or** one specific interpretation may have been discussed with an attempt at a conclusion (4–6 marks). In other words, there is a line of reasoning/**discussion** which has some relevance to the stimulus.
3	An **adequate** but **underdeveloped** attempt to discuss the stimulus showing different viewpoints about which is more important, prayers or good deeds, which are supported with reference to sources of wisdom and authority, and the student has made some comments on them. In other words, there is a discussion of the stimulus supported with evidence of comparison and criticism along with a judgement/conclusion (7–9 marks). A line of reasoning has been presented and **discussed** which is mostly relevant.
4	A **good** attempt which has shown a structured **discussion** while comparing/contrasting and criticising/commenting on the different ideas about which is more important, prayers or good deeds (10–12 marks). The student has offered a well-developed and sustained **discussion** which is coherent, relevant and well structured. The student **might** suggest: – after the comparisons and contrasts, that both prayer and doing good deeds are important, or the student may argue for the importance of one or the other – that submission to the will of Allah involves both, and that both are rewarded according to the intention behind them; it may be that both are worthless if carried out with the wrong intention – that prayer might lead to a frame of mind in which a Muslim then carries out good deeds, thereby connecting the two

Hints and tips

➤ Read the stimulus carefully and identify its significance in your response, making sure you stick to the wording in the stimulus and do not divert into a concept that you would prefer to discuss.

➤ Refer to different beliefs and teachings and evaluate the importance of these differences.

➤ Remember that your response should be a **discussion** – try to present viewpoints for both sides as if you were having a conversation. Do not just list all the ideas for the stimulus in one paragraph and then all the ideas against in another paragraph.

➤ Remember that you do not have to express a personal view – if you want to, you can, but make sure you justify your point of view with evidence and argument.

➤ Support your statements/ideas/information with reference to sources of wisdom and authority, e.g. teachings from the Qur'an or Hadith.

➤ Do not fall into the trap of saying 'An atheist does not believe in Allah and therefore would not agree with the religious point of view'. You are not adding to the argument/discussion at all.

Paper 2: Religion, philosophy and ethics in the modern world

Student responses

This section shows sample answers from two students. One set (Student A) is stronger, the other (Student B) is weaker. The answers are followed by examiner-style commentary (shown by the icon ⓔ) that indicates where credit is due. In the weaker answers, it also points out areas for improvement, specific problems and common errors.

Christianity: relationships and families

Question 1

Student A

(a)   1   Sacrament – they want their marriage blessed by God

      2   'Go forth and multiply' – they want to have children to obey God

      3   Mutual comfort – Eve was created to be Adam's companion

ⓔ **All three of these reasons are valid and so gain 1 mark each – total 3 marks. They are specific Christian reasons why a couple want to get married.**

(b)   Some Christians believe that Jesus accepted everyone no matter who they were. For example, the parable of the good samaritan shows Christians that no matter who you are, love and kindness is the ultimate aim of Christian behaviour. Therefore, they would practise agape and believe that same-sex marriages should happen, especially as it is now legal (13 March 2014). In August 2017, the Episcopal Church of Scotland became the first Anglican denomination to conduct a same-sex marriage. This was a result of the Scottish Church voting to allow same-sex marriages, in order to express the view that everyone is made equally in the eyes of God. 'There is neither Jew nor Greek, slave nor free…' possibly including the idea of heterosexual nor homosexual.

However, other Christians – for example Roman Catholics – are totally against same-sex marriages because they believe that marriage is between a man and woman because God created Adam and Eve to be one flesh, and that it goes against the sanctity and sacrament of marriage. Also the Old Testament teaches, 'do not lie with a man as one lies with a woman; that is detestable'. St Paul in his letter to the Corinthians taught that homosexuals will not go to heaven. So these Christians would have the attitude that although it is wrong to be homophobic, a Christian would say they can live together but they should be celibate and thus a marriage is not needed.

ⓔ **The student responds to the trigger word 'attitudes' and shows two different responses/ attitudes to same-sex marriages. The student selects appropriate material to support these different views and explains their views with reference to biblical teachings and relevant terminology (agape/sacrament/sanctity).**

(c) Christians would look back on the vows made during their wedding because they are important promises. They would remember that they promised God and their family and friends that they would stay together 'for better or worse' until death ended their marriage. So therefore it would be wrong to break these vows as the ceremony is seen as a sacrament, which is an inner sign of an outward grace. Only God can break up their marriage because the priest states during the ceremony that what God joins together no man should put asunder (separate). Therefore they would ask God to help them to work through their problems and help them to return to the love they felt for each other on their wedding day. They would know that God will help them with whatever difficulties they are facing because St Paul in his letter to the Corinthians said: 'God will not let you be tempted beyond what you can bear.' Therefore it is a matter of faith and trust in God that they will work at their marriage.

They might reflect on the idea that the minister outlined the teaching that marriage is given by God so that a husband and wife may comfort and help each other. So instead of indulging in petty quarrels or giving up on the marriage because it seems too difficult, they would try and support each other through the crisis because this is what they promised God they would do at their wedding. Thus, by reflecting on the important events and teachings of the ceremony, it would help them work through their difficulties.

(e) **The student makes a good attempt by responding to the trigger word 'why', giving ideas of what happens in a wedding ceremony (vows, sacrament and teaching) and explaining why these would help them in times of difficulty. The student also emphasises that God will help those who believe in him. They reach a conclusion that these ideas are important.**

(d) Some Christians, especially Catholics, are against divorce because they see marriage as a sacrament. It is done in the eyes of God and therefore it would be wrong to break the sanctity of marriage and also break the vows made before God. In the ceremony, the couple promise to stay together, whatever happens, until one of them dies, which is when God's will breaks the marriage. Jesus was against divorce, he taught that what God joins together no man should separate. Yet there is a passage in the New Testament in which he refers to the laws of Moses in the Old Testament which say that a man can divorce his wife if she commits adultery (breaking the seventh commandment). Some Christians have interpreted this to mean that Jesus would allow divorce, but others say it has been taken out of context and he indicated that it was only because men were not happy with the idea of no divorce that the laws of Moses had included that provision. Jesus went on to say that if a divorced man remarried and had sex with his new wife, he was in fact committing adultery against the wife he had divorced. It could be suggested that Jesus was against divorce for silly reasons, but if it was serious enough, like breaking one of the Ten Commandments, then perhaps it could be allowed. This would be relevant even today because Christian couples who are thinking about divorce are encouraged to go to counselling, like RELATE, and this might help them get back on track.

(e) **The student demonstrates good knowledge and understanding about why some Christians are against divorce. Support is given to the explanations with reference to church and biblical teachings. The student draws a conclusion as to why there appear to be different interpretations, and application to today's society is made.**

A non-Christian would say that there are too many contradictions within the teachings of the Christian faith and so divorce can happen, especially if there is abuse within the marriage. The Anglican Church would agree because they will allow people to become divorced as the 'lesser of two evils'. Yet the Catholic Church will not allow divorce but will allow annulment under specific reasons, such as lack of understanding of the nature of marriage or where one of the couple is unable to fulfil the conditions of marriage. An annulment states that the marriage never actually happened and so the concept of divorce is not being addressed, although the couple would still have to go to the legal courts to get a secular divorce before their annulment became fact, which could seem hypocritical. But Pope Francis, leader of the Catholic Church, who is seen as God's authority on earth, says divorce is always wrong – marriage is an indissoluble sacrament but annulment is not the same as divorce – either the marriage existed and thus divorce cannot happen or the marriage did not exist and therefore divorce is not required. The Quakers (Society of Friends) are saddened if a marriage fails because they believe it is also a failure of the meeting (congregation), but they will allow it. So a Christian would respond to the argument that the teachings between the different churches/denominations are contradictory by stating that the churches recognise that sometimes marriages do fail and thus they allow some form of ending.

(e) **The student responds to a secular consideration of the contradictions within the teachings of the Catholic and Anglican churches with Christian viewpoints.**

When Jesus was on earth he taught love and forgiveness and many Christians interpret this to mean that he would not like a couple to be unhappy, especially if it was an abusive relationship, and therefore it would be the loving thing to do to allow a divorce to take place. It should also be considered that in today's world, views on divorce have totally changed and with many couples not actually becoming legally married, divorce is no longer seen as the sin it was. However, if a truly committed Christian couple believed in the sanctity of their marriage, they would try to put their marriage right or perhaps just live apart and not go through a legal process. Divorce can be considered wrong if it is done for frivolous reasons or the couple did not consider the responsibilities of marriage seriously enough, yet if there are difficulties within a marriage which cannot be overcome, like one of the partners becoming addicted to drugs, surely a loving God would understand, especially if children were at risk. After all, in the Lord's Prayer, Christians ask God for forgiveness. Surely this extends to forgiveness for a failed marriage that ends in divorce.

(e) **In the conclusion the student discusses the concept of Christian love in respect of the stimulus and comes to a balanced conclusion.**

Question 1
Student B

(a) Christians want to get married to show their love for each other, to make their love known in front of friends, family and God, and to have children.

(e) **The first two of these reasons are interlinked and thus only 1 mark is awarded. The final reason, although not wrong, is too generic – in other words, it could relate to any couple, not specifically a Christian couple. If the student had supported the final part with reference to the Bible quote 'go forth and multiply', then it would be credited.**

(b) Christians do not believe in same-sex marriages because Adam and Eve were created by God as man and woman, not two people of the same gender. Two people of the same sex cannot have children and for Christians this is one of the purposes of marriage. Also any children adopted by the couple would be teased at school and this would not be fair. The Bible is against homosexuality and says they should be killed.

(e) **The student does not respond to the trigger word 'attitudes' and gives a one-sided view only. This means that full marks cannot be achieved. However, the student attempts to explain why there is opposition to same-sex marriages but the ideas are not developed fully with supporting quotes, and the school issue, although not incorrect, is too general and therefore would not achieve any marks.**

(c) If Christians were having problems with their marriage by having rows and facing the temptation of adultery, they might think back to their wedding day when they were really happy to announce their love to all their guests and to promise God they would be together for ever. They promised God they would be faithful to each other, 'forsaking all others'. Therefore they would not want to disappoint God by breaking their promises to him. They would remember that the vicar told them at their wedding that marriage is a responsibility and should not be taken without serious thought so they would try to work through their problems. Therefore, looking back on their wedding would be a great help.

(e) **The student responds in a narrative way but does address the trigger word 'why', although not in great detail. They reach a conclusion about the statement but it needs to be developed in more detail, with more discussion and more support through the use of specific biblical/Christian quotes.**

(d) Most of the Christian churches believe that divorce is wrong because the Bible teaches that God said 'he hates divorce'. Also Jesus taught that once a man and a woman were joined together in marriage, no one should break up that marriage. Catholics are against divorce, Pope Francis says that marriage is a sacrament carried out in the eyes of God and should never be broken. Catholics follow the teachings of the Pope because he is head of the church and is God's representative on earth and is therefore telling the people what God wants the people to do. St Paul taught that a man should not divorce his wife. Therefore, if a Christian believes that the Bible is the true word of God, they will not get a divorce.

(e) **The student just lists various Christian ideas and teachings about divorce being wrong. They attempt to comment on these ideas but there is no real discussion.**

However, other Christians are more liberal. Although they believe that marriage should be for ever, they do recognise that in some circumstances divorce should take place as a last resort when all ways to make the marriage work have broken down. This is because Jesus showed love and compassion to everyone when he was on earth. His message was of love and it would be wrong to make an unhappy couple stay together for the rest of their lives instead of allowing them to divorce. In the past it was very difficult to get a divorce – you had to be rich to do so – and therefore it did not happen very often. However, in today's times, divorce is not considered to be wrong by people who are not religious, it is considered to be the best way out of a marriage in which someone is being badly hurt, either mentally or physically.

(e) **The student attempts to discuss why some Christians will allow divorce to take place and to analyse why divorce is more common today. It lacks direct knowledge of sources of wisdom and authority. There is also a lack of direct knowledge of denominational points of view.**

Marriage is a gift from God and therefore should not be broken. Vows are said at the wedding in which the couple promise God they will stay together for ever. Therefore, if a couple were true Christians, they would not consider getting a divorce.

(e) **The student draws a conclusion but it is not balanced. In order to have a developed discussion the student could have addressed the contradictions within the teachings of Jesus, or they might have discussed and evaluated why there are different attitudes within the various churches.**

Mark scheme

1 (a) 1 mark is awarded for each correct response up to a maximum of three. The student **might** refer to:
- the purposes of marriage: procreation (extend family life), avoid casual sex, companionship
- St Paul's teaching in 1 Corinthians 7:9, 'for it is better to marry than to burn with passion'
- love and commitment (lifelong commitment)
- sacrament of marriage ordained by God, God's blessing, obedience to God

Social or generic reasons would need to be shown to fit in with Christian teachings.

Hints and tips

Your response must include three specific points. Do not spend too long on this question because it is only worth 3 marks, but remember to include Christian ideas and not generic ones, i.e. ideas which would be relevant to any religion or non-religious person.

(b) This response is marked by levels of response according to the student's knowledge and understanding of the question (AO1)

Knowledge and understanding AO1

Level	Description
1	A **weak** response with limited understanding (1–2 marks): the student may have given only one attitude/idea about how Christians respond to same-sex marriage with an attempt to explain but in a simplistic way. **Or** the student may have listed two different attitudes. **Or** the student may have given some misinformation or the response may be too generic (not specific to Christianity).
2	An **adequate** but **underdeveloped** response (3–4 marks): the student may have shown a selection of different ideas on Christian responses to same-sex marriages and explained and supported them in a brief or descriptive way rather than showing the full depth of their understanding.
3	A **good** response (5–6 marks): the student may have given various denominational responses to the concept of same-sex marriages which are supported and explained with reference to biblical and church teachings. The student wll have shown a sound understanding of the issues surrounding same-sex marriages. The student **may** refer to: – biblical teachings on homosexuality such as Leviticus 20:13, Romans 1:27 or 1 Corinthians 6:9–10 – Christian teachings on agape – Adam and Eve – one flesh – marriage is a sacrament – the fact that same-sex marriages are now legal in the UK (13 March 2014) but church teachings on same-sex weddings vary: the Church of England will offer blessings but will not conduct a wedding service, the Roman Catholic Church prohibits same-sex weddings, and some churches in America, such as the United Church of Christ, will perform the service. Reference may be made to the first same-sex couple to get married in the Scottish Episcopal in August 2017. – the case of Hazelmary and Peter Bull who refused to let civil partners Steven Preddy and Martyn Hall stay in a double room at Chymorvah House in Marazion in Cornwall in 2008

Hints and tips

➤ Read the question carefully and note the trigger/command words 'describe' and 'attitudes'.

➤ Responses to this question should be purely knowledge based–all 6 marks are awarded for AO1.

(c) This response is given **two** separate marks, both of which are determined by levels of response. Only **one** response is written but two different sets of **skills** are assessed by the examiner. The first mark is given for knowledge and understanding (AO1) and the second mark is awarded for the student's analysis and evaluation of the question (AO2). If the student simply writes down all they know about a specific topic, then the marks will be limited to the maximum marks for AO1. The examiner is assessing how the student uses their knowledge and understanding to relate to the specifics of the question/stimulus.

Knowledge and understanding AO1

Level	Description
1	**Some** demonstration of knowledge and understanding which is given 1 mark. This might include a little information and understanding on the importance of the vows or reference to teachings within the ceremony.
2	**Good** demonstration of knowledge and understanding which is given 2 marks. This might include different ideas on the importance of various aspects of the wedding ceremony, such as: – relating the vows to specific marital difficulties – reflecting on fidelity, 'forsaking all others' – God's presence/blessing at the wedding and His presence during times of difficulties – relating the ceremony to the purposes of marriage – reflecting on the belief that the wedding is a sacrament – supporting ideas with specific biblical or denominational teachings

Analysis and evaluation AO2

Level	Description
1	A **weak** response – the student may have only given a single viewpoint or the response is simply a description of different parts of the wedding ceremony rather than offering comments which demonstrate a judgement (1 mark).
2	A **limited** response – the student has perhaps given different descriptions of what happens during a wedding ceremony and how these relate to marriage difficulties but these have not been developed by any comment and as such the analysis is limited. **Or** the student may have attempted to comment and show judgement on one specific view (2 marks). This might include reference to various parts of the wedding service along with either biblical or church teachings. **Or** one particular part of the wedding service may have been discussed in detail. There may be some inaccuracies or misunderstanding of the stances taken.
3	An **adequate** but **underdeveloped** response – the student has given different ideas on how looking back to the wedding service would help and has attempted to show some judgement/ analysis on them, but the ideas and comments are not developed enough to reach the highest level (3 marks). This might include reference to specific parts of the wedding service and how they relate to the purposes of marriage and the couple's role in the marriage, but no conclusion has been suggested and the explanations were not in sufficient depth to reach Level 4.
4	A **good** understanding of the question – the student has responded with a variety of viewpoints on specific aspects of the wedding service and how these relate to marital problems, which are explained and analysed, and a conclusion/judgement on the question has been made (4 marks). For instance, the student **might**: – compare and contrast different viewpoints on marriage being for life in today's modern world – present analysis and comments on whether or not specific aspects of the service, e.g. the vows, have any relevance in helping the couple to work through difficulties in their marriage – compare and contrast different viewpoints on traditional vows, e.g. obedience, and those the couple want to make in today's modern world – comment on the intention of marriage for life coming up against obstacles such as severe injury, couple not being able to have children, abuse, addiction, etc.

Hints and tips

➤ Make sure you address all aspects of the question. The command words are 'explain' and 'why'.

➤ If you are explaining you should use the word 'because' or the phrase 'for the reason that'.

➤ Include some comments/analysis on the explanations.

➤ Remember that this question is asking you to support your ideas with sources of wisdom and authority.

➤ Keep in mind that the majority of the marks in this part (c) question are for AO2. Therefore knowledge is less important than your evaluative skills.

(d) This response is given **two** separate marks, both of which are determined by levels of response. Only **one** response is written but two different sets of **skills** are assessed by the examiner. The first mark is given for knowledge and understanding (AO1) and the second mark is awarded for the student's analysis and evaluation of the question (AO2). If the student simply writes down all they know about a specific topic, then the marks will be limited to the maximum marks for AO1. The examiner is assessing how the student uses their knowledge and understanding to relate to the specifics of the question/stimulus.

Knowledge and understanding AO1

Level	Description
1	A **limited/weak** demonstration of knowledge and understanding which is given 1 mark. This might include information and understanding about the teachings on divorce which are explained in a simplistic manner. The ideas are presented in the form of a list. There will be weak knowledge of different views within Christianity.
2	An **adequate** but **underdeveloped** demonstration of knowledge and understanding which is given 2 marks. This might include different denominational teachings and/or biblical teachings on divorce which have a superficial explanation.
3	A **good** demonstration of knowledge and understanding which is given 3 marks. This might include different example of biblical or denominational teachings on divorce which are explained and show understanding of how these views influence individuals, communities and societies. The student **might** refer to: – biblical teachings on divorce: Matthew 5:31, Mark 10:2–12, Deuteronomy 22:19, Malachi 2:16, 1 Corinthians 7, etc. – different church teachings: Church of England, Roman Catholic, Methodist, etc. – Catholic view on annulment – secular or legal views

Analysis and evaluation AO2

Level	Description
1	A **weak** response – the student may have given only a single viewpoint or the response is simply a description of events rather than offering comments which demonstrate a judgement (1–3 marks). This might include a descriptive/simplistic account of one interpretation of biblical or denominational teachings on divorce. No attempt to offer a judgement/conclusion will have been made. In other words, the information is communicated in a basic way and there is no evidence of a **discussion** taking place.
2	A **limited** response – the student has perhaps given different examples of biblical or denominational teachings on divorce but they have not been developed and there is little evidence of a conclusion. **Or** the student may have attempted to comment and show judgement on one specific example/teaching (4–6 marks). There may be some inaccuracies or misunderstandings of the teachings. In other words, there is a line of reasoning/**discussion** which has some relevance to the stimulus.
3	An **adequate** but **underdeveloped** response – the student has perhaps given different views and has attempted to show some judgement/analysis on them but the ideas and comments are not developed enough to reach the highest level. This might include different biblical and denominational teachings on divorce which the student may have commented on or compared and contrasted. However, they have not been discussed or analysed in sufficient depth to reach Level 4. A line of reasoning has been presented and **discussed** which is mostly relevant.
4	A **good** understanding of the question – the student has responded with a variety of viewpoints or different denominational teachings which are explained, analysed, compared and contrasted. There is evidence of a conclusion/judgement on the question (10–12 marks). The student has offered a well-developed and sustained discussion which is coherent, relevant and well structured. The student **might**: – refer to the fact that people do not get married with the intention to divorce but sometimes circumstances make divorce the only viable option (a necessary evil), e.g. abuse, addiction, mental or physical health problems – refer to the life span of people today being far longer than those centuries ago – compare and contrast and comment on the impact of biblical and denominational teachings – come to a balanced conclusion/judgement

Hints and tips

➤ Read the stimulus carefully and identify its significance in your response, making sure you stick to the wording in the stimulus and do not divert into a concept that you would prefer to discuss.

➤ Remember that your response should be a **discussion** – try to present viewpoints for both sides as if you were having a conversation. Do not just list all the ideas for the stimulus in one paragraph and then all the ideas against in another paragraph.

➤ Refer to different beliefs and teachings and evaluate the importance of these differences.

➤ Try to refer back to what you studied in Part 1 of this course: beliefs and teachings and practices.

➤ Compare and contrast the religious views with secular views.

> Remember that you do not have to express a personal view – if you want to, you can, but make sure you justify your point of view with evidence and argument.

> Do not fall into the trap of saying 'An atheist does not believe in God and therefore would not agree with the religious point of view'. You are not adding to the argument/discussion at all.

Question 2

Student A

(a) A teaching on equality is when St Paul said in his letter to the Galatians: 'There is neither Jew nor Greek, there is neither slave nor free, there is neither male nor female, for you are all one in Christ Jesus.' This means that everyone, no matter who they are, is the same in the eyes of God, so everyone should be treated the same.

ℓ **The first mark is given for the teaching 'neither/nor', and the development comes before the teaching where the teaching is put into context, St Paul's letter for the second mark, and the third mark is given for the explanation of the teaching, saying what it means.**

(b) Some Christians look to the traditional roles of men and women in the family because they believe the Bible is inerrant. They believe the wife is a helper to her husband because Eve was created to be a helper to Adam, and that she is the one to look after the children because her punishment for eating the fruit of the forbidden tree was to suffer painful childbirth. Also her punishment was to have her husband rule over her. This coincides with St Paul's teaching, 'wives submit to your husbands'. All these teachings show that women have the lesser role in family life while the husband is more superior. Traditionally he is seen as the breadwinner and this again relates to Adam's punishment for disobeying God, which is have 'painful toil'.

However, because the Bible was written in patriarchal times there is a more modern view which states that both the wife and husband have equal status. This view is known as egalitarianism. The creation story in Genesis 1 indicates that both were made in God's image. The wife can stay at home if she wants or can go to work while the husband stays at home to bring up the children or both may go out to work. Both men and women have equal opportunities to succeed and both will ensure their children are brought up in the faith and take them to church and have them baptised.

ℓ **The student responds to the trigger word 'teachings' and links different teachings to the traditional and modern roles of men and women in the family.**

(c) Celibacy is to not indulge in the act of marriage or sex. But is this an unrealistic and outdated viewpoint in this modern world? The Bible presents different views on whether or not it is right to be celibate. St Paul was celibate and in his first letter to the Corinthians he said, 'it is good for them to stay unmarried as I am'. Yet in the next verse he also said, 'if they cannot control themselves they should marry'. Although this might sound contradictory, it demonstrates the Christian view that casual sex is the wrong approach because sex is a gift from God and should be done in the correct setting, which is marriage. Marriage is deemed to be important by Christians because Proverbs teaches that 'he who finds a wife finds what is good and receives favour from the Lord', and the letter to the Hebrews states 'marriage should be honoured by all'. The letter goes on to condemn adultery, which is against the seventh commandment. This again shows that casual sex or infidelity are considered to be a sin. So if the Bible is promoting the act of sex within marriage, why is celibacy thought to be so important? Catholic priests are celibate because it is believed they should devote themselves to living a Christ-like life. Jesus was celibate in spite of the infamous novel *The Da Vinci Code*. Also St Paul taught why celibacy is important in his first letter to the Corinthians when he said an unmarried person could focus on the Lord's affairs but a married person will focus on worldly matters. It seems as though celibacy is a matter of personal choice for a Christian: marriage is not wrong, nor is celibacy, but it is just a personal preference and an understanding of the dictates of the conscience whether or not a person can be married and also focus on God.

(e) **The student makes a good attempt at a response by showing deep knowledge and understanding of the different Christian attitudes to celibacy. They support their ideas with many biblical references and show analysis throughout the response.**

(d) Some women would be outraged at this statement because they view themselves as equal to their husbands – egalitarianism. Some women might even go so far as to declare that they are better than their husbands. The reason this statement is made is that it is from a teaching of St Paul when he declared: 'wives submit yourselves to your husbands' in his letter to the Colossians. It also reflects the vow which used to be made by every woman in the marriage service to 'obey' her husband. Nowadays it is not obligatory to make this vow and Catherine, the Duchess of Cambridge, did not make the vow in her wedding to Prince William. However, it could be argued that while women do not have to make the vow, some do because they believe that it is important to have a head of the household because it prevents arguments. Marriage is a mutual contract between a husband and wife and even though they are equal spiritually, there has to be someone to make the final decision. Just as a head of state makes the final decision on a matter of law or whether a country should go to war, in a marriage a decision can be made by the husband after collaboration and input by both. This view closely reflects the idea of complementarianism, the idea that men and women have been created by God to be different and to have different roles in life.

(e) **The student indicates the modern-day feminist view on obedience in marriage in regard to the traditional biblical teaching but shows that they understand the implications of having someone to make the final decision on which action to take.**

St Paul is not the only person in the Bible to teach that wives should obey their husbands. Peter also did in his first epistle, which taught that wives should be submissive but that also husbands should be considerate and treat their wives with respect. As a result, this appears to indicate that marriage is not about the man saying 'do this' and 'do that or else', but that it is a mutual collaboration between two people who are spiritually equal in the eyes of God (Genesis 1:27). Traditionalists who believe in the inerrant word of God in the Bible might argue that women are not equal to men because of the Bible teachings which show that Eve was created second to be a helper to man (Genesis 2:7). Also St Paul in his first letter to the Corinthians taught that 'man does not originate from women but women from men'. This is all very well but today, the Genesis stories are seen by many as myths, they are just explanations of the purpose of God's creation and it should not be taken literally that Eve was made from the rib of a man. All people know that it takes a man and a woman to make a baby and although perhaps the woman has a major part in the pregnancy and birth, the baby is a product of both parents. Therefore perhaps it is important to show that obedience has nothing really to do with the idea of whether men are more important than women or vice versa.

(e) **The student discusses the difference between obedience/submission and sexism – the belief that one sex is more important than another.**

Of course there are instances in which obedience by the wife is not practical. If the husband is abusive or gambling away the couple's savings, then it might be considered acceptable for the wife to oppose the husband. Unfortunately, there are no biblical teachings about such matters. The only time divorce is allowed is on the occurrence of infidelity by the wife, and even then there are contradictory interpretations of whether Jesus meant divorce could happen. So a Christian who believes in the Bible as being the true word of God and suitable for 'teaching and training in righteousness' may choose to live in an unacceptable marriage purely because she had promised to obey her husband in the wedding ceremony. This seems to be wrong.

(e) **The student indicates that there are pertinent occasions when a wife should not obey her husband but states that there are no biblical teachings which would support this.**

Surely, for a Christian, God is the one who should be obeyed? It should not matter who 'wears the trousers' in a marriage. As St Peter taught, 'we must obey God rather than men'. This is not referring to the male gender but to authorities who made rules. So today, Christians should focus on the purpose of God's creation and the underlying message of Jesus which is agape love, and reject man-made rules which would try to reject the message. This idea can be applied to wives and husbands in that if there are disagreements, instead of focusing on who should have the final word or who should obey whom, the couple should reflect on what Jesus would want them to do. Surely this is more important than worrying about whether wives should obey their husbands.

(e) **The student discusses the importance of obedience to God and comes to a balanced judgement at the end of the response.**

Question 2

Student B

(a) In the book of Genesis, which tells how God created human beings, Christians are taught that God made everyone in his image.

(e) **The first mark is given for Genesis and creation, and the second mark is given to the specific teaching 'in his image'. No link is made to the question but it is implicit in the response. To achieve the third mark the student could have added an explanation of what 'made in his image' means and a link to the question.**

(b) Women are supposed to stay at home, bring up the children and make sure her husband comes home to a clean house and cooked evening meal. The husband goes out to work and is the wage earner. This is an old-fashioned view and nowadays there are such things as house-husbands who stay at home while the wife goes out to work. St Paul taught that women should be silent in church and even today the Catholic Church will not allow women priests because Eve was the first to sin, and Jesus was a man and his Apostles were men so women are not allowed to fulfil that role.

(e) **The student gives implicit knowledge about the traditional and modern roles of Christian husbands and wives in the family but this is not supported by any direct teachings. Unfortunately the student then diverts into talking about women priests, which is not what the question is asking for.**

(c) Celibacy is when someone does not have sex or get married. However, is this going against God's command to Adam and Eve to 'go forth and multiply'? Having children is one of the main purposes of marriage and it allows the Christian faith to be promoted and spread because the Christian family will ensure that the children are brought up in the faith. Yet monks and nuns are celibate, such as Mother Teresa, because they devote themselves to worshipping God and helping others. Jesus taught that 'others have renounced marriage because of the Kingdom of Heaven', implying that people should focus on spiritual matters rather than on worldly matters. However, this brings us back to the point that if people do not have children, what will happen to the faith? The Shakers, so called because they danced and spoke in tongues during worship, had as one of their basic rules that everyone should be celibate. There are now only a few members left, which is an obvious result of not having sex. Some Christians also believe that it is all right for someone to be in a homosexual partnership as long as they are celibate, which seems unfair.

🅔 **The student shows some knowledge and understanding of the different attitudes on celibacy, which are supported directly by two specific teachings. They have made an attempt at analysis but further development is needed, with more reference to specific teachings to gain the 4 marks that are available for AO2.**

(d) I would say that wives should not have to obey husbands because at no time throughout the centuries did husbands ever agree to obey their wives. Marriage should be an equal partnership and if there is true love and respect in the marriage it will not matter as to whether either one of the couple is considered to be the 'one in charge'. Bible teachings do indicate that women should obey their husbands but very few people believe that today, anyway.

🅔 **The student offers a generic response but it does reflect some understanding of the implications of the statement.**

Of course everyone has to obey someone in their lives. Children obey their parents, students obey their teachers, and everyone has to obey the laws of the land. One of the Ten Commandments is to 'honour your father and mother', which suggests obedience. So is it entirely wrong that wives should have to obey their husbands? Perhaps in traditional times when males were the only breadwinners it could be said that the men should have complete authority because they were providing the necessities for life.

🅔 **The student makes reference to obedience in biblical teachings. They make a valid point that obedience is not the only vow. Although there is an attempt at discussion, it is limited.**

St Paul has a contradictory view on women. Sometimes he proclaims that 'everyone is equal in the eyes of God: there is neither Jew nor Greek, there is neither slave nor free, there is neither male nor female, for you are all one in Christ Jesus'. But at the same time he is telling women to be silent in church and that wives should submit to their husbands. So it is difficult for a Christian bride to know whether or not she should include the vow of obedience in her promises. I suppose a traditionalist Christian who believes that every word in the Bible is true would view women as second-class citizens because Eve was created after Adam and as a helper for him, not because she would be a woman in her own right. So therefore these Christians would agree that wives should obey their husbands.

Based on everything I have said I think women do not need to obey their husbands because the Bible is pointless because of all the contradictions in it.

🅔 **The student refers to the contradictory teachings of St Paul and links them into the discussion on obedience. The analysis is superficial – it has no real depth. The student gives a personal judgement but it too is limited.**

Mark scheme

2 (a) Marks are awarded for three points which relate to each other, not three separate ideas. A mark is given for the teaching requested, and a further 2 marks are given for explanation or development which could put the teaching in context. The student **might** refer to:
   – teachings: Genesis 1:27, Matthew 7:12, John 13:24, Galatians 3:28, 1 Corinthians 6:19, Acts 10:34, Acts 17:26.

Hints and tips

➤ The question is asking for one teaching so make sure you give only one.

➤ This is a three-point question, so state the teaching, then show further detail and development for the second and third marks.

(b) This response is marked by levels of response according to the student's knowledge and understanding of the question (AO1).

Knowledge and understanding AO1

Level	Description
1	A **weak** response with limited understanding (1–2 marks): the student may have listed two teachings about the role of men and women in the family. **Or** the student may have given one teaching about the role of men and women in the family which has been developed and explained, but in a simplistic way. **Or** the student may have given some misinformation or the response may be too generic (not specific to Christianity).
2	An **adequate** but **underdeveloped** response (3–4 marks): the student may have given different teachings on the roles of men and women in the family and explained and supported them in a brief or descriptive way rather than showing the full depth of the understanding of the student.
3	A **good** response (5–6 marks): the student may have given various teachings on the roles of men and women in the family which are supported and explained with reference to biblical and church teachings. The student will have shown a sound understanding of the issues surrounding the roles of men and women in the family. The student **may** refer to: – traditional teachings – the husband is the breadwinner and wife stays at home, references: Genesis 2:18, Genesis 3:6, Genesis 3:16–17, Colossians 3:18, Ephesians 5:21–24 – modern and social views: equal roles, references: Genesis 1:27, Galatians 3:28. – Christian egalitarianism and Christian complementarianism

Hints and tips

➤ Read the question carefully and note the trigger/command words: 'different teaching', 'roles', 'family'.

➤ Responses to this question should be purely knowledge based – all 6 marks are awarded for AO1.

➤ Make sure your ideas are Christian and if you give a generic idea such as 'breadwinner', make sure you link it to a Christian teaching.

(c) This response is given **two** separate marks, both of which are determined by levels of response. Only **one** response is written but two different sets of **skills** are assessed by the examiner. The first mark is given for knowledge and understanding (AO1) and the second mark is awarded for the student's analysis and evaluation of the question (AO2). If the student simply writes down all they know about a specific topic, then the marks will be limited to the maximum marks for AO1. The examiner is assessing how the student uses their knowledge and understanding to relate to the specifics of the question/stimulus.

Knowledge and understanding AO1

Level	Description
1	**Some** demonstration of knowledge and understanding which is given 1 mark. This might include a little information and understanding of the different attitudes on celibacy.
2	**Good** demonstration of knowledge and understanding which is given 2 marks. This might include ideas on the different teachings within the Bible and the church on celibacy. The student **might** refer to: – a definition of celibacy – specific teachings: Genesis 1:28, Proverbs 18:22, Matthew 19:10–12, 1 Corinthians 7:8–9, 1 Corinthians 7:32–24, Hebrews 13:4–7 – St Paul being celibate contrasted with St Peter who was married, Jesus viewed as a celibate (possible connection to the Essenes), the Shakers

Analysis and evaluation AO2

Level	Description
1	A **weak** response – the student may have given only a single viewpoint or the response is simply a description of the different attitudes to celibacy rather than offering comments which demonstrate a judgement (1 mark).
2	A **limited** response – the student has perhaps given different attitudes to the concept of celibacy but these have not been developed by any comment and as such the analysis is limited. **Or** the student may have attempted to comment and show judgement on **one** specific view (2 marks).
3	An **adequate** but **underdeveloped** response – the student has given different ideas on the different attitudes to celibacy and has attempted to show some judgement/analysis on them but the ideas and comments are not developed enough to reach the highest level (3 marks).
4	A **good** understanding of the question. The student has responded with a variety of viewpoints on the different attitudes to celibacy, which are explained and analysed, and a conclusion/judgement on the question has been made (4 marks). For instance, the student **might**: – consider whether or not celibacy is appropriate in today's world – compare and contrast the two views of whether or not a person can devote themselves to God while at the same time being involved in worldly matters: 'You cannot serve two masters' – comment on the view that the Bible teachings were written in a completely different age – comment on St Paul's seemingly contradictory attitudes

Hints and tips

➤ Make sure you address all aspects of the question. The command words are 'explain' and 'different attitudes'.

➤ If you are explaining, you should use the word 'because' or the phrase 'for the reason that'.

➤ Include some comments/analysis on the explanations.

➤ Remember that this question is asking you to support your ideas with sources of wisdom and authority.

➤ Keep in mind that the majority of the marks in this part (c) question are for AO2. Therefore knowledge is less important than your evaluative skills.

(d) This response is given **two** separate marks, both of which are determined by levels of response. Only **one** response is written but two different sets of **skills** are assessed by the examiner. The first mark is given for knowledge and understanding (AO1) and the second mark is awarded for the student's analysis and evaluation of the question (AO2). If the student simply writes down all they know about a specific topic, then the marks will be limited to the maximum marks for AO1. The examiner is assessing how the student uses their knowledge and understanding to relate to the specifics of the question/stimulus.

Knowledge and understanding AO1

Level	Description
1	A **limited/weak** demonstration of knowledge and understanding which is given 1 mark. This might include information and a little understanding about the biblical teachings on wives obeying their husbands which are explained in a simplistic manner. The ideas are presented in the form of a list. There will be weak knowledge of the different views within Christianity.
2	An **adequate** but **underdeveloped** demonstration of knowledge and understanding which is given 2 marks. This might include different biblical teachings on whether a wife should obey her husband which have a superficial explanation.
3	A **good** demonstration of knowledge and understanding which is given 3 marks. This might include different examples of biblical or denominational teachings on whether a wife should obey her husband which are explained and show understanding of how these views influence individuals, communities and societies. The student **might** refer to: – biblical teachings on obedience: 1 Peter 3:1, 1 Peter 3:7, Galatians 3:28, Acts 5:29, Genesis 2:7, 1 Corinthians 11:8, 2 Timothy 3:16, Genesis 1:27 – Sarah obeying Abraham – marriage vows – examples of when obedience should not be a priority

Analysis and evaluation AO2

Level	Description
1	A **weak** response – the student may have given only a single viewpoint or the response is simply a description of events rather than offering comments which demonstrate a judgement (1–3 marks). This might include a descriptive/simplistic account of one or two different interpretations of biblical teachings on obedience. No attempt to offer a judgement/conclusion will have been made. In other words, the information is communicated in a basic way and there is no evidence of a discussion taking place.
2	A **limited** response – the student has perhaps given different examples or biblical or denominational teachings on obedience but they have not been developed and there is little evidence of a conclusion. **Or** the student may have attempted to comment and show judgement on one specific example/teaching (4–6 marks). There may be some inaccuracies or misunderstandings of the teachings. In other words, there is a line of reasoning/discussion which has some relevance to the stimulus.
3	An **adequate** but **underdeveloped** response – the student has perhaps given different views and has attempted to show some judgement/analysis on them but the ideas and comments are not developed enough to reach the highest level (7–9 marks). This might include different biblical and denominational teachings on obedience which the student may have commented or compared and contrasted. However, they have not been discussed or analysed in sufficient depth in order to reach Level 4. A line of reasoning has been presented and discussed which is mostly relevant.
4	A **good** understanding of the question. The student has responded with a variety of viewpoints or different denominational teachings on obedience which are explained and analysed and a conclusion/judgement on the question has been made (10–12 marks). The student has offered a well-developed and sustained **discussion** which is coherent, relevant and well structured. The student **might** refer to: • feminist or modern views contrasted with traditionalist views • whether marriage is just about obedience or whether other purposes of marriage are more important • the times when obedience is not practical • a balanced conclusion/judgement

Hints and tips

➤ Read the stimulus carefully and identify its significance in your response, making sure you stick to the wording in the stimulus and do not divert into a concept that you would prefer to discuss.

➤ The trigger word is 'always'.

➤ Remember that your response should be a **discussion** – try to present viewpoints for both sides as if you were having a conversation. Do not just list all the ideas for the stimulus in one paragraph and then all the ideas against in another paragraph.

➤ Refer to different beliefs and teachings and evaluate the importance of these differences.

➤ Try to refer back to what you studied in Part 1 of this course: beliefs and teachings and practices.

➤ Compare and contrast the religious views with secular views.

➤ Remember that you do not have to express a personal view – if you want to, you can, but make sure you justify your point of view with evidence and argument.

➤ Do not fall into the trap of saying 'An atheist does not believe in God and therefore would not agree with the religious point of view'. You are not adding to the argument/discussion at all.

Christianity: the existence of God, gods and the ultimate reality

Question 3

Student A

(a) Christians believe that God is good because:

1 He came down in the form of Jesus to save us from sin.

2 He allows miracles to happen.

3 He is the source of all good behaviour – the moral code in the Bible.

ⓔ **The student gives three correct reasons and so achieves the full 3 marks.**

(b) The cosmological argument put forward by St Thomas Aquinas, sometimes called the first cause argument, states that the universe must have been started by some being and that this being is God. Christians base this belief on the opening chapter in the Bible, Genesis, which states, 'In the beginning God created the heavens and the earth'. Aquinas came up with five ways to prove God exists, and the first three are those associated with the cosmological argument. The first way is motion – God has to be the prime mover, the one who begins everything, because there cannot be infinite regress. The second way is based on the idea of cause and effect, which means there has to be a first cause – the one who begins the effects – and this must be God. The third way states that because everything in the world is an effect, everything is contingent, God has to be a necessary being – one that is not contingent does not need a cause.

ⓔ **The student outlines the first three ways of St Thomas Aquinas's arguments for the existence of God and shows understanding by explaining the technical terms, thus reaching the top level, but not necessarily the highest mark in this level. They make reference to biblical authority.**

(c) Christians believe that a miracle is when God overturns the laws of nature. It is when God reveals himself and does things which science cannot explain. An example is when God fed his chosen people with manna in the desert during the exodus. This particular miracle showed the Israelites that God will provide for them when they are in times of need, thus strengthening their faith in him.

Miracles are important to Christians because they believe that God's greatest miracle was Jesus dying on the cross and then being resurrected three days later. Fundamentalist Christians believe this miracle literally happened because the Bible is the true word of God – it is the breath of God, he inspired the writers. The significance of the miracle of resurrection is that Jesus paves the way for Christians to enter heaven. The resurrection proves that Jesus's death atoned for the wrongdoing of Adam and Eve. St Paul says that if the resurrection didn't happen then Christian preaching is in vain.

Some might question whether a Christian who does not believe that miracles happened in the Bible, such as the birth of Christ to a virgin, are really Christians. The birth of Christ is one of the cornerstones of the faith. Liberal Christians, however, do believe that some of the miracles are symbolic; they are stories which contain a spiritual truth. For instance, the feeding of the 5,000 is seen to hold the message of agape love and that Christians should share as the early Christians did in Acts. Looking at the resurrection, although this holds the core spiritual truth that God overcomes evil and that Christ rising from the dead shows that death has been conquered and there is eternal life in heaven, it must also be said that if a Christian holds doubts that it literally happened then they have no real faith.

ⓔ **The student responds well to the question and evaluates different attitudes through the concepts of literal and symbolic interpretations of miracles. Although they give no specific biblical quotes, they use plenty of biblical examples of miracles. The student draws the conclusion that if Christians question the ideas of miracles then their faith is suspect.**

(d) A religious experience is when God reveals himself to a person. It can happen in many ways: through prayer, meeting inspirational people, seeing God through the beauty of this world or experiencing a miracle. Because there are many different ways, some of which are personal or private and others which are more general – anyone could experience them – then perhaps the statement should be modified to say that a personal or private experience is more difficult to prove to be true than something which happens to a lot of people.

ⓔ **The student begins by explaining what religious experiences are and then responds to the statement, showing they have understood the implication that because of the difficulty in proving the truth behind these experiences, the statement is in itself unfair.**

For instance, if just one person claimed to have had a vision then people could claim it happened because the person was drunk or mad. St Teresa of Avila had an experience which she described as God piercing her heart with a dart. But how is it possible for her to prove to others this is what happened? Even her contemporaries wanted to dissuade her from telling others about her experiences because they believed they were delusions from the devil. So if they could not believe her, why should anyone, especially atheists, believe they happened? Others might claim that because she was brought up as a strong Catholic to believe in such experiences, she deluded herself in her illnesses that this was what was happening. For Teresa, the experiences brought her closer to God, she was surrendering herself to his will. So to her they were true even if she could not prove them. She did not question her faith. But as the question is suggesting, just because she believed them to be true it might not be possible for her to prove their existence to other people.

ⓔ **The student discusses the concept of personal/private experiences by citing the example of Teresa of Avila and returns to the statement by stating that it is difficult to prove beyond doubt.**

The Toronto Blessing is an example of where many people have undergone an experience at the same time. In 1994 there was a gathering when many of the congregation were overcome by laughing and shaking. Some fell to the ground as they experienced the presence of God. This would suggest that because lots of people felt God's presence at the same time this is a form of proof. However, critics or atheists would deny this, saying it could be a matter of group hysteria or peer pressure because people were trying to show that their faith was the same as the others who were rolling around on the floor, or did not want to feel as if they had been excluded. However, others would argue that this type of experience happens on many occasions and is still happening and therefore it is a form of proof. They would say that because a religious experience has a religious dimension and can change people spiritually then the changes in the people who have undergone this experience, positive religious changes, mean that it is wrong to say that God has not expressed himself to these people in this form. The philosopher David Hume would say that oral testimony is always suspect, no matter how many people say it is true. This is perhaps going a step too far because if 1,000 people claim to have seen a beached whale on the seashore and one person says it was not a whale, it appears to be common sense to say that the 1,000 people are correct.

ℯ **The student discusses the Toronto Blessing, which is an example of a public corporate religious experience, linking it to the statement.**

Another personal example is that of Nikki Cruz, who was a New York gangster, reliant on drugs, who was converted to Christianity when he attended a meeting led by David Wilkerson. Nikki changed his life to become an evangelist and he also ran groups which tried to get young people off drugs. This experience, although personal, which in itself cannot perhaps be proved because Nikki claimed he opened his mouth but the words which came out were not his own, can perhaps be proved by what happened to Nikki afterwards – his change in attitude and his Christian approach to 'love thy neighbour'.

ℯ **The student offers another private example of religious experience through the case study of Nikki Cruz and attempts to analyse the significance of the experience.**

One of the claims of religious experience is that it is ineffable – it is nearly impossible to put the event into words. It is personal and subjective. Therefore it could be true to say that it is difficult to prove them to be true. The emphasis is on 'difficult' rather than the statement which states they 'can never' be proven. Religion is faith, you believe because you believe. When Jesus called Peter to be one of his fishermen, Peter just left his life to follow him. That surely is a personal religious experience – it is life – changing, both physically and spiritually. People read about that story in the New Testament and they too feel that they can follow Christ, just like Peter. They do not question whether the story is true, they just believe it is. So perhaps the statement is wrong to say that religious experiences can never be proven to be true because it does not really matter. A religious experience is where God reveals himself and his wishes to you or to lots of people and it is just a matter of a person's choice as to whether to accept the experience or not.

ℯ **The student concludes by discussing the statement and coming to a judgement.**

Question 3

Student B

(a) Christians believe that God is good because:
1 The world he created was all good – it was Adam and Eve who let evil enter the world.
2 He performed miracles to save his chosen people – like parting the Red Sea.
3 Some Christians might say he is not all good because of the Angel of Death in the Old Testament.

ℯ **The student's first two reasons are correct and gain 2 marks, but the last one gives a point that goes against the question asked.**

(b) The cosmological argument is all about cause and effect. When we look at the world we see that there has to be a cause for everything – an acorn grows into a tree. So the question is asked, how did the world come into existence because you cannot get something from nothing? People say the world just came about with the Big Bang, but you then have to ask, what caused the Big Bang? Aquinas said that the cause of the world had to be God because God does not need a cause to exist and therefore only God could be the one who began everything. Aquinas argued that you cannot go on going backwards and backwards looking for something which began everything, you had to stop somewhere and that you had to stop at God.

e **The student outlines the cosmological argument but it is a simplistic explanation and as such is underdeveloped.**

(c) Christians believe that miracles happen today. They often pray for them in church or go to places such as Lourdes in France to hopefully undergo a miraculous healing event. If a miracle happens it has to be proclaimed a miracle after an investigation by the Vatican. To become a saint in the Catholic Church you have to have miracles done in your name. Some attend healing services where charismatic Christians, using the power of the Holy Spirit, will perform the laying on of hands and speak in tongues. They believe in the miracles of the Bible, such as the parting of the Red Sea and Jesus calming the storm when his disciples were frightened. However, perhaps because of modern science and the advance of technological inventions, some people might say that miracles do not happen as frequently today. They might say that people have more faith in science than in God. Jesus told the leper after healing him not to tell anyone because he wanted people to listen to his message rather than have people follow him because he cured people.

e **The student responds to the question in a narrative way rather than exploring in depth the different attitudes which are held about miracles. The information is correct and there is reference to biblical miracles but the explanations are simplistic and there is no analysis or evaluation. The student has not drawn any conclusion. There were only 2 marks available for knowledge and understanding for this question, and the student has not addressed their answer to focus on the 4 marks available for evaluation and why miracles are important to Christian belief.**

(d) Religious experiences are difficult to prove to be true because they can happen through prayer or meditation and it is thus a personal and private experience. It is difficult to sometimes convince your friends that a certain programme on the television is the best programme you have ever seen, because everyone has different opinions. Therefore, trying to convince someone that you have spoken to God would probably result in being ridiculed or mocked or even being called mad. The Yorkshire Ripper believed that God had told him to go and kill prostitutes, but he was declared insane.

e **The student responds to the statement by agreeing that it is difficult to prove religious experiences are true and develops this response by using the case study of the Yorkshire Ripper.**

In the Bible, Saul is on his way to Damascus when he is blinded by a bright light and hears the voice of Jesus speaking to him. As a result, he becomes a Christian and spreads the belief in Christ over his many journeys. He is also willing to die for his belief in Jesus, and as a result many see this conviction as evidence of an experience with God. But critics have claimed that this is not a convincing argument because there are three different accounts of this event in the book of Acts.

e **The student attempts to discuss Saul's conversion as an example of religious experience, giving arguments for why it might be true and why it might not. However, these arguments are not discussed in enough detail to form a conclusion.**

A Christian might pray for a miracle, such as the healing of a loved one, and his or her prayers might be answered by that person becoming well again. They would then claim that this miracle is proof that religious experiences happen – God has revealed himself to be benevolent. However, critics would claim that perhaps the person became well again because the doctors had discovered some new medicine which was the real cure. Many of the miracles in the Bible have now been explained by science, such as the turning of water into wine was through a chemical reaction.

(e) **The student uses the example of miracles as a way of discussing whether they are proof or not of a religious experience. As with the previous example, the criticisms are not developed – it could be argued that God had inspired the doctors' hands.**

It is difficult to prove a lot of things and religious experiences are probably one of the most difficult things to prove. Most people don't believe something unless they experience it for themselves, therefore the statement could be argued to be true,

(e) **The student attempts to draw a conclusion and although the construct of the argument is valid, it is underdeveloped.**

Mark scheme

3 (a) 1 mark is awarded for each correct response up to a maximum of three marks. Students **might** refer to:
- miracles
- God as people's strength and comfort
- the incarnation and the reason for it
- the Bible as a source of moral authority
- the creation being good
- end of time theology: God's goodness will conquer all evil

Hints and tips
Do not spend too long on this question as it is only asking for knowledge, so keep your answers brief.

(b) This response is marked by levels of response according to the student's knowledge and understanding of the question (AO1).

Knowledge and understanding AO1

Level	Description
1	A **weak** response with limited understanding (1–2 marks): the student may have explained one idea about the argument from cause (cosmological argument) but it is lacking in detail.
2	An **adequate** but **underdeveloped** response (3–4 marks): the student may have given and explained different aspects of the argument from cause (cosmological argument). These ideas will be presented in a brief or descriptive way rather than showing the full depth of the student's understanding.
3	A **good** response (5–6 marks): the student may have shown knowledge and understanding in detailed explanations of the variations of the argument from cause (cosmological argument). The student **might** refer to: – Aquinas' first cause argument – Genesis – cause and effect/infinite regress

Hints and tips

➤ Responses to this question should be purely knowledge-based – all 6 marks are awarded for AO1.
➤ Don't worry about the perceived strengths and weaknesses of the first cause argument for the existence of God, simply outline the argument in as much detail as possible.

(c) This response is given **two** separate marks, both of which are determined by levels of response. Only **one** response is written but two different sets of **skills** are assessed by the examiner. The first mark is given for knowledge and understanding (AO1) and the second mark is awarded for the student's analysis and evaluation of the question (AO2). If the student simply writes down all they know about a specific topic, then the marks will be limited to the maximum marks for AO1. The examiner is assessing how the student uses their knowledge and understanding to relate to the specifics of the question/stimulus.

Knowledge and understanding AO1

Level	Description
1	**Some** demonstration of knowledge and understanding which is given 1 mark. This might include information and explanations of the importance of miracles to some Christians.
2	**Good** demonstration of knowledge and understanding of information which is given 2 mark. This might include, examples and explanations of the importance of miracles to some Christians. The student **might** refer to: – a definition of a miracle, scientific and/or religious – examples: modern-day/biblical, pilgrimage places such as Lourdes and Walsingham – different interpretations of miracles: literal or symbolic, with an understanding as to why the different interpretations are held – the Bible: how some scholars believe some miracles were added, such as Jesus calming the storm, in order to encourage the early Christians who were undergoing difficulties

Analysis and evaluation AO2

Level	Description
1	A **weak** response – the student may have given only a single viewpoint or the response is simply a description of events (a list) rather than offering comments which demonstrate a judgement (1 mark).
2	A **limited** response – the student has perhaps given different Christian views but has not shown any comment and as such the analysis is limited. **Or** the student may have attempted to comment and show judgement on one specific view (2 marks).
3	An **adequate** response – the student has given different Christian views and has attempted to show some judgement/analysis on them but the ideas and comments are not developed enough to reach the highest level (3 marks).
4	A **good** understanding of the question. The student has responded with a variety of viewpoints or different schools of thought, which are explained and analysed, and a conclusion/judgement on the question has been made (4 marks). The student **might**: – discuss the implications of the different interpretations of miracles – compare and contrast and come to a judgement on the different Christian attitudes – come to a balanced conclusion/judgement

Hints and tips

➤ Make sure you read the question carefully and identify sources of wisdom and authority.
➤ Remember that the majority of marks in this part (c) question are for AO2. Therefore, be less descriptive and more evaluative about the different points of views on whether or not miracles are important for Christian faith.

(d) This response is given **two** separate marks, both of which are determined by levels of response. Only **one** response is written but two different sets of **skills** are assessed by the examiner. The first mark is given for knowledge and understanding (AO1) and the second mark is awarded for the student's analysis and evaluation of the question (AO2). If the student simply writes down all they know about a specific topic, then the marks will be limited to the maximum marks for AO1. The examiner is assessing how the student uses their knowledge and understanding to relate to the specifics of the question/stimulus.

Knowledge and understanding AO1

Level	Description
1	A **limited/weak** demonstration of knowledge and understanding of religious experiences which are listed and not explained in detail. There will be weak knowledge of the different views within Christianity. This is given 1 mark.
2	An **adequate** but **underdeveloped** demonstration of knowledge and understanding of religious experiences which is given 2 marks.
3	A **good** demonstration of knowledge and understanding about religious experiences which is given 3 marks. The student **might** refer to: – different examples of religious experiences such as biblical ones (St Paul), John Wesley, Nikki Cruz, Teresa of Avila, Julian of Norwich, the Toronto Blessing or any other valid examples – conversion, miracles, prayer, mysticism, visions and meditation – types of religious experience: public/general, private/personal, corporal

Analysis and evaluation AO2

Level	Description
1	A **weak** response – the student may have given only a single viewpoint or the response is simply a description of what happens in a religious experience rather than offering comments which demonstrate a judgement (1–3 marks). In other words, the information is communicated in a basic way and there is no evidence of a **discussion** taking place.
2	A **limited** response – the student has perhaps given different examples of ideas on proving religious experiences but has not shown any in-depth comments and as such the analysis is limited. **Or** the student may have attempted to comment and show judgement on one specific type and/or example (4–6 marks). In other words, there is a line of reasoning/**discussion** which has some relevance to the stimulus.
3	An **adequate** but **underdeveloped** response – the student has perhaps given different views on the validity of religious experiences and has attempted to show some judgement/analysis on them but the ideas and comments are not developed enough to reach the highest level (7–9 marks). A line of reasoning has been presented and **discussed** which is mostly relevant.
4	A **good** understanding of the question. The student has responded with a variety of viewpoints or different schools of thought which are explained and analysed, and a conclusion/judgement on the question has been made (10–12 marks). The student has offered a well-developed and sustained **discussion** which is coherent, relevant and well structured. The student **might** have: – compared and contrasted the different types/examples of religious experiences and made a balanced judgement on the findings – explained David Hume's sceptic views and applied them to various examples before coming to a conclusion – examined scientific or secular views on religious experiences before coming to a conclusion – evaluated the difficulties in proof

Hints and tips

➤ Read the stimulus carefully and identify its significance in your response, making sure you stick to the wording in the stimulus and do not divert into a concept that you would prefer to discuss.

➤ Remember too that your response should be a **discussion** – try to present viewpoints for both sides as if you were having a conversation. Do not just list all the ideas for the stimulus in one paragraph and then all the ideas against in another paragraph.

➤ Refer to different beliefs and teachings and evaluate the importance of these differences.

➤ Try to refer back to what you studied in Part 1 of this course: beliefs and teachings and practices.

➤ Compare and contrast the religious views with secular views.

➤ Remember that you do not have to express a personal view – if you want to, you can, but make sure you justify your point of view with evidence and argument.

➤ Do not fall into the trap of saying 'An atheist does not believe in God and therefore would not agree with the religious point of view'. You are not adding to the argument/discussion at all.

Question 4

Student A

(a) The relationship between God and the world is that he created everything through his power of command and that he sustains it. This is confirmed in the Psalms when it is asked 'who makes lightnings for the rain, who brings forth the wind…'

🄮 **The first mark is given for the relationship, God the creator and sustainer of the world. The second mark is given for the development that everything happened through the divine fiats (commands) and the third mark is given for the supporting quote from the Psalms.**

(b) There are various forms to this argument but basically the argument centres on the belief that because everyone has some sense within themselves of the difference between 'right' and 'wrong' actions, this sense indicates that people have a sense of morality. Since the ideas about morality have to come from somewhere, they believe that the only possible source is God. Therefore this argument's conclusion is that God exists.

Cardinal Newman called this sense of morality our conscience, our inner voice, and he believed the inner voice was from God. Of course, there are many criticisms of this view because of the immorality which exists in the world and the fact people often do not follow their conscience.

Kant, a philosopher in the 18th century, did not believe anyone could actually prove the existence of God, but he felt that it was reasonable to assume that God exists because of this idea of morality within people. Even a small child knows the difference between good and bad. Kant based his argument on the one proposed by St Aquinas.

🄮 **The student outlines three of the different interpretations of the moral argument showing an understanding of the significance of each.**

(c) Christians believe the anthropic principle is important because it is a logical way of demonstrating that the world was designed in such a way for human existence and survival and that it did not happen by chance or an accident and so therefore this proves the existence of God. This principle was first put forward by F.R. Tennant, who suggested that the universe is perfect, designed to ensure the development of life which is evolution, and is the result of God's creation.

Some fundamentalist Christians would not support the claim of evolution because they believe that God literally created Adam from the dust (Genesis 2:7) and gave him a soul with the breath of life, and Eve was created from Adam's rib. However, Professor John Polkinhorne, an Anglican minister, would support Tennant's theory because he believes that everything had to be just so in order for life to begin and to survive. The gravity has to be exact, the protons have to be larger than the electrons – any bigger or smaller and human life would not exist. So the Big Bang, which liberal Christians and secularists believe was the start of the world, was not by chance, as would be stated by atheists such as Richard Dawkins. Liberal Christians believe the accounts in Genesis are just ways of explaining why God created the world, and thus the third verse of Genesis when God said 'Let there be light' refers to the explosion which commenced the start of the building process of the earth and then the process of evolution. The importance of the anthropic principle is that it is reflecting the teachings in Genesis 1, whether taken literally or figuratively, that God created a world for humans and as such the principle shows that the belief of Christians is justified and entirely reasonable.

(e) **The student responds well to the question and demonstrates good knowledge and understanding of the anthropic principle while linking their ideas to an explanation of why this principle is of religious importance.**

(d) Ultimately this statement might be true, but it has not stopped many philosophers from trying to do just that, prove that God exists. St Thomas Aquinas' cosmological argument is based on observations of world around us. Aquinas states that everything that exists is moved, caused and contingent (depends) on something else for its existence. Aquinas argues that we cannot have a chain of infinite causes. He claims that there must be a first cause that itself is uncaused by anything else. He argues that if there was an infinite chain of causes they would not find within themselves the cause of themselves, there would therefore be nothing in the world. However, we know there are many things in the world. He calls this uncaused causer, God. The reasons he argues that this can be God is because Christians emphasise that God is omnipotent (all powerful), transcendent (outside of this space and time), and eternal (he is uncreated and always existed). However, an atheist might disagree with the cosmological argument because even if the universe does need a first cause, why does it need to be the God of classical theism? People who criticise this argument – like Richard Dawkins – would say that we use 'God' to fill the gaps in our knowledge of the universe. Therefore, Aquinas has not proven the existence of God, far from it. Ultimately the premise of the cosmological argument makes us realise how contradictory Christians can be because they say that nothing can come from nothing, except God. Why can't the universe exist in this way if it is possible for God to?

(e) **The student refers to the first cause argument for God's existence. They outline the argument but don't get caught up in purely descriptive writing. The student asks some important questions about this argument and makes a judgement on the success of the argument.**

Another argument for God's existence comes from William Paley and is called the teleological argument. Paley tells a story about a watch. If you went for a walk in the woods and saw a watch, you would not think it had just made itself. You would think someone had made it. Paley thought that natural objects, like eyes, are so complex and well put together, that they must have been designed. They couldn't just have happened by chance. Paley thought that natural objects must have a designer – God. Someone might agree with Paley's argument because when we study the world around us it does looked designed, or 'finely tuned'. For example, the electric charge on the electron: if it was a bit different, then life would not develop. However Hume might argue that, if God is the intelligent designer then why do we have parts of the world that suffer from earthquakes? Did God design the earthquakes? Why are some parts of the world stricken by drought? Did God design parts of the world to be so dry that humans suffer death as a result? A Christian might respond and say that evil was not part of God's original design, but that Adam and Eve in their disobedience ruined God's design. However, does this undermine God's omniscience? Would it be right to suggest that God isn't all-knowing to preserve his omnipotence? It could be argued that a God that isn't omniscient isn't worth worshipping.

(e) **The student offers a second 'proof' for the existence of God. They present a discussion on whether or not this actually proves God.**

Most Christians might agree that God cannot be proved but would focus instead on the idea that it is faith which matters, not physical proof. The epistle of James teaches 'but when you ask, you must believe and not doubt'. The gospel of St John tells the story of doubting Thomas, who refused to believe in Jesus's resurrection until he had physical proof, and how Jesus told him to 'stop doubting but believe'. The miracle of Jesus calming the storm as told in the gospel of St Mark is said by some scholars to have been inserted at a later date as not a literal account of a miracle but as a symbolic means of encouraging the early Christians who were undergoing persecution. So in conclusion it can be said that perhaps no one has yet proved beyond a shadow of doubt that God exists but in reality it does not matter because faith in him is all about a leap into the dark.

ⓔ **The student focuses on how faith is more important than proof and comes to a balanced judgement.**

Question 4
Student B

(a) Christians believe that the relationship between God and the world is that he came down in human form as Jesus to die on the cross so as to atone for the broken relationship through the sin of Adam and Eve.

ⓔ **The student has made a common mistake by misreading the question and states the relationship between God and humanity instead of the world. Therefore, no marks are awarded.**

(b) The moral argument is based on the idea that everyone has a conscience and can determine the difference between good and bad. Some might argue that this conscience comes from our environment, it reflects how we are brought up. If we are taught by our parents that it is not wrong to steal then of course a child will steal. However, the moral argument claims that the conscience is the voice of God. It is like a tiny voice inside us which directs us to do what is right. If we choose to not listen to the voice then we are choosing to disobey God. The moral argument says that the conscience can only come from God, there is no higher authority because God is all-good and therefore this means that if the conscience can only come from God, this means God exists.

ⓔ **The student outlines the moral argument but in a simplistic way. The student could have given either the names of the philosophers who put forward the moral argument or alternative versions. Although it is tempting, this question is not asking for an evaluation of the moral argument.**

(c) The anthropic principle is built on the concept that the world/universe was designed. Everything has to be just so for human survival. The Goldilocks principle, which compares earth to its two nearest neighbouring planets, shows that too much of the greenhouse effect or too little of it would mean that life could not exist. Venus is too hot, Mars is too cold, but earth is just right – just as baby bear's chair, porridge and bed were just right for Goldilocks. However, who is to say that there was not life on those two planets before life on earth began? So this is important for Christians because it supports their belief in the teachings of the creation story in Genesis that God created the world for humanity.

e The student responds to the question showing some knowledge and understanding of the anthropic principle and supports the principle with the Goldilocks principle. The student offers some evaluation, but it is rather superficial, and they address the religious importance at the end of the response. Further details on the principle, more evaluation and more reference to sources of wisdom and authority are required.

(d) Many people have tried to prove that God exists. There are the arguments from design, the cosmological arguments, and the moral argument. There are also people who have had religious experiences who claim that they have had a vision or a message from God, or even undergone a miraculous event, and thus this proves he exists. Unfortunately, although there are many claims and arguments for God's existence, they are all heavily criticised, especially by people who rely on science to explain the unexplainable things which happen in this world. Many of these arguments are more compelling than the ones put forward to prove God and so therefore it can be argued that no one can prove the existence of God.

e The student responds to the statement by agreeing that it is so difficult to prove the existence of God that perhaps the statement is correct. However, this idea is underdeveloped.

Christians believe that God interacts with the world and that he helps people in time of need through miracles. But non-believers would argue that sometimes the miracles can be explained by science. Also they wonder why, in times of horrific disasters such as the collapse of the Twin Towers, God first of all allowed that to happen and secondly why so few survivors were pulled from the rubble when over 3,000 people were killed and many more were injured. A Christian response that this is all part of God's plan and purpose or perhaps a test of faith as in the book of Job would not be well received. However, some Christians may argue that God did intervene with a miracle in that the Twin Towers did not collapse immediately so that thousands of the people inside could escape. But does this fact alone prove God?

e The student discusses whether or not miracles can prove God.

Some Christians would argue that trying to prove God is not necessary. They believe that if God wanted to reveal himself, he would if he wanted. In fact, he has already done so through the personhood of Jesus when God came down in human form in order to repair the relationship between humankind and himself: 'For God so loved the world.' Christians believe that physical proof is not needed as Paul's second letter to the Corinthians taught 'for we live by faith not by sight'. So these Christians view the idea of proof as non-essential because God wants people to use their free will and have faith in him through their own choice, not because they are given irrefutable proof.

e This is an acceptable response: the student shows knowledge and understanding and understands the significance of the statement. In order to achieve further marks, the student needs to support more of their ideas with references to sources of wisdom and authority and demonstrate the full depth of their understanding through more detailed evaluation and analysis.

Mark scheme

4   **(a)** Marks are awarded for three points which relate to each other, not three separate ideas. A mark is given for a statement of the meaning of God's relationship with the world, and a further 2 marks are given for explanation or development or a biblical teaching to support it. The student **might** refer to:

- God as the creator and sustainer of the world
- even if the creation stories are seen as myths they still show that the world is dependent upon God for its existence
- biblical teachings: Genesis 1 and 2, Psalm 135:6–7, Psalm 147:8, Job 38:33–37, Ecclesiastes 3:1, Colossians 1:17.

Hints and tips

➤ Read the question correctly – it is asking about God's relationship with the world, not humanity.

➤ Do not spend too long on this question as it is only asking for knowledge, so keep your answer brief.

  (b) This response is marked by levels of response according to the student's knowledge and understanding of the question (AO1).

Knowledge and understanding AO1

Level	Description
1	A **weak** response with limited understanding (1–2 marks): the student may have listed two teachings/ideas about the moral argument. **Or** the student may have given one teaching/idea about the argument which has been developed and explained, but in a simplistic way. **Or** the student may have given some misinformation or the response may be too generic.
2	An **adequate** but **underdeveloped** response (3–4 marks): the student may have given and explained different aspects of the moral argument. These ideas will be presented in a brief or descriptive way rather than showing the full depth of the student's understanding.
3	A **good** response (5–6 marks): the student may have shown knowledge and understanding in detailed explanations of the variations of the moral argument. The student **might** refer to: – a generic description of the argument, Cardinal Newman, Kant – but make sure it is made clear that Kant was not trying to prove the existence of God because he knew that was impossible from a material world view – possible biblical support for conscience: 1 Timothy 1:19, 1 Timothy 3:9, Hebrews 10:22, Romans 2:14–15

Hints and tips

➤ Make sure you read the question carefully and identify sources of wisdom and authority, and in this particular case relevant scholars associated with the moral argument.

➤ Responses to this question should be purely knowledge-based – all 6 marks are awarded for AO1.

➤ Don't worry about the perceived strengths and weaknesses of the moral argument for the existence of God, simply outline the argument in as much detail as possible.

(c) This response is given **two** separate marks, both of which are determined by levels of response. Only **one** response is written but two different sets of **skills** are assessed by the examiner. The first mark is given for knowledge and understanding (AO1) and the second mark is awarded for the student's analysis and evaluation of the question (AO2). If the student simply writes down all they know about a specific topic, then the marks will be limited to the maximum marks for AO1. The examiner is assessing how the student uses their knowledge and understanding to relate to the specifics of the question/stimulus.

Knowledge and understanding AO1

Level	Description
1	**Some** demonstration of knowledge and understanding which includes information and explanations of the religious importance of the anthropic principle. This is given 1 mark.
2	**Good** demonstration of knowledge and understanding of information, examples and explanations of the religious importance of the anthropic principle supported by reference to sources of wisdom and authority. This is given 2 marks. The student **might** refer to: – an explanation of the anthropic principle, F.R. Tennant, Professor John Polkinhorne – support from the Goldilocks principle – biblical support: creation stories in Genesis 1 and 2, Genesis 1:3, Genesis 2:7, Genesis 2:21–22, John 1:1–4, Colossians 1:16 – the religious importance: proof of God's existence in a logical way, confirms a Christian belief, reflects the teachings of the Bible, forms a basis of discussion between other religions and secularists/atheists

Analysis and evaluation AO2

Level	Description
1	A **weak** response – the student may have given only a single viewpoint or the response is simply a description of events (a list) rather than offering comments which demonstrate a judgement (1 mark).
2	A **limited** response – the student has perhaps given different ideas on the religious importance of the anthropic principle but has not shown any comment and as such the analysis is limited. **Or** the student may have attempted to comment and show judgement on one specific view (2 marks).
3	An **adequate** response – the student has given different views on the religious importance of the anthropic principle and has attempted to show some judgement/analysis on them but the ideas and comments are not developed enough to reach the highest level (3 marks).
4	A **good** understanding of the question. The student has responded with a variety of viewpoints or different schools of thought on the religious importance of the anthropic principle, which are explained and analysed and a conclusion/judgement on the question has been made (4 marks). The student **might**: – discuss the implications of the different interpretations of the Bible in connection with either supporting the anthropic principle or disagreeing with it – come to a judgement on whether the anthropic principle has religious importance or not – discuss whether or not the anthropic principle supports scientific views

Hints and tips

➤ Read the question carefully – this question is asking about the religious importance of the principle, so do not just give an account of the principle by itself. Explain why the argument may be convincing to Christians.

➤ Support your statement by referring to sources of wisdom and authority.

(d) This response is given **two** separate marks, both of which are determined by levels of response. Only **one** response is written but two different sets of **skills** are assessed by the examiner. The first mark is given for knowledge and understanding (AO1) and the second mark is awarded for the student's analysis and evaluation of the question (AO2). If the student simply writes down all they know about a specific topic, then the marks will be limited to the maximum marks for AO1. The examiner is assessing how the student uses their knowledge and understanding to relate to the specifics of the question/stimulus.

Knowledge and understanding AO1

Level	Description
1	A **limited/weak** demonstration of knowledge and understanding of whether or not people can prove the existence of God, but the ideas are listed and not explained in detail. This is given 1 mark.
2	An **adequate** but **underdeveloped** demonstration of knowledge and understanding of whether or not people can prove the existence of God, which is given 2 marks.
3	A **good** demonstration of knowledge and understanding presented which helps to address whether or not people can prove the existence of God, which is given 3 marks. The student **might** refer to: – classical/theological proofs: cosmological, design, moral and religious experience – examples of religious experiences – arguments which disprove God: argument of the problem of evil, science, an arbitrary God (sometimes not responding), unanswered prayers, Richard Dawkins – use of specific examples – biblical sources: Matthew 24:27, Mark 4:35–41, John 3:16, John 20:24–29, 1 Corinthians 2:9, 2 Corinthians 5:7

Analysis and evaluation AO2

Level	Description
1	A **weak** response – the student may have given only a single viewpoint or the response is simply a description about whether or not people can prove the existence of God, rather than offering comments which demonstrate a judgement (1–3 marks). In other words, the information is communicated in a basic way and there is no evidence of a **discussion** taking place.
2	A **limited** response – the student has perhaps given different ideas about whether or not people can prove the existence of God, but has not shown any comment in depth and as such the analysis is limited. **Or** the student may have attempted to comment and show judgement on one specific type and/or example (4–6 marks). In other words, there is a line of reasoning/**discussion** which has some relevance to the stimulus.
3	An **adequate** but **underdeveloped** response – the student has perhaps given different views of the validity of whether or not people can prove the existence of God, and has attempted to show some judgement/analysis on them but the ideas and comments are not developed enough to reach the highest level (7–9 marks). A line of reasoning has been presented and **discussed** which is mostly relevant.
4	A **good** understanding of the question. The student has responded with a variety of viewpoints or different schools of thought, which are explained and analysed and a conclusion/judgement on the question has been made (10–12 marks). The student has offered a well-developed and sustained **discussion** which is coherent, relevant and well structured. The student **might** have: – compared and contrasted proofs and disproofs for the existence of God and made a balanced judgement on the findings – analysed and commented in detail on one specific aspect of proving or not proving God's existence – analysed the meaning of faith – analysed God revealing himself through the world, the Bible and the incarnation

Hints and tips

➤ Read the stimulus carefully and identify its significance in your response, making sure you stick to the wording in the stimulus and do not divert into a concept that you would prefer to discuss.

➤ Remember that your response should be a **discussion** – try to present viewpoints for both sides as if you were having a conversation. Do not just list all the ideas for the stimulus in one paragraph and then all the ideas against in another paragraph.

➤ Refer to different beliefs and teachings and evaluate the importance of these differences.

➤ Try to refer back to what you studied in Part 1 of this course: beliefs and teachings and practices.

➤ Compare and contrast the religious views with secular views.

➤ Remember that you do not have to express a personal view – if you want to, you can, but make sure you justify your point of view with evidence and argument.

➤ Do not fall into the trap of saying 'An atheist does not believe in God and therefore would not agree with the religious point of view'. You are not adding to the argument/discussion at all.

Question 5

Student A

(a) 1 Poverty

2 Religious injustice – avenging attacks on their religious beliefs

3 Moral beliefs – e.g. animal rights

ⓔ **The student gives three valid causes of terrorism and so achieves the full 3 marks.**

(b) An absolute pacifist is someone who believes that war and violence are always wrong, even in self-defence. They believe this because of the sixth commandment: 'Do not murder.' Also Jesus taught that 'those who live by the sword shall die by the sword', meaning that if you live your life in a violent way, sometime or another you will die through violence. In the Sermon on the Mount he told people to 'turn the other cheek' and to 'love your enemies'. Quakers are pacifists because they believe that within everyone is the Holy Spirit, part of God, and therefore it is wrong in any way to harm God.

A conditional pacifist is against war and violence in principle but accepts that in certain circumstances there may be no other alternative but to resort to war – they see it as the lesser of two evils. Jesus told his followers that they should kill his enemies who did not want to acknowledge him as the son of God, which could suggest that Jesus knew that sometimes violence had to be used to overcome evil. Dietrich Bonhoeffer was a pacifist but took part in the plot of the attempted assassination of Hitler. He believed that to take no action at all would be to condone evil. Pope Francis has recently stated that he supports peace but not pacifism because he believes action must be taken to stop aggression. So pacifism appears to be a concept which is more of an ideal because sometimes the values of a pacifist have to be overruled because violence is a necessary evil.

ⓔ **The student outlines two aspects of pacifism, 'absolute' and 'conditional', and develops the explanations by supporting them with biblical quotes and examples of people who are pacifists. They also make reference to Pope Francis and draw a conclusion.**

(c) Christians base their ethical actions on teachings from the Bible, the word of God, and from their church. War features a lot in the Old Testament but there are conflicting teachings. In the book of Micah it talks of peace not war when people will 'beat their swords into ploughshares and their spears into pruning hooks'. Yet in the book of Joel it says to 'prepare for war. Raise the warriors'. Even the New Testament contains different ideas. Jesus in the Sermon on the Mount praises the peacemakers and tells his followers to 'turn the other cheek' rather than using violence. Yet he also said, 'I bring a sword' and tells his disciples to sell their cloaks to buy a sword. Yet it could be said that Christians would probably want to follow a peaceful stance rather than war because of the sixth commandment.

ⓔ **The student is focusing on biblical teachings about war showing that there appear to be different ideas or interpretations of the teachings.**

The churches also have different teachings about war. Catholics follow the authority of their Pope and will look to the just war theory in order to see whether it is appropriate to wage war or not. There are various criteria or rules which have to be met before war can begin: *jus ad bellum*, whether it is good to go to war, *jus in bello*, how people should behave in war, and *jus post bellum*, the rules which people must follow in order to ensure peace after a war. However, Quakers do not believe in war at all, they are absolute pacifists and follow the peace testimony which their founder, Charles Fox, sent to Charles II, stating that no Quaker will ever use weapons or fight in a war. In the First World War, many Quakers were conscientious objectors but they assisted the wounded in the war by being stretcher bearers.

(e) The student shows how two different denominations approach the idea of war and suggests the idea that they follow the commands of authority from their leaders when coming to a decision.

(d) All people, whether secular or religious, would say that the world is full of violence in everyday happenings: domestic, social and political. Yet although everyone desires peace and a world in which violence does not exist, it seems to be a sweeping statement to assert that violence is always wrong since there are times when violence has to be used to overcome evil.

(e) The student begins by showing that they have understood the significance of the statement and are focusing on the trigger word 'always'.

Pacifists, such as Quakers, would state that violence is always wrong. They believe that it is going against God's wishes and that within everyone there is the light of God which makes every individual special – the sanctity of life. Yet while they themselves would not do a violent action, they do help others in times of war. In the First World War many of them were stretcher bearers in the trenches and when the Second World War broke out they were ready to volunteer to do the same. So it could be said that although they are against violence, they will help others who are performing violence because they recognise that perhaps it is a necessary evil in order to make a better world. They are following St Paul's command in his letter to the Romans to 'not be overcome by evil, but to overcome evil by good'. However, is this a hypocritical stance because overcoming evil with violence is surely not a good thing to do, and similarly by helping soldiers on the battlefield to get better and fight again, is this not just a way of condoning violence?

(e) The student discusses the Quaker stance on violence and attempts to analyse whether or not it is a practical stance.

Terrorists believe that the only way to make their cause known and to succeed is by using violence, for example the IRA in the past, and ISIS today. The Catholic priest Camillo Torres renounced his priesthood to become a terrorist in order to fight against the oppression of the poor in Colombia. He believed that if Christ was on earth today he would be a guerrilla because the Old Testament prophesised that the Messiah would come to help the poor and the oppressed. Yet in contrast, Oscar Romero in San Salvador, who was also against social injustice, refused to use violence and tried to find justice through non-violent means. He based his actions on the parable of the sheep and the goats. Yet, similar to Martin Luther King who stood up against segregation and the political inequality of black Americans, both were killed in their struggles. This could suggest that non-violence does not really achieve what it sets out to do and that violence ends the same: 'those who live by the sword, die by the sword'. Many people, not just religious ones, believe that terrorism is wrong because of the innocent people who are killed through bomb attacks and horrible actions on individuals. Yet how does one overcome terrorism? Justin Welby supported the UK bombing of Syria against ISIS because he believed the actions met the just war theory criteria. He saw the action as being one which was a necessary evil. So it would appear as if violence is not always wrong because how else can the spreading of terrorist activities be stopped? However, he also pointed out that violence should not be the only action but a holistic approach should be taken.

(e) The student discusses terrorism by contrasting the beliefs of two Catholics, Torres and Romero, and evaluating which is the better method. The student develops this idea by citing Justin Welby's support of the bombing in Syria but analyses that it should not be the only response in the war on terrorism.

Sometimes violence has to be used in order to protect oneself and one's family. Dietrich Bonhoeffer did not believe in violence but he saw it as the only way to rid Germany of Hitler and so joined in the plot to assassinate him. However, Jesus blessed the peacemakers and taught his followers to 'turn the other cheek', and he also criticised Peter for cutting off the soldier's ear when they arrested him in the garden of Gethsemane. If a person is a member of the Salvation Army, they can be either a pacifist, conscientious objector or serve in the military. Some are even military chaplains. General Booth was against war but today the Salvation Army recognises that sometimes violence has to be used in order to overcome the threat of something worse. Thus it would seem that however much a Christian wants to follow the example of Jesus, sometimes in this world of conflict today there is no choice but to use the weapons of violence in order to bring about peace.

e The student gives various teachings and examples of people for and against violence and suggests that however great the desire for a peaceful world, it just cannot happen.

The Old Testament portrays God as a warrior and he is seen condoning acts of violence in order to protect his chosen people, such as the parting of the Red Sea and then allowing it to drown all the Egyptians. Jesus is seen as a pacifist who preaches the message of peace. He rode into Jerusalem on the back of a donkey. Yet he committed violence himself in righteous anger when he cleared the temple of the money lenders. The world is not the good place it was at the beginning of creation. Adam and Eve opened the floodgates to violence and evil when they took the forbidden fruit and fell under the influence of Satan. So in order to defeat the evil which is now inherent, perhaps violence is necessary as the lesser of the two evils. It is too simplistic to believe that violence is always wrong.

e The student stays focused throughout the response and does not divert into discussing war in detail instead of violence. They conclude by discussing the portrayal of God as a warrior versus Jesus the pacifist and return to the statement, coming to a judgement that violence must happen at times.

Question 5
Student B

(a) 1 Social and political injustice
     2 Unfair treatment
     3 Religious extremism

e Although the second point is a cause, it is too generalised/generic – it could refer to anything, such as a whole class being in detention because of the wrongdoings of one student, therefore it will not be awarded a mark. The other two points are valid causes – 2 marks awarded.

(b) There are different Christian attitudes to pacifism. Some believe that Jesus himself was a pacifist and thus will not use violence at any time because they wish to follow in his footsteps. They remember his teachings in the Sermon on the Mount which was to 'turn the other cheek' and to not follow the Old Testament teaching of 'an eye for an eye'. Christians also have just war theory which gives rules which allow Christians to go to war in certain cases, if the correct authority told them that they could, and if there was a really good reason for it, such as getting rid of evil like getting rid of a tyrant such as Hitler. The Archbishop of Canterbury believes that the war against ISIS is a just war and so he supported the bombing in Syria. Yet Martin Luther King was a pacifist and he campaigned about social injustice through non-violent demonstrations. So some Christians believe in pacifism while others do not.

e Student B interprets the question slightly differently to Student A and has outlined why a Christian might be a pacifist and why they might not. This is a valid interpretation and so

can be credited, but since the emphasis of the question is on pacifism, the student needs to develop more details on that concept. Also the response reads more like a list of ideas than a response focused on answering the question.

(c) There are many different Christian beliefs on war because there are different teachings in the Bible and also from the different Christian denominations. The Old Testament gives two beliefs: one that war is good, such as when God helps Joshua win in the battle of Jericho. The other belief is that war is wrong and that peace should be aimed for, such as in the book of Micah when everyone will sit under their fig trees and God will sort out problems.

The New Testament gives the message of peace, not war. Some Christians believe Jesus was a pacifist because he spoke out about violence when he was arrested in the garden of Gethsemane even though he resorted to violence with the traders in the temple.

(e) **The student gives an adequate but underdeveloped response and so does not achieve the top level. They have referred to sources of wisdom and authority to answer the question but could improve their response by including denominational views. The student attempts to respond to the trigger phrase 'explain why' but does not do so in depth.**

(d) If you are a pacifist you would insist that violence is always wrong. Martin Luther King believed in using non-violent methods to try and achieve equality for black Americans. He believed you should confront evil with love. He used sit-ins, freedom marches and the famous bus boycott. However, although his actions resulted in many of the inequalities being stopped, he did not stop racism so people might wonder what would have happened if he had used violence.

(e) **The student responds to the statement by using the example of Martin Luther King. They make a brief attempt to evaluate the outcome of non-violence.**

The UN attempts to end conflict and bring peace by sending in troops to a place to stop violence from happening. They are not allowed to use violence themselves unless it is for self-protection. Jesus taught: 'Blessed are the peacemakers for they will be called children of God.' He stood up to violence by refusing to let his disciples fight when he was arrested in the garden of Gethsemane. The book of Isaiah says he is the prince of peace. So it would appear as if violence is always wrong.

(e) **The student attempts to show that violence is wrong by using the examples of the UN and Jesus. However, there is a missed opportunity for further discussion on the fact that the UN can use violence in self-defence and that Jesus himself used violence in the temple.**

Yet many Christians will fight in wars, especially if the war meets the criteria of the just war theory as set down by Aquinas. If the war has been authorised by the correct authority, if it is a last resort, and if it aims to bring about peace, then a war can happen. God is seen as a warrior in the Old Testament and he helps Joshua defeat his enemies by making the sun stand still in the sky and sending down hail stones. Quakers, however, do not believe in war at all because they see killing as wrong, it is against the sixth commandment and because the light of God is within everyone.

(e) **The student diverts into discussing different beliefs about war. This could have been a valid interpretation if it had been tied into the use of violence.**

It is indeed difficult to believe that violence can never happen because we live in a world of violence. It could be suggested that the only thing to stop violence is violence.

(e) **The student attempts to draw a conclusion but although the construct of the argument is valid, it is underdeveloped.**

Mark scheme

5   (a) 1 mark is awarded for each correct response up to a maximum of three. Students **might** refer to:
- social injustice (such as poverty)
- political injustice (such as territory being overrun by an occupying power or not having the freedom to vote)
- religious injustice (such as China's treatment of the Tibetan Buddhist monks) or religious extremism (such as ISIS)
- moral beliefs (such as people fighting for animal rights or being against abortion)

Hints and tips

Do not spend too long on this question as it is only asking for knowledge. The trigger word is 'name', so keep your answer brief and do not spend too long trying to explain the terms.

(b) This response is marked by levels of response according to the student's knowledge and understanding of the question (AO1).

Knowledge and understanding AO1

Level	Description
1	A **weak** response with limited understanding on the concept of pacifism within the Christian religion (1–2 marks). There may be factual errors. Points might be listed with no development.
2	An **adequate** but **underdeveloped** response showing some knowledge and understanding on the different Christian attitudes to pacifism (3–4 marks). The information will be presented in a brief or descriptive way rather than showing the full depth of the understanding of the student.
3	A **good** response showing good knowledge and understanding of the different Christian attitudes to pacifism (5–6 marks). The student **might** refer to: – absolute, conditional, and preferential pacifism – biblical teachings: Ten Commandments, Sermon on the Mount, example of Jesus, or use teachings from the different denominations – specific case studies such as Dietrich Bonhoeffer, Martin Luther King, Francis of Assisi, the Quakers/the Society of Friends, the Amish, the Mennonites or any other valid example – the early Christians being pacifists – Aquinas' just war theory or war being a necessary evil – as long as the focus is on pacifism

Hints and tips

➤ The question is asking about 'attitudes', which means different viewpoints within the Christian religion about the concept of pacifism.
➤ Responses to this question should be purely knowledge-based – all 6 marks are awarded for AO1.

(c) This response is given **two** separate marks, both of which are determined by levels of response. Only **one** response is written but two different sets of **skills** are assessed by the examiner. The first mark is given for knowledge and understanding (AO1) and the second mark is awarded for the student's analysis and evaluation of the question (AO2). If the student simply writes down all they know about a specific topic, then the marks will be limited to the maximum marks for AO1. The examiner is assessing how the student uses their knowledge and understanding to relate to the specifics of the question/stimulus.

Knowledge and understanding AO1

Level	Description
1	**Some** demonstration of knowledge and understanding which is given 1 mark. This might include information and understanding on the different biblical ideas of war and peace or the different church teachings on war and peace, but this will be superficial.
2	**Good** demonstration of knowledge and understanding of Christian viewpoints on waging war which is given 2 marks. The student **might** refer to: – different interpretations of the various biblical teachings: Joel versus Micah, Old Testament contrasted with New Testament – the example of Jesus: his arrest in the garden of Gethsemane contrasted with the expulsion of the traders at the temple, or teachings on peace contrasted with the teaching to 'sell your cloak and buy a sword', or Matthew 10:34. – different churches/denominational teachings: Quakers/the Society of Friends, Catholic (just war), Church of England/Justin Welby, the Mennonites – the just war theory and holy war – the role of army chaplains – specific case studies, e.g. Iraq, Afghanistan, Falklands War, the Second World War or civil wars in such countries as Syria and the Lebanon, ISIS

Analysis and evaluation AO2

Level	Description
1	A **weak** response – the student may have given only a single viewpoint or the response is simply a description of different Christian views/attitudes on war rather than offering comments which demonstrate a judgement (1 mark).
2	A **limited** response – the student has perhaps given different Christian teachings but these have not been developed by any comment and as such the analysis is limited. **Or** the student may have attempted to comment and show judgement on one specific view (2 marks). There may be some inaccuracies or misunderstanding of the stances taken.
3	An **adequate** response – the student has compared and contrasted different Christian views on whether or not war is a good or bad thing and has attempted to show some judgement/analysis on them but the ideas and comments are not developed enough to reach the highest level (3 marks).
4	A **good** understanding of the question. The student has responded with a variety of viewpoints or different schools of thought, which are explained and analysed, and a conclusion/judgement on the question has been made (4 marks). The student **might** have: – commented on the different interpretations of the conflicting biblical teachings – commented on whether Jesus was a pacifist or not/the early church being pacifist – compared and contrasted and commented on realist Christian thought versus pacifism – applied and commented on the differing views to specific examples/case studies such as Afghanistan, ISIS, the Second World War, etc.

Hints and tips

➤ Read the question carefully and respond to the command words, which are 'explain why' and 'different beliefs'.

➤ Remember that this question is asking you to support your ideas with sources of authority and wisdom.

(d) This response is given **two** separate marks, both of which are determined by levels of response. Only **one** response is written but two different sets of **skills** are assessed by the examiner. The first mark is given for knowledge and understanding (AO1) and the second mark is awarded for the student's analysis and evaluation of the question (AO2). If the student simply writes down all they know about a specific topic, then the marks will be limited to the maximum marks for AO1. The examiner is assessing how the student uses their knowledge and understanding to relate to the specifics of the question/stimulus.

Knowledge and understanding AO1

Level	Description
1	A **limited/weak** demonstration of knowledge and understanding which is given 1 mark. This might include information and understanding about the use of violence and non-violence which is simplistic or just a list of ideas.
2	An **adequate** but **underdeveloped** demonstration of knowledge and understanding on Christian teachings on violence and/or secular views which is given 2 marks.
3	A **good** demonstration of knowledge and understanding on different Christian teachings on violence along with secular views or examples which is given 3 marks. The student **might** refer to: – definition of violence – how it is not just war but could refer to social violence, riots, domestic abuse, political demonstrations, etc. – biblical and denomination teachings on violence, sanctity of life, Decalogue, Quaker/Society of Friends' teachings – contrasting violence with a pacifist view – Jesus as a pacifist or not – secular views on violence – diverse views within a denomination, such as the Salvation Army, Church of England – specific examples: Martin Luther King, Dietrich Bonhoeffer, Camillo Torres, Oscar Romero, or any other valid example – liberation theology

Analysis and evaluation AO2

Level	Description
1	A **weak** response – the student may have only given a single viewpoint of Christian teachings on violence or the response is simply a description of events rather than offering comments which demonstrate a judgement (1–3 marks). In other words, the information is communicated in a basic way and there is no evidence of a **discussion** taking place.
2	A **limited** response – the student has perhaps given different examples or biblical or denominational teachings on violence but they have not been developed and there is little evidence of a conclusion. **Or** the student may have attempted to comment and show judgement on one specific example/teaching (4–6 marks). In other words, there is a line of reasoning/ **discussion** which has some relevance to the stimulus.
3	An **adequate** but **underdeveloped** response – the student has perhaps compared and contrasted different views on violence and has attempted to show some judgement/analysis on them but the ideas and comments are not developed enough to reach the highest level (7–9 marks). A line of reasoning has been presented and **discussed** which is mostly relevant.
4	A **good** understanding of the question. The student has responded with a variety of viewpoints or different schools of thought on violence, which are explained and analysed and a conclusion/ judgement on the question has been made (10–12 marks). The student has offered a well-developed and sustained **discussion** which is coherent, relevant and well structured. The student **might**: – compare and contrast different Christian teachings before commenting on them and then coming to a balanced conclusion, e.g. the Sermon on the Mount with Old Testament teachings, just war theory with teachings on pacifism, Quakers/Society of Friends with Justin Welby, etc. – compare and contrast different case studies of people and their views on violence before commenting on them and then coming to a balanced conclusion, e.g. Martin Luther King with Dietrich Bonhoeffer or Malcolm X, Camillo Torres with Oscar Romero, secular or generic examples – make generic or secular comments on threats to peace today (e.g. riots and terrorism) and whether or not violence is the answer to these threats

Hints and tips

➤ Read the stimulus carefully and identify its significance in your response, making sure you stick to the wording in the stimulus and do not divert into a concept that you would prefer to discuss.

➤ Remember that your response should be a **discussion** – try to present viewpoints for both sides as if you were having a conversation. Do not just list all the ideas for the stimulus in one paragraph and then all the ideas against in another paragraph.

➤ Refer to different beliefs and teachings and evaluate the importance of these differences.

➤ Try to refer back to what you studied in Part 1 of this course: beliefs and teachings and practices.

➤ Compare and contrast the religious views with secular views.

➤ Remember that you do not have to express a personal view – if you want to, you can, but make sure you justify your point of view with evidence and argument.

➤ Do not fall into the trap of saying 'An atheist does not believe in God and therefore would not agree with the religious point of view'. You are not adding to the argument/discussion at all.

Question 6

Student A

(a) A Christian teaching on forgiveness is 'if you forgive people when they sin against you, you will also be forgiven by God'. This teaching comes from the gospel of St Matthew, which is an account of Jesus preaching the Sermon on the Mount in which he gives details on how to live a moral life and so get to heaven.

e **The first mark is given for the teaching 'forgive others, God will forgive you'. The development of where this teaching comes from, the Sermon on the Mount, achieves the second mark. The third mark is given for the explanation of what the Sermon on the Mount is all about.**

(b) Christians have a problem with war because they believe taking human life is wrong, it goes against the sanctity of life, yet sometimes it is believed that there is a need for war because it is the right thing to do if they are defending their country and ensuring that justice is done. St Thomas Aquinas proposed a theory, based on the teachings of Augustine, which would try to defend the idea of going to war on certain occasions. He came up with three rules: there must be a very compelling reason to go to war, it must be started by someone in authority, and good must result from the war, not evil. Other conditions have been added by later theologians, such as proportionality and last resort. There are also rules on how the war should be fought and what must happen at the end of the war.

Quakers though would disagree with the just war theory, whatever the reason. They believe that no war could be just or a good thing. They believe that within everyone is a part of God, since humans are made in 'God's image and likeness'.

Other Christians might argue that there is no such thing as a just war – no wars ever comply with all of the conditions. For example, although the Allies in the Second World War were fighting for justice and peace, did this justify the horrific bombing of Dresden or the dropping of the atomic bombs on Japan? Some Catholics would firmly state 'no' because such acts violated the condition that an act which contributes to the indiscriminate destruction of cities is a crime against God and so must not be done (CCC 2314).

e **The student outlines the teachings and establishment of the just war theory, indicating that for some Christians this allows them to go to war. Then they show the opposing attitude that wars can never be just, as taught by the Quakers and some Catholics with regard to CCC 2314.**

(c) Christians believe that the promotion of justice is one of the main core commands of God in the Bible and the mission of Christ. The Prophet Amos taught 'to let justice roll in like a river, righteousness like a never failing stream'. This is important because it indicates what Christians should be striving for. The gospel of St Luke tells how at the start of his ministry Jesus referred to the teachings from Isaiah and proclaimed that he had been sent to 'preach the good news to the poor' and 'release the oppressed'. This is important because it shows the purpose of the incarnation: he came to earth to atone for the original sin as well as to ensure fair treatment and justice for all, because this is what God wants and what is taught by the Ten Commandments.

The Bible teaches the need to aim for peace and to maintain justice in both the Old and the New Testament. Isaiah teaches people to 'learn to do good and seek justice' and because the idea of justice is incorporated within Christian love, which is agape, this extends to social justice. James teaches 'to look after the orphans and widows', which is restating the teaching in Exodus to 'not take advantage of' them. Justice also extends to restorative justice and criminal justice. Psalm 11 teaches that God is righteous, which means he is moral and good, because 'he loves justice'.

Finally, God, who is seen as a judge by Christians, he judges, condemns and punishes people who abuse others, such as when he punished the Egyptians for making the Hebrew people their slaves. Therefore all teachings about justice are important to Christians because they are a code for righteous living and ensure that everyone is included.

(e) **The student focuses on the 'importance' of the teachings and indicates that there is more than one type of justice. They use and explain biblical teachings and offer analysis throughout.**

(d) Jesus never said it would be easy to follow him. In fact, he told his disciples that if they wanted to follow him 'they must deny themselves and take up the cross'. In those days the cross symbolised death so Jesus was actually telling his disciples that life was going to be very difficult. So when he taught in the Sermon on the Mount that people 'must forgive others' if they wanted God to forgive their sins, he was not just saying forgive those people you can forgive but if there are others who have totally upset you then you need not forgive them, he was saying you must forgive everybody. In fact, when Peter asked him how many times you should forgive someone and Peter suggested seven times, which symbolises the perfect ideal, Jesus said you must go even further and forgive 77 times, which indicated that there is no end to forgiveness. So the statement is saying that it is not possible to forgive all the time, but Christians would interpret this as meaning it might seem that it is not possible, but with the help of God and by following the example of Jesus, it is possible.

(e) **The student begins by saying that it appears as though the statement is a valid one but when looking at Jesus's teachings on forgiveness, they are indicating that whatever the difficulties, a Christian must always forgive, no matter what the emotional cost.**

A Christian would focus on the fact that Jesus suffered horribly and died on the cross to atone for all sins. By doing that he restored the relationship between humankind and God and reopened the way to heaven so that it was possible for there to be eternal life: 'For God so loved the world that He gave his one and only Son, that whoever believes in Him shall not perish but have eternal life.' So if God was prepared to forgive the horrendous sins of man, symbolised by the horrendous crucifixion, then why should people falter at forgiving others? However, many would argue that it is impossible to forgive some crimes. Should Hitler be forgiven for the Holocaust? In 2005, Anthony Walker was killed by two racists for no reason. His mother Gee Walker publicly forgave her son's killers, saying that it was her duty as a Christian to do so because if Jesus could ask God to forgive his tormenters while he was on the cross, then so she should follow his example. However, just recently one of the killers applied for early release, saying he was only 17 at the time of the crime. Gee Walker was very upset about this and said if he were to be released early then it would mean that her son had died for nothing. So has she really forgiven them? Perhaps as time goes on and all she has are the memories of her son and the realisation that he cannot fulfil his potential, she has found that total forgiveness is too hard. She believes that in order to break the chain of hate, forgiveness has to be given, but it does seem as though it is an awfully difficult thing to do in such a case.

(e) **The student discusses God's forgiveness for humanity and the forgiveness of Gee Walker and analyses and comments on the implications of the statement.**

Jesus taught about forgiveness in the Sermon on the Mount. He said that when confronted with someone else's bad action towards us, instead of reacting badly we need to look at ourselves first and decide whether we are in fact sinning ourselves: 'speck of sawdust'. He also showed the importance of God's forgiveness in the parable of the lost son. St Augustine taught that we must hate the sin but not the sinner, which was repeated by Gandhi and Martin Luther King. All of these show that forgiveness is an important aspect of being a Christian. It might seem impossible to forgive someone for a dreadful crime, but instead of just giving a nod to the idea of forgiveness by grudgingly saying 'I forgive', surely it would be more Christian-like to say that it is too hard for you to offer forgiveness at that point and then turn to God to ask him for his help. Because if forgiveness is not possible, what is going to happen to you? You will become bitter and twisted inside and as a result it will be even more difficult to be a disciple of Jesus.

(e) **The student gives some more teachings on forgiveness and then focuses on the implications of not forgiving and how that affects the person who has been wronged. The final statement returns to the opening of the response about the difficulties of being a disciple.**

Question 6
Student B

(a) One Christian teaching on forgiveness is when Peter asked Jesus how many times should he forgive a sinner and Jesus replied, 'not seven times but seventy-seven times'. Another teaching is the parable of the unmerciful servant.

(e) **The teaching of 'not seven but seventy-seven' is given the first mark and the development of putting that teaching into context receives the second mark. Because the student states that the parable was another teaching, it cannot be credited, but if the student had suggested that Jesus then told the parable to exemplify what he was teaching about 'not seven but seventy-seven', it could have been credited.**

(b) There are different Christian attitudes to the just war theory. One attitude supports it while the other is the absolute pacifist stance which rejects war and violence altogether. There are seven rules which must be obeyed if a war is to be declared a just one. The war must be declared by a legitimate authority, there must be a good reason for going to war (it can't be to expand your country or get the resources of another country), the war must promote good and defeat evil, the main aim of the war is to achieve a just and lasting peace, it can only start as a last resort after all different ways of preventing the war from happening have been tried, no innocent civilians should be killed, and lastly only enough force judged to be necessary should be used.

(e) **The student demonstrates a sound knowledge of the rules and conditions of a just war but the question is asking for different attitudes. Although this is simplistically addressed in the opening statement, the student does not explore the absolute pacifist stance.**

(c) There are many different types of justice and Christians believe that all of them are important. Christians follow the teachings within the Old and the New Testament. Isaiah teaches that 'the Lord loves justice'. This is important because it is showing Christians what God wants them to do. Catholics are taught that it is their duty to aim for peace, which has to be built upon truth, justice, love and freedom, which are all essential requirements to work for in the Christian faith. The Psalms teach that 'righteousness and justice are the foundations' of God's throne. So if God's qualities are the perfect ideal of righteousness and justice, a Christian must at least attempt to copy them. When Jesus preached the Sermon on the Mount, he proclaimed the Beatitudes and other codes of correct living, which all work to ensure that there is fair treatment for everyone, which is the key idea of justice.

(e) **The student gives an adequate but underdeveloped response and so does not achieve the top level. They list a number of sources of wisdom and authority but do not demonstrate a deep understanding of why justice is so important. The majority of marks in this question are for evaluation and comment upon the beliefs and teaching of Christianity. This answer doesn't keep this in mind.**

(d) When Jesus was dying on the cross he said, 'Father forgive them, they know not what they do.' So if Jesus was prepared to forgive people in spite of the dreadful agony he was experiencing, it means that Christians should forgive all the time. A non-believer would agree with the statement and say that it is not possible to forgive all the time because if a person has murdered someone, they have chosen to take a life away. They were not forced to do so and may have even enjoyed the power they felt, so why should they be forgiven, especially if they have not shown that they were sorry? One of the mothers of one of Myra Hindley's victims said she could never forgive Myra and would do all she could to keep Myra in jail. She said she could not even say the line in the Lord's Prayer, 'forgive us our trespasses as we forgive the trespasses of others'. This surely shows that it is not possible to forgive all the time.

ⓔ **The student discusses the Christian view of forgiveness contrasted with a secular view and one of a Christian who felt she was unable to forgive. This is a strong opening to the answer.**

It does seem impossible to forgive all the time. It could be argued that it might be impossible to forgive straight away because of the hurt and anguish felt but that as time went on forgiveness might be possible.

ⓔ **The student discusses the idea that forgiveness may come slowly. However, this would be better if it was supported with a specific case study, for example the case of Mary Foley. It would be even better if the student had used a specific quote on forgiveness to support the action, such as Colossians 3:13.**

Jesus taught in parables and in the parable of the lost son Jesus tells how God will forgive anyone if they turn to him and repent. Does this mean that if someone is not sorry for what they have done then you do not have to forgive them? It seems as though it would be very difficult to forgive someone for random shootings which have happened recently in America, such as at the nightclub when gays were deliberately targeted. How can anyone forgive someone who did that? Even if they are mentally ill, it does seem to be very difficult.

ⓔ **The student discusses the parable of the lost son and concludes that sometimes it is difficult to forgive someone. However, greater knowledge of the parable could be shown. After a strong start to this essay the student loses their way, but they have shown religious literacy and offered various viewpoints on the statement.**

Mark scheme

6   **(a)** Marks are awarded for three points which relate to each other, not three separate ideas. A mark is given for a specific teaching on forgiveness and then a further 2 marks are given for an explanation of the teaching and/or specific details of the context of the teaching. The student **might** refer to:

- 'forgive others', Matthew 6:14–15, and the Sermon on the Mount which exemplify moral teachings
- 'not seven but seventy-seven': Matthew 18:22, parable of the unmerciful servant: Matthew 18:21–35
- the Lord's Prayer/Pater Noster
- any other valid teaching

Hints and tips

➤ Do not spend too long on this question as it is only asking for knowledge, so keep your answer brief.

➤ The question is asking for one teaching, so make sure you do not penalise yourself by giving more than one teaching.

➤ Give the teaching, then explain it and/or put it into context: who said it and when.

(b) This response is marked by levels of response according to the student's knowledge and understanding of the question (AO1).

Knowledge and understanding AO1

Level	Description
1	A **weak** response with limited understanding of the concept of the different attitudes to the just war theory (1–2 marks). There may be factual errors. Points might be listed with no development.
2	An **adequate** but **underdeveloped** response showing some knowledge and understanding of the different Christian attitudes to the just war theory (3–4 marks). The information will be presented in a brief or descriptive way rather than showing the full depth of the student's understanding.
3	A **good** response showing good knowledge and understanding of the different Christian attitudes to the just war theory (5–6 marks). The student **might** make reference to: – the three parts of the theory: going to war, conduct during the war and what should happen after the war – Augustine, Aquinas, later additions to the theory – the opposition of the just war theory: no war is ever just, absolute pacifism, Quakers – why they do not believe in violence, sixth commandment, Jesus was a pacifist (although there are contradictory teachings) – specific examples: the Second World War (Dresden and Hiroshima versus Nazism and Japanese expansion), Iraq War (tyranny of Saddam Hussein, possible WMD versus conditions not met, false information)

Hints and tips

➤ The question is asking about 'attitudes', which means different viewpoints within the Christian religion about the concept of the just war theory.

➤ Try to be selective with your information.

➤ Do not be tempted to discuss war in general and the contradictory teachings in the Bible – focus on the just war theory.

(c) This response is given **two** separate marks, both of which are determined by levels of response. Only **one** response is written but two different sets of **skills** are assessed by the examiner. The first mark is given for knowledge and understanding (AO1) and the second mark is awarded for the student's analysis and evaluation of the question (AO2). If the student simply writes down all they know about a specific topic, then the marks will be limited to the maximum marks for AO1. The examiner is assessing how the student uses their knowledge and understanding to relate to the specifics of the question/stimulus.

Knowledge and understanding AO1

Level	Description
1	**Some** demonstration of knowledge and understanding which is given 1 mark. This might include information and understanding on the different Christian teachings on justice.
2	A **good** demonstration of knowledge and understanding of why Christian teachings on justice are so important, which is given 2 marks. The student **might** refer to: – different types of justice: social, legal/criminal, restorative, retributive – an explanation of what justice is/means – biblical support: Exodus 6:6, Exodus 14, Exodus 22:22, Psalm 11:7, Psalm 97:2, Psalm 106:3, Leviticus 23:22, Isaiah 1:17, Isaiah 61:1–2, Isaiah 61:8–9, Amos 5:24, Micah 4, Matthew 5–7, Luke 4:16–19, James 1:27, or any other valid teaching

Analysis and evaluation AO2

Level	Description
1	A **weak** response – the student may have given only a single viewpoint or the response simply lists different Christian teachings on justice rather than offering comments which demonstrate a judgement (1 mark).
2	A **limited** response – the student has perhaps given different Christian teachings on justice but these have not been developed with any comment and as such the analysis is limited. **Or** the student may have attempted to comment and show judgement on **one** specific view (2 marks). There may be some inaccuracies or misunderstanding of the stances taken.
3	An **adequate** response – the student has compared and contrasted different Christian teachings on justice and has attempted to show some judgement/analysis on them, but the ideas and comments are not developed enough to reach the highest level (3 marks).
4	A **good** understanding of the question. The student has responded with a variety of viewpoints or different schools of thought, which are explained and analysed, and a conclusion/judgement on the question has been made (4 marks). The student **might** have commented on: – the multitude of teachings on justice, perhaps reflecting on whether or they are an essential component of the ministry of Christ – God being the ideal role model for justice, giving examples – the view that justice is not just for Christians but should be applied to everyone – the Universal Declaration of Human Rights – the view that although there are many teachings, there are other priorities, or the view that justice will never be achieved by all

Hints and tips

➤ Read the question carefully and respond to the command term, which is 'explain the importance of'.

➤ This question is referring to justice in general, so although there are many different types, you could focus on just one, i.e. social justice, **as long as** you indicate to the examiner that you are aware that there are different types.

➤ There are so many teachings within the Bible and church decrees that it would be impossible for you to refer to all of them – just select a few that you are able to comment on and analyse why this particular teaching is important.

➤ Remember that this question is asking you to support your ideas with sources of wisdom and authority

(d) This response is given **two** separate marks, both of which are determined by levels of response. Only **one** response is written but two different sets of **skills** are assessed by the examiner. The first mark is given for knowledge and understanding (AO1) and the second mark is awarded for the student's analysis and evaluation of the question (AO2). If the student simply writes down all they know about a specific topic, then the marks will be limited to the maximum marks for AO1. The examiner is assessing how the student uses their knowledge and understanding to relate to the specifics of the question/stimulus.

Knowledge and understanding AO1

Level	Description
1	A **limited/weak** demonstration of knowledge and understanding which is given 1 mark. This might include information and understanding about the act of forgiveness which is simplistic or just a list of ideas.
2	An **adequate** but **underdeveloped** demonstration of knowledge and understanding on different Christian teachings on the act of forgiveness which is given 2 marks. There may be superficial use of sources of wisdom and authority.
3	A **good** demonstration of knowledge and understanding on different Christian teachings on the act of forgiveness along with examples, which have developed explanations. This is given 3 marks. The student **might** refer to: – definition of forgiveness, what it entails, what happens if you do not forgive – biblical and denominational teachings on forgiveness: Matthew 5:39, Matthew 6:14–15, Matthew 7:1–5, Matthew 16:24, Matthew 18:21–35, Matthew 26:28, Luke 15:11–31, Luke 16:24, Colossians 3:13, or any other valid quote – specific cases: Gee Walker 2005, Mary Foley

Analysis and evaluation AO2

Level	Description
1	A **weak** response – the student may have given only a single viewpoint of Christian teachings on forgiveness or the response is simply a description of events rather than offering comments which demonstrate a judgement (1–3 marks). In other words, the information is communicated in a basic way and there is no evidence of a **discussion** taking place.
2	A **limited** response – the student has perhaps given different examples or biblical or denominational teachings on forgiveness but they have not been developed and there is little evidence of a conclusion. **Or** the student may have attempted to comment and show judgement on one specific example/teaching (4–6 marks). In other words, there is a line of reasoning/ **discussion** which has some relevance to the stimulus.
3	An **adequate** but **underdeveloped** response – the student has perhaps compared and contrasted different teachings on forgiveness and has attempted to show some judgement/ analysis on them but the ideas and comments are not developed enough to reach the highest level (7–9 marks). A line of reasoning has been presented and **discussed** which is mostly relevant.
4	A **good** understanding of the question. The student has responded with a variety of viewpoints or different schools of thought on forgiveness which are explained and analysed and a conclusion/judgement on the question has been made (10–12 marks). The student has offered a well-developed and sustained **discussion** which is coherent, relevant and well structured. The student **might**: – compare and contrast different ideas on whether forgiveness should be given straight away, later, or at all – analyse the impossibility of forgiveness all the time and what it does to the wronged person – analyse and comment on God's forgiveness and human forgiveness

Hints and tips

➤ Read the stimulus carefully and identify its significance in your response, making sure you stick to the wording in the stimulus and do not divert into a concept that you would prefer to discuss.

➤ Remember that your response should be a **discussion** – try to present viewpoints for both sides as if you were having a conversation. Do not just list all the ideas for the stimulus in one paragraph and then all the ideas against in another paragraph.

➤ Refer to different beliefs and teachings and evaluate the importance of these differences.

➤ Try to refer back to what you studied in Part 1 of this course: beliefs and teachings and practices.

➤ Compare and contrast the religious views with secular views.

➤ Remember that you do not have to express a personal view – if you want to, you can, but make sure you justify your point of view with evidence and argument.

➤ Do not fall into the trap of saying 'An atheist does not believe in God and therefore would not agree with the religious point of view'. You are not adding to the argument/discussion at all.

Christianity: dialogue between religious and non-religious beliefs and attitudes

Question 7
Student A

(a) 1 There are religious representatives in the House of Lords
2 Public holidays are based around Christian festivals, e.g. Christmas
3 Faith schools receive public funding

(e) **The student gives three correct ideas and thus achieves the full 3 marks.**

(b) Great Britain is seen to be mainly Christian, although there are many other different religions within its multicultural society. As a result, some Christians are exclusivists, and believe that only their religion is true and that the others are false. They base this belief on the incarnation of Christ and the Bible because it is the true word of God. So they think that only those who have a personal faith in Jesus and accept that he is their saviour can go to heaven. Anyone else will be sent to hell. They believe this because Jesus said: 'I am the way, the truth and the life. No one comes to the Father except through me.' They would reject the idea of pluralism, which accepts all the different religions as being valid because they say there are many ways to God, on the grounds that there can only be one true faith. Exclusivists would also reject the idea of inclusivism, which argues that although Christianity is the one true religion, there can be anonymous Christians who are people who through their actions show they are following the way of Christ even though they may not have had the opportunity to have knowledge of Christ. Exclusivists of course reject this idea and believe you must have accepted Christ into your life in order to be saved. The Roman Catholic Church traditionally were exclusivists, although more modern teachings will allow for some non-Catholics and non-Christians to be saved. Pope Benedict XVI declared other religions were in a 'gravely deficient situation'. Some exclusivists go as far as stating that other religions are only partially true or are controlled by Satan.

(e) **The student responds to the instructions in the question throughout the response by acknowledging that Great Britain has diverse religious traditions. They outline what exclusivism is and support their explanations with biblical quotes. They contrast exclusivism with pluralism and inclusivism but return to exclusivism in the concluding statement.**

(c) Christians believe that marriage is a sacrament and it is a ceremony that should be done in the 'eyes of God' in order for God to show his blessing. At the beginning of the ceremony, the priest or vicar tells the congregation how Christ was at a wedding when he performed his first miracle and that marriage is 'a gift of God in creation'. Therefore, to a Christian the ceremony is an eventful and spiritual occasion. However, a secular marriage is not a sacrament nor is it spiritual but just an event with no reference to God. Therefore, although some Christians would accept that the couple are pronouncing their love for each other, they would not believe that it had any religious significance or was binding, and so therefore was not an important part of their beliefs. God would not have joined the couple into the 'one flesh' which he did for Adam and Eve.

Another point of disagreement is that secular marriages can take place anywhere, it does not have to be in a registered set place, and there are no set rules on how the ceremony proceeds, the couple can decide what they want to say. So Christians would be against this because they believe that it should take place in a religious building which is the house of God and therefore special. Also the vows which are said at a Christian marriage, 'for better or worse, in sickness or health', are said in front of God and therefore are sacred and should not be broken. They can act as a guide if the couple run into difficulties during the marriage. A Christian will see these vows as a reminder that marriage is meant to be a life-long commitment. If these vows aren't present at a secular marriage then it might encourage people to see marriage as something that isn't permanent, and lead to divorce, which a lot of Christians wouldn't agree with. Yet secularists would disagree and believe that their promises or statement are special and binding because they are said in front of witnesses.

(e) The student focuses their response on the idea of marriage being a sacrament which requires God's presence and blessing. This is developed by contrasting it to secular beliefs. The student uses biblical teachings and quotes from a Christian wedding service to support the Christian views. This is important because the examiner will be assessing the student's ability to refer to sources of wisdom and authority. There is balance and attempts at analysis.

(d) Whatever stance Christians take on abortion, whether it should be the mother's choice or the father's, or whether it is a matter of the sanctity of life or the quality of life, all Christians would agree that it is a religious matter. They believe this because they believe that all life is created by God. The Psalms tell them that God 'created my inmost being'. Humanists would agree with the statement that it is not a religious matter because they have no belief in a divine entity, and they would weigh up the evidence as to why the abortion was being considered and try to come to a conclusion about which would be the kindest course of action. In fact, they would follow the golden rule 'to treat others as you would like to be treated', which is Jesus's own second great commandment, 'to love thy neighbour as thyself'. So although there is a distinct dividing line between the two – one states abortion is a religious matter while the other side states it is not – there is still the idea that compassion should be considered when considering the idea of abortion. And since Jesus taught his central message of love, 'love others as I have loved you', perhaps it could be said that the dividing line is not as apparent between the two views as at first thought.

(e) The student opens the discussion by showing that although there are two distinct views on the statement, there is a bridge between them, which is compassion.

Members of the Salvation Army would also state that the dilemma of abortion is a religious matter. They believe in the sanctity of life, 'God created man in his image'. Although they do not condone abortion, they do recognise that it is acceptable in certain circumstances, such as rape or if medical procedures determine the foetus has something severely wrong with it. They would suggest that each case merits prayer and careful thought and after the procedure they would support and show love and compassion, which Jesus taught, to the mother involved. Hence abortion is a matter of religion because the dilemma focuses on the core of their ethical belief which is that all life belongs to God.

(e) The student states that abortion is a religious matter by giving the Salvation Army view and supports and develops the response with biblical quotes and reference to their ethical code.

However, for people who are not religious then of course it is not a religious matter. They would base their decision on whether to have an abortion or not on the quality of life of both the mother and the baby. The parents may not be able to afford a child or to give it the love it requires and as such they would feel justified to make the decision dependent on their own personal moral and ethical code. Supporters of pro-choice would agree and while supporters of pro-life would argue for the right of the unborn child, but it does not mean that their disagreement is down to religious reasons. Science has developed to such a state that many abnormalities which would disadvantage both the family and the unborn child can be detected early on in the pregnancy and therefore many would consider an abortion to be the best possible and compassionate action to take. They would argue that bringing religion into the discussion, such as by citing the sixth commandment, it is just making the decision harder and trying to emotionally blackmail the mother at a time when she should be supported, not criticised.

(e) The student gives reasons as to why abortion is not a religious matter. By referencing religion, they argue that it could be seen as a form of emotional blackmail.

People who are religious will of course state that the ethical dilemma of abortion is a religious matter. Christians will argue for the sanctity of life and that God told Adam and Eve to 'go forth and multiply'. Catholics see abortion as a mortal sin because they believe the soul is present from the moment of conception and thus their decisions will be advised by their beliefs and the teachings of the church. However, it is too simplistic to believe there is a clear dividing line between religious and non-religious people. People who are not religious often base their ethical decisions on religious teachings. Many societies today base their legal code on the Ten Commandments, such as 'do not murder' and 'do not steal'. Therefore, perhaps it could be stated that abortion is a matter for the conscience of the individual and whether they base that on religious or secular teachings/beliefs is purely a matter of what they personally believe.

ⓔ **The student ends the discussion with a balanced conclusion. The student has not been tempted to write a response about whether abortion or not should be allowed but focuses on the statement about whether it is a religious matter or not.**

Question 7
Student B

(a) 1 Christmas

2 Remembrance services are Christian services

3 Sunday trading laws are based on the fact that Sunday is the Christian holy day

ⓔ **This response would achieve only 2 marks because the first point needs further elaboration. The student needs to say that public holidays are based around Christian holidays, for example, Christmas.**

(b) Most people are supposedly Christians in the UK and they have different beliefs about the other religions which can be found in the UK. Exclusivist Christians do not accept other religions as being true, they believe that Christians are the only ones to go to heaven if they accept Jesus in their lives and believe that he was sent to save them. They base this on the teaching of St John's Gospel, which says: 'For God so loved the world that He gave his one and only Son that whoever believes in Him shall not perish but have eternal life'.

Also Jesus said that only he was the way and the truth, meaning that only those who believe in him can reach God. So anyone who believes in another religion, such as Islam or Hinduism, will go to hell, they cannot be saved.

ⓔ **The student opens the response by recognising the instructions in the question about the diversity within British religious traditions. They outline what exclusivists believe and support their response with two biblical quotes from the gospel of St John. The student develops the response to reject other religions and even some Christian denominations. However, the response is underdeveloped. In order for the student to achieve the top level they could include further ideas on exclusivism, or a contrast with other schools of thought.**

(c) Secularists believe that religion and state should not mix. As such they would see marriage as a right of all people, and that religion should not come into someone's decision to get married.

A secularist can have a civil marriage. This is a legally recognised union of two people. The civil marriage must not be religious, or contain any form of worship, or be conducted by a minister of any religion.

Christians will disagree with a civil marriage because it excludes God from the marriage. Christians believe that God is an important part of a couple's marriage. Ecclesiastes 4:12 says 'Though one may be overpowered, two can defend themselves. A cord of three strands is not quickly broken'.

This emphasises that God is involved in a Christian marriage. The couple have additional help in their marriage that a civil marriage won't. Christians will be able to withstand difficulties in their marriage in a way that secularists won't.

A secular marriage is more about telling witnesses why they are choosing to get married and why their relationship is special to them. Christians get married in a place of worship to get blessed by God and to make their vows in front of him as a witness to make sure they do not break them.

(e) **The student's response is more implicit than explicit on why Christians disagree with humanist marriages. As such the analysis is also implicit and so this is an underdeveloped response. The student supports their statements with biblical references, thus addressing the instructions in the question about referring to sources of wisdom and authority.**

(d) Christians have different views on abortion. Some believe it is always wrong, while others believe it can happen in special circumstances such as rape, or if the baby will have severe medical issues when it is born. They might base their decision on whether the sanctity of life is more important than the quality of life or whether it is a matter of agape love. Thus the question about whether to have an abortion or not is a religious one. To people who do not have any religious faith or follow any religious teachings then the question of abortion is a matter of personal choice. They would consider why they might need an abortion and what the possible consequences might be. There would be no reference to religion whatsoever.

(e) **The student opens the response by stating that there is a clear dividing line between religious and non-religious people.**

Catholics are usually pro-life Christians. They believe that life is created by God for a special purpose, that life begins at conception and this is the time when God plants the soul of the person: 'I knew you in the womb.' So for them abortion is usually wrong. Similarly, the General Synod of the Church of England stated that while they oppose abortion they recognise that there are strictly limited conditions when it might take place. So whether they say no or yes to an abortion is based on religious teachings.

(e) **The student specifies in a descriptive manner the views on abortion of the Catholic Church and the Church of England but demonstrates that they are responding to the statement in the final sentence. The student could include knowledge of some of the instances in which abortion might be allowed in the Church of England,**

Pope Francis is firmly against abortion, believing it to be a symptom of today's 'throw-away culture'. Yet even though most Catholics will follow the teachings of their church and the Pope, the Catholic Church has stated that it is a matter for each Catholic to follow his or her own conscience, even when it conflicts with church teaching. So some Catholics are pro-choice.

(e) **This could have been a valid point if the student had indicated how it linked into the statement. They could have developed the response by discussing whether conscience is a religious construct or a secular one.**

Secular or non-religious people obviously do not consider a religious teaching when they are thinking about having an abortion. They will base their decision on social and economic means – whether they can afford to have the child, whether it will interfere with their career, whether the child will be loved. They might consider the people who target abortion clinics as wicked and who have no right to condemn anyone who has had to come to the decision to have an abortion. They believe the decision is purely down to personal choice.

(e) **Although the student begins well, they fail to demonstrate throughout the response that they have understood the significance of the statement. The analysis is more implicit than explicit and areas of the answer needed to be developed further.**

Mark scheme

7 **(a)** 1 mark is awarded for each correct response up to a maximum of three. Students **might** refer to:
- religious representatives in parliament – House of Lords
- faith schools
- Christian services to mark key events, e.g. remembrance services
- public holidays based on Christians celebrations
- the Queen is the head of the Church of England
- the Queen appoints the Archbishop of Canterbury

Hints and tips

Do not spend too long on this question as it is only asking for knowledge, so keep your answer brief.

(b) This response is marked by levels of response according to the student's knowledge and understanding of the question (AO1). The examiner will also determine whether the student has responded to the instructions in the question about the diversity of religious traditions in Great Britain.

Knowledge and understanding AO1

Level	Description
1	A **weak** response with limited understanding of what the term exclusivism means and how it relates to the Christian religion. There may be factual errors. Points might be listed with no development. (1–2 marks).
2	An **adequate** but **underdeveloped** response on what the term exclusivism means and how it relates to Christian thought (3–4 marks). These ideas will be outlined in a brief or descriptive way rather than showing the full depth of the student's understanding. There is a selection of appropriate sources of wisdom and authority – but this may be superficially used.
3	A **good** response showing knowledge and understanding of what the term exclusivism means and how it relates to Christian thought (5–6 marks). The student **might**: – have indicated that they recognise that religious traditions in Great Britain are diverse, but mainly Christian – have given a definition of the term exclusivism and may have contrasted it with the term inclusivism – support the definition of exclusivism with biblical quotes and/or teachings from the different Christian denominations, e.g. John 14: 6, John 3: 16–18, Romans 10: 13–15, Acts 10: 4–12, or any other valid quote – support the definition of inclusivism with biblical quotes and/or teachings from the different Christian denominations, e.g. parable of the sheep and the goats, John 14: 2, agape

Hints and tips

➤ The command word is 'outline', which is asking you to set out the main characteristics of exclusivism. You should include a definition of what it is, plus an explanation showing what it means, biblical support for the belief, and perhaps a contrast with other beliefs to show you have full understanding of the term.

➤ Remember that the instructions with the question ask you to consider that 'religious traditions in Great Britain are diverse, but mainly Christian', so you must make reference to this in your response.

(c) This response is given **two** separate marks, both of which are determined by levels of response. Only **one** response is written but two different sets of **skills** are assessed by the examiner. The first mark is given for knowledge and understanding (AO1) and the second mark is awarded for the student's analysis and evaluation of the question (AO2). If the student simply writes down all they know about a specific topic, then the marks will be limited to the maximum marks for AO1. The examiner is assessing how the student uses their knowledge and understanding to relate to the specifics of the question/stimulus.

Knowledge and understanding AO1

Level	Description
1	**Some** demonstration of knowledge and understanding of Christian disagreements with secular marriages which is given 1 mark.
2	**Good** demonstration of knowledge and understanding of Christian views in relation to secular marriages which is given 2 marks. The student **might** refer to: – the Christian views of marriage being a sacrament, God's presence, holy, until death, vows are religiously binding, supported with biblical quotes or references to a particular denominational service – a comparison between Christian views and secular views, that a secular service is seen as special, no reference to God, unique because the couple can decide on what happens – it is not a set service – the legal aspects

Analysis and evaluation AO2

Level	Description
1	A **weak** response – the student may have given only a single viewpoint or the response simply lists different views/attitudes on why Christians might criticise a secular marriage rather than offering comments which demonstrate a judgement (1 mark).
2	A **limited** response – the student has perhaps given different Christian views on why they do not agree with secular marriages but these have not been developed by any comment and as such the analysis is limited. **Or** the student may have attempted to comment and show judgement on **one** specific view (2 marks). There may be some inaccuracies or misunderstanding of the stances taken.
3	An **adequate** response – the student has given different Christian views on why they do not agree with secular marriages and has attempted to show some judgement/analysis on these views, but the ideas and comments are not developed enough to reach the highest level (3 marks). There may be evidence of a conclusion but this is not in sufficient depth to reach Level 4.
4	A **good** understanding of the question. The student has responded with a variety of viewpoints on why Christians are against secular marriages. These are explained and analysed and a conclusion/judgement on the question has been made (4 marks). The student **might** comment and come to a conclusion on the view that: – Christian marriage is a sacrament/spiritual experience, ordained and blessed by God, 'one flesh', vows are a guide for married life, 'marriage an honourable estate' – secular marriages are an event to declare love and explain why couples want to get married, non-legal, same-sex marriages accepted, divorce accepted

Hints and tips

➤ Remember that if you are explaining, you should use the word 'because' or the phrase 'for the reason that'.

➤ Include some comments/analysis on the explanations.

➤ Remember that this question is asking you to support your ideas with sources of wisdom and authority.

➤ Keep in mind that the majority of marks in this part(c) question are for AO2. Therefore, make sure you comment upon and evaluate the Christian views you present, in relation to secular marriages

(d) This response is given **two** separate marks, both of which are determined by levels of response. Only **one** response is written but two different sets of **skills** are assessed by the examiner. The first mark is given for knowledge and understanding (AO1) and the second mark is awarded for the student's analysis and evaluation of the question (AO2). If the student simply writes down all they know about a specific topic, then the marks will be limited to the maximum marks for AO1. The examiner is assessing how the student uses their knowledge and understanding to relate to the specifics of the question/stimulus.

Knowledge and understanding AO1

Level	Description
1	A **limited/weak** demonstration of knowledge and understanding which is given 1 mark. This might include information and understanding about Christian beliefs and/or secular ideas on abortion which are simplistic or just a list of ideas.
2	An **adequate** but **underdeveloped** demonstration of knowledge and understanding which is given 2 marks. This might include different examples of church or denominational teachings on the ethics of abortion, e.g. sanctity of life, sixth commandment, biblical teachings, etc. However, the use of these sources of wisdom and authority may be superficial. These will have been contrasted with simplistic secular ideas.
3	A **good** demonstration of knowledge and understanding which is given 3 marks. This might include different examples of church or denominational teachings on the ethics of abortion supported by reference to specific quotes while being contrasted with secular ideas. The student **might** refer to: – the sanctity of life (referring back to what they learned in Part 1 (beliefs and teachings and practices) contrasted with quality of life, pro-choice versus pro-life, scientific or secular views – biblical quotes: Psalm 139: 13, sixth commandment, Psalm 137: 3–5, Genesis 1: 28, Jeremiah 1: 5, 1 Corinthians 6: 19, Job 1: 21, etc. – compassion/agape – Catholic teachings: papal encyclicals, Pope Francis, doctrine of double effect – the Didache – legal requirements/secular/scientific views

Analysis and evaluation AO2

Level	Description
1	A **weak** response – the student may have given only a single viewpoint or the response is simply a description of ideas on whether abortion is a religious matter or not rather than offering comments which demonstrate a judgement (1–3 marks). In other words, the information is communicated in a basic way and there is no evidence of a **discussion** taking place.
2	A **limited** response – the student has perhaps given different examples of biblical or denominational teachings on abortion contrasted with secular views but they have not been developed and there is little evidence of a conclusion. **Or** the student may have attempted to comment and show judgement on a specific Christian idea contrasted with secular beliefs (4–6 marks). In other words, there is a line of reasoning/**discussion** which has some relevance to the stimulus.
3	An **adequate** but **underdeveloped** response – the student has perhaps given different views on whether abortion is a religious concern and has attempted to show some judgement/analysis on them, but the ideas and comments are not developed enough to reach the highest level (7–9 marks). A line of reasoning has been presented and **discussed** which is mostly relevant.
4	A **good** understanding of the question. The student has responded with a variety of viewpoints or different schools of thought on whether abortion is a religious concern, which are explained and analysed, and a conclusion/judgement on the question has been made (10–12 marks). The student has offered a well-developed and sustained **discussion** which is coherent, relevant and well structured. The student **might**: – compare and contrast Christian and secular views on whether the decision of abortion should be made according to religious teachings or secular ones and then comment or make a judgement – consider the idea of personal choice only, which could be determined by religious or some other thought and how religion can be seen as emotional blackmail – consider the after-effects of abortion – emotional and physical – consider that science has gone too far and that often medical personnel may make a judgement on the viability of the embryo and later be proved wrong – consider the view that following religious teachings helps in the decision making

Hints and tips

➤ Read the stimulus carefully and identify its significance your response, making sure you stick to the wording in the stimulus and do not divert into a concept that you would prefer to discuss.

➤ Remember too that your response should be a **discussion** – try to present viewpoints for both sides as if you were having a conversation. Do not just list all the ideas for the stimulus in one paragraph and then all the ideas against in another paragraph.

➤ Refer to different beliefs and teachings and evaluate the importance of these differences.

➤ Try to refer back to what you studied in Part 1 of this course: beliefs and teachings and practices.

➤ Compare and contrast the religious views with secular views.

➤ Remember that you do not have to express a personal view – if you want to, you can, but make sure you justify your point of view with evidence and argument.

➤ Do not fall into the trap of saying 'An atheist does not believe in God and therefore would not agree with the religious point of view'. You are not adding to the argument/discussion at all.

Question 8

Student A

(a) A secularist may have an issue with church schools because most of the funding for faith schools come from public funds. They might argue that in some ways this is state-sponsored evangelisation, and that religion is a private thing, and that if people want church schools they should have to pay for these themselves.

ⓔ The first mark is given for stating that church schools receive funds, from the public purse, the second mark is given for explaining why the first point is an issue, and the third point is for suggesting what a secularist would prefer to be the case.

(b) Although there are many other different religions within its multicultural society, Britain is usually described as being a Christian country. Religion – Christianity – does play a big role in the public life in the UK. The monarch is the head of the Church of England and 15 other commonwealth countries. The official title of the monarch is 'His/Her Majesty, by the Grace of God, of the United Kingdom of Great Britain and Northern Ireland… Defender of the Faith'. In this case the faith is the Church of England, a denomination within Christianity. In fact the Archbishop of Canterbury – the Primate of the Church of England – is the person who actually crowns new monarchs, showing just how interlinked state and religion are in the UK.

In the UK there are two Houses of Parliament. The second of these houses is known as the House of Lords. In the House of Lords there are 26 Lords Spiritual. These are all bishops of the Church of England. This means that bishops of the Church of England can play a significant role in the running of the UK. At the current time, the House of Lords are debating the Brexit legislation that the government is trying to bring into law.

In the UK there are many public events that are marked by Christian services. For example, when Prince William and Kate Middleton got married, it took place in Westminster Abbey and the Archbishop of Canterbury conducted the service. Another example is that every November, a National Service of Remembrance takes place in London to remember the contribution of service personnel in the two world wars. The service is essentially a Christian service as it includes Christian prayers and hymns, for example 'Abide with me'.

ⓔ The student shows knowledge of the various ways in which religion – specifically Christianity – plays a role in public life in the UK. Their knowledge is accurate and developed to a good extent.

(c) A forced marriage is when one of the couple has not consented to be married. During the wedding service both the groom and then the bride are asked individually whether they give their consent to the marriage before they state their vows. This underlines the importance that consent is crucial and if consent is not given then the ceremony will be cancelled. Catholics are against forced marriages so much that they will allow an annulment, which states the marriage never happened, if it is discovered either the bride or groom were forced to give consent. It is also illegal in this country for a marriage to take place if it is a forced one and it is against the Universal Declaration of Human Rights. However, even in this modern age, there are many countries which allow very young girls to be married to much older men. This is not only physically dangerous for the young girl but also emotionally and spiritually dangerous, and is in fact child abuse. Christians are against these marriages because they believe that marriage is between a man and a woman, not a young girl who has no real idea about what marriage entails. Jesus repeated the teaching from Genesis that marriage is when a man leaves his home to take a wife and they become 'one flesh'. For a Christian, marriage is not just about the physical union but about the spiritual union and as such marriage is a sacrament. Thus a forced or child marriage is making a mockery of this. It is insulting God in asking for his blessing on an immoral act, especially when in the service, marriage is described as an 'honourable estate'. Some Christians who live in different countries to the UK believe in arranged marriages, which are usually said to have the consent of the couple but sometimes one of the couple may not have much choice because of pressure from the parents. The Bible refers to an arranged marriage between Isaac and Rebecca in Genesis, in which Rebecca goes willingly. However, since this occasion was written in times of a patriarchal society, when women were considered to be the property of their husbands, it could be argued that she did not have much choice. Therefore, Christians are against forced marriages, whichever type, because it is both legally and morally wrong and it does not fulfil God's purpose.

ⓔ **The student addresses various types of forced marriages and explains why they are wrong in the eyes of a Christian. They offer biblical support and also church teachings, as well as analysis and comment.**

(d) There is the view that Great Britain is becoming a secularised society due to the dwindling church attendances (in some churches) and the fact that there are many other religious faiths. As a result, some believe that the church is not wanted in today's society and should not be involved in political decisions such as education because they see faith schools as being divisive. They believe everyone should have the right to form their own opinion on whether they want to follow a faith or not. However, in order to form a decision, a person does need to have all the facts. France does not allow the teaching of religious education in their schools, but because of the recent horrific events in which people have been killed, many are now questioning this because they believe that knowledge of other faiths promotes tolerance and stops ignorance. Yet the religious tradition of Great Britain is predominantly Christian. This is because of the historical tradition when the church and kings ruled together. In fact, William the Conqueror used the church to subdue the English. The common people were threatened by the church to obey the king or go to hell. This is perhaps one of the reasons why secularists believe that religion should not be involved in the ruling of society. So it is difficult to say whether religion is wanted or not because there are pros and cons on both sides.

ⓔ **The student opens the discussion by showing that the statement is complex and that perhaps there can be no clear answer. They use historical and modern examples.**

In 2011 the High Court sided with Derby City Council in a case where an anti-homosexual couple were barred from being foster parents. Two judges declared that there was 'no place in British law for Christian beliefs'. Christians were outraged and stated that many of society's values and laws are based on some of the Ten Commandments: do not steal, do not murder, etc. But when referring to biblical authority it can be suggested that perhaps the church and the law should be kept separate. Jesus taught that no one can serve two masters – God has to come first. So what does this mean for society? A Christian would argue that it is a good thing because God is omniscient and he created the world for a special purpose for humans to live in harmony and do good works. So by following Christian teachings such as agape, and God's commands in the Bible, this will enable people to live in peace. However, an atheist such as Richard Dawkins would argue that 'faith is one of the world's great evils' because religion supplies false answers to scientific questions and also it gives false hope, such as miracles. Nietzsche stated 'God is dead', referring to the fact that we no longer need a fantasy figure in our lives as a comfort blanket because science can provide the answers and humans are mature enough to make decisions for themselves without relying on a book written hundreds of years ago. It is debatable whether humans are mature enough when you look at the atrocities committed in the world, some of which are done in the name of religion. Again, it looks as though the arguments for both sides of the statement have good and bad points.

ⓔ **The student again discusses the complex implications of the statement but using the example of the High Court ruling in 2011 and then comparing and contrasting biblical authority. They use Dawkins and Nietzsche to argue for secularism but also criticise these views.**

In Peter's first epistle he tells people to 'submit yourselves for the Lord's sake to every authority instituted among men…show proper respect to everyone'. This mirrors Paul's letter to the Romans in which he states 'let every person be subject to the governing authority' because God had placed them in power. This might indicate that religion and society should be separate because we are told to follow the laws of men, but on the other hand it is also saying that the authorities are only there because God has put them in power. This then raises the question, if God puts governments in power, why are there tyrannical governments in Syria and North Korea? It seems as though when one problem is answered about the statement another one comes into being. Thus it is impossible to state whether or not religion is wanted in a secular society. Obviously the secularists say no, religion is not wanted, because freedom of thought and conscience should not be dictated by religion. Christians would argue otherwise because they would look to countries which have tried to do away with religion, e.g. communist countries, and state that although religious belief is suppressed by the governments in power, they have not been able to wipe out religious belief. Therefore it could be stated that everyone has free will and if they want to be religious then that is okay, and if they do not then that is okay. But it still does not answer the question which is then raised — should religious values have an impact on legal laws?

ⓔ **The student uses biblical sources to discuss whether or not people should obey secular laws or religious ones. They come to the conclusion that there is no clear answer to the statement.**

Question 8
Student B

(a) A problem with church schools is that they have a religious character.

ⓔ **The phrase 'religious character' is inherent within the concept of a church school, so this would not receive any marks. The student would have to explain why a secularist would have an issue with the values of a church school.**

(b) Religion, more specifically Christianity, has a big role in public life in the UK. For example, in the UK there are restrictions in the hours that shops are allowed to be open on a Sunday. Sunday has traditionally been the Christian day of rest, and these restrictions reflect the commandment 'keep the Sabbath day holy'.

In both Houses of Parliament, their meetings begin with Christian prayers, despite the fact that parliament is now very multicultural, for example in 2017 the first female Sikh was elected to parliament.

Public holidays are also based around Christian festivals. For example, two of the major school holidays are at Christmas and Easter time. This wouldn't be the case if the UK was a Muslim country.

ⓔ **The student gives some valid ways in which religion plays a role in public life in the UK. However, the final two ways are underdeveloped and lack both breadth and depth.**

(c) During the wedding ceremony, the vicar or priest will ask the congregation if anyone knows of any impediment to the marriage taking place. This gives people a chance to speak out if they believe that the marriage should not take place, for instance if they think either the bride or groom is being forced into the marriage against his or her will. In the ceremony both the bride and the groom are asked if they are willing to marry the other person and they say 'I will'. This all goes to show that forced marriages are considered to be bad by Christians. Christians would also be against child marriages, which happen in many countries around the world, even though scholars would argue that Mary would only have been a young teenager when she was engaged to Joseph.

ⓔ **The student addresses both arranged and forced marriages. They use support from the wedding service and a scholarly argument about Mary's age. However, their analysis is very simplistic.**

(d) Do secularists want religion involved in society? The answer is no. Do religious people, such as Christians, want religion involved in society? The answer is yes. But who should have the final say? The religious people or the secularists? Secularists want to protect the different religions from one another in this country. Yet what happens when a person's religious rights clash with another religion? Who is to say which religion should take precedence? Should the country in which there is a major religion, such as Great Britain, which is predominantly Christian, allow Christianity to have the final say? Case studies say no: the High Court ruling in 2011 stated there was 'no place in British law for Christian beliefs' and so this is saying Christianity is not wanted in a secularised society. But is Great Britain a secular society? There is a multitude of different religions which would indicate that it is not. Secularists and all the different religions share core values such as compassion, human dignity and the importance of the individual. So who is to say it is not a matter of 'wanting', but in fact it is a matter that both views should work in harmony because both have something valuable to say.

ⓔ **The student demonstrates an understanding of the implications within the statement, indicating that perhaps the trigger word 'wanting' is wrong and religion should in fact be about mutual cooperation.**

Many of the biblical teachings are contradictory about whether to obey God or the government in charge. Jesus taught that the Roman taxes should be paid, 'render unto Caesar', but he also taught 'you can't obey two masters'. Peter in Acts says 'we must obey God rather than men', but in his first letter to the early church he told them to submit themselves 'to every authority instituted among men'. So it is difficult to say whether or not religion is wanted in a secular society.

ⓔ **The student introduces the idea of contradictory teachings but does not develop them in any way to indicate a discussion. They attempt to link them to the statement but not very satisfactorily.**

Some people believe that religion has impeded science. Catholic views on IVF have stated that it is wrong. Genetic engineering has been criticised. The Christian church is against the legalisation of same-sex marriages because they believe God created man and woman to be in a marriage and nothing else. So these people do not want religion in their society because they do not agree that there is a God in the first place and therefore the teachings which are put forward against the progress of science are false. Therefore it could be stated that due to the negativity that religion sometimes brings to society, and because we are constantly evolving and inventing new technology, religion is not wanted in society.

ⓔ **The student argues for the statement in the conclusion but they could have also presented the value of religious ideas in society before coming to a judgement.**

Mark scheme

8 **(a)** Marks are awarded for three points which relate to each other, not three separate ideas. A mark is given for a specific reason why a secularist might be against faith schools, and a further 2 marks are given for an explanation or example of the reason. The student **might** refer to:

- the fact that church schools receive most of their income from public funds.
- church schools might select students based on their religion (discrimination)
- in church schools acts of worship will be Christian
- it is wrong that children should not be allowed to attend what might be their local school because of their (or their parents') religion.

Hints and tips

➤ Do not spend too long on this question as it is only asking for knowledge, so keep your answer brief.

➤ The command word is 'one reason', so do not give more than one as the examiner will consider only the first reason.

(b) This response is marked by levels of response according to the student's knowledge and understanding of the question (AO1).

Knowledge and understanding AO1

Level	Description
1	A **weak** response with limited understanding of ideas on the role of religion in public life in the UK. There may be factual errors. Points might be listed with no development. (1–2 marks).
2	An **adequate** but **underdeveloped** response on the role of religion in public life in the UK (3–4 marks). These ideas will be given in a brief or descriptive way rather than showing the full depth of the student's understanding.
3	A **good** response showing knowledge and understanding of the role of religion in public life in the UK (5–6 marks). The student **might** refer to: – Christian services to mark key events, e.g. remembrance services – public holidays based on Christian celebrations – the Queen as the head of the Church of England – the Queen appoints the Archbishop of Canterbury – the spiritual lords in the House of Lords – the Queen's role in the General Synod – Sunday trading laws to refer Christians beliefs in 'keeping the Sabbath holy' – the fact that sittings in both Houses of Parliament begin with Christian prayers

Hints and tips

➤ The command word is 'describe', which is asking you to set out the main characteristics of the role of religion in public life in the UK.

➤ Responses to this question should be purely knowledge-based - all 6 marks are awarded for AO1.

(c) This response is given **two** separate marks, both of which are determined by levels of response. Only **one** response is written but two different sets of **skills** are assessed by the examiner. The first mark is given for knowledge and understanding (AO1) and the second mark is awarded for the student's analysis and evaluation of the question (AO2). If the student simply writes down all they know about a specific topic, then the marks will be limited to the maximum marks for AO1. The examiner is assessing how the student uses their knowledge and understanding to relate to the specifics of the question/stimulus.

Knowledge and understanding AO1

Level	Description
1	**Some** demonstration of knowledge and understanding of Christian views on forced marriages which is given 1 mark.
2	**Good** demonstration of knowledge and understanding of Christian views on forced marriages which is given 2 marks. The student **might** refer to: – different types of forced marriage: arranged, lack of consent, child marriage (no understanding of what marriage means) – consent through the vows – historical traditions when people in power used marriage to establish relationships between other ruling factions – the 12th-century monk who made Catholic law on consent, rules of the Catholic Church on annulment – biblical support: Genesis 2: 24, Matthew 19: 4–6, Isaac's marriage, Genesis 24: 57–60, Ephesians 6: 2 (fifth commandment) – authority: Universal Declaration of Human Rights, Forced Marriage Act 2007, wedding vows, Gratian – Catholic law *Decretum Gratiani* – consent

Analysis and evaluation AO2

Level	Description
1	A **weak** response – the student may have given only a single viewpoint or the response simply lists different views/attitudes on why Christians are against forced marriages rather than offering comments which demonstrate a judgement (1 mark).
2	A **limited** response – the student has perhaps given different Christian views on why they are against forced marriages but these have not been developed by any comment and as such the analysis is limited. **Or** the student may have attempted to comment and show judgement on one specific view (2 marks). There may be some inaccuracies or misunderstanding of the stances taken.
3	An **adequate** response – the student has given different Christian views on why thcy do not agree with forced marriages and has attempted to show some judgement/analysis on these views, but the ideas and comments are not developed enough to reach the highest level (3 marks).
4	A **good** understanding of the question. The student has responded with a variety of viewpoints on why Christians are against forced marriages, these are explained and analysed and a conclusion/judgement on the question has been made (4 marks). The student **might**: – comment and come to a conclusion on the view that Christian marriage is a sacrament/spiritual experience, ordained and blessed by God, 'one flesh', consent, 'marriage an honourable estate' and a 'holy mystery' – comment and come to a conclusion on the view that consent is obligatory – comment on the physical, emotional and spiritual harm child marriage entails and how it opposes basic human rights – similar to rape

Hints and tips

➤ Remember that if you are explaining, you should use the word 'because' or the phrase 'for the reason that'.

➤ Include some comments/analysis on the explanations.

➤ Remember that this question is asking you to support your ideas with sources of wisdom and authority.

(d) This response is given **two** separate marks, both of which are determined by levels of response. Only **one** response is written but two different sets of **skills** are assessed by the examiner. The first mark is given for knowledge and understanding (AO1) and the second mark is awarded for the student's analysis and evaluation of the question (AO2). If the student simply writes down all they know about a specific topic, then the marks will be limited to the maximum marks for AO1. The examiner is assessing how the student uses their knowledge and understanding to relate to the specifics of the question/stimulus.

Knowledge and understanding AO1

Level	Description
1	A **limited/weak** demonstration of knowledge and understanding which is given 1 mark. This might include information and understanding about whether or not religion is wanted in a secular society which are simplistic or just a list of ideas.
2	An **adequate** but **underdeveloped** demonstration of knowledge and understanding which is given 2 marks. This might include some understanding on the different ideas about whether or not religion is wanted in a secular society. The use of sources of wisdom and authority may be superficial.
3	A **good** demonstration of knowledge and understanding which is given 3 marks. This might include different ideas about whether or not religion is wanted in a secular society. The student **might** refer to: – positive religious contributions: the Ten Commandments as basic rules for society, agape, Christian core values of love, peace and harmony, e.g. France debating on whether to have RE in the curriculum – negative religious contributions: impeding science, against same-sex weddings, Nietzsche, Richard Dawkins, crimes by the church, ISIS, statistics which show that there are more divorces in religious marriages – specific examples: High Court ruling 2011, community nurse suspended for offering to pray for a patient, woman lost her job for refusing to remove her cross, idea that church and state working together forces people to leave the church – biblical references: Matthew 22: 21, Luke 16: 13, John 18: 36, Acts 5: 29, Romans 13: 1, 1 Peter 2: 13–17

Analysis and evaluation AO2

Level	Description
1	A **weak** response – the student may have given only a single viewpoint or the response is simply a description of ideas about whether or not religion is wanted in a secular society rather than offering comments which demonstrate a judgement (1–3 marks). In other words, the information is communicated in a basic way and there is no evidence of a **discussion** taking place.
2	A **limited** response – the student has perhaps given different examples or biblical or denominational teachings about whether or not religion is wanted in a secular society contrasted with secular views, but they have not been developed and there is little evidence of a conclusion. **Or** the student may have attempted to comment and show judgement on a specific Christian idea contrasted with secular beliefs (4–6 marks). In other words, there is a line of reasoning/ **discussion** which has some relevance to the stimulus.
3	An **adequate** but **underdeveloped** response – the student has perhaps given different views on whether or not religion is wanted in a secular society and has attempted to show some judgement/ analysis on them, but the ideas and comments are not developed enough to reach the highest level (7–9 marks). A line of reasoning has been presented and **discussed** which is mostly relevant.
4	A **good** understanding of the question. The student has responded with a variety of viewpoints or different schools of thought about whether or not religion is wanted in a secular society, which are explained and analysed, and a conclusion/judgement on the question has been made (10–12 marks). The student has offered a well-developed and sustained **discussion** which is coherent, relevant and well structured. The student **might**: – compare and contrast Christian and secular views about the value or otherwise of religion or Christianity within a society and then comment or make a judgement – consider the idea of what might happen if religion is excluded – consider the view that religion is more divisive than unifying, or vice versa – focus on the Christian teaching that you cannot serve two masters – how does this relate to society? And if human rights are paramount, whose religious rights take priority?

Hints and tips

➤ Read the stimulus carefully and identify its significance in your response, making sure you stick to the wording in the stimulus and do not divert into a concept that you would prefer to discuss.

➤ Remember that your response should be a **discussion** – try to present viewpoints for both sides as if you were having a conversation. Do not just list all the ideas for the stimulus in one paragraph and then all the ideas against in another paragraph.

➤ Refer to different beliefs and teachings and evaluate the importance of these differences.

➤ Try to refer back to what you studied in Part 1 of this course: beliefs and teachings and practices.

➤ Compare and contrast the religious views with secular views.

➤ Remember that you do not have to express a personal view – if you want to, you can, but make sure you justify your point of view with evidence and argument.

➤ Please do not fall into the trap of saying 'An atheist does not believe in God and therefore would not agree with the religious point of view'. You are not adding to the argument/discussion at all.

Paper 2: Religion, philosophy and ethics in the modern world

Islam: relationships and families

Student responses

This section shows sample answers from two students. One set (Student A) is stronger, the other (Student B) weaker. The answers are followed by examiner-style commentary (shown by the icon ⓔ) that indicates where credit is due. In the weaker answers, it also points out areas for improvement, specific problems and common errors.

Question 1
Student A

(a) Pre-marital sex is considered to be wrong and leads to other sinful acts. The Qur'an teaches 'illicit sexual intimacy is immoral', therefore it should only take place in marriage.

ⓔ **The student states that pre-marital sex is wrong and leads to other sinful acts (first mark), and this is developed with reference to the Qur'an (second mark), with the development that the only place for sex is within marriage (third mark).**

(b) One of the main purposes of a Muslim marriage is to have children. This is following the example of the Prophet Muhammad (pbuh) who had several wives and children, and also to ensure the continuance of the faith. Although the father plays an important role in the religious education of any children, it is the mother who goes through pregnancy and is the one who contributes mainly to instilling religious and ethical beliefs through her examples and by living her life by Muslim values. In many cases the wife stays at home while the husband, seen as the provider, goes out to work, but in today's society this is not always the case – it depends on the arrangement within each family and society. A wife should be faithful and honest to her husband and protect his property; just as he must do the same for her, respecting her rights and freedoms. Some Muslims take this to mean that a wife must not be alone with another male without her husband's consent. A wife may accept her husband's protection because the Qur'an teaches that 'men have a degree of responsibility over them'. Some of these beliefs have led to some misunderstandings about the role of women in Islam, but the males and females are seen as individuals who are not identical but complementary to each other.

ⓔ **The student shows good knowledge and understanding of the role of wives in a Muslim marriage. They demonstrate understanding of why there are misconceptions about the role of wives.**

(c) In 2004 civil partnerships were legalised, thus recognising the rights of same-sex couples in a union similar to a civil marriage. Homosexual and lesbian relationships are forbidden by many Muslims because they regard them as being unnatural. Sexual intercourse is a way of procreation and thus is how a man and a woman can contribute to Allah's creation. The Qur'an teaches that it is a sin if 'you practise your lusts on men in preference to women'. The Muslim Council of Britain launched a website called 'Muslims Defending Marriage', which described civil partnerships as attacking traditional marriage because the system endorses the facts that same-sex couples have the same rights as heterosexual couples. The Muslim Council of Scotland was also against the introduction of civil partnerships because it feared that it would lead to same-sex marriages, which in fact has happened. It stated that marriage is a sacred event and not a social contract. It is an institution defined as the union of a man and a woman to create the ideal environment for raising children. Yet it should be recognised that the system is only a civil one and not a religious one and so it could be said that it is merely a safeguarding of a same-sex couple's rights rather than an endorsement of their lifestyle. There are some Muslims who have entered into civil partnerships and believe there are different ways of interpreting the sources of authority to allow for more flexibility in lifestyles. The Muslim group Imaan was set up by gay Muslims to provide support for and justification for Muslims who wish to practise same-sex partnerships, including through civil partnerships.

ⓔ The student outlines Muslim attitudes on civil partnerships. These attitudes are supported by reference to the Qur'an and also to the Muslim Council of Britain and the Muslim Council of Scotland. There is awareness of diversity of opinion.

(d) Equality can refer to either gender equality, financial equality, political equality, etc. Article 1 of the Universal Declaration on Human Rights states that 'all human beings are born free and equal in dignity and rights'. This may be the ideal value to uphold but in reality it is very difficult to treat everyone in exactly the same way. A person may have physical or learning difficulties, and it would be silly to try and treat a baby the same as an adult. Muslims follow the teachings of the Prophet Muhammad (pbuh) in his last sermon when he said, 'all humankind is descended from Adam and Eve', and no person is better than the other. The ummah, the whole community of Muslims, which is bound together through religious values and beliefs, is an example that all Muslims should be treated equally. When a pilgrim goes on the Hajj, they dress simply in a white cloth, underlining the fact that no one is more important than the other. But everyone is different, they have qualities and features which are unique to them. People may share the same beliefs and values but it does not mean that they are the same. So should everyone be treated equally if that were possible?

ⓔ The student indicates from the start of the response that they have recognised the significance of the statement. They explain the idea of equality and support the idea with a Muslim teaching and practice. However, the implication is that equality is just a principle and as such it is not a possibility.

Although Muslims teach equality, there are gender distinctions which sometimes give the idea that women are not treated as equals. The Qur'an teaches that wives have the same rights as their husbands, but 'in certain situations men would have the final word' (Surah 2:229). This could be said to show that in reality men are more superior. However, Islam teaches that both the male and the female are accountable for their respective actions and so will be judged equally by Allah. The Hadith teaches: 'Allah does not look upon your outward appearance, he looks upon your hearts and your deeds.' Therefore it might be fair to state that although men and women are accountably equal through their actions, they cannot be treated the same because they are physically different and traditionally they have had different purposes: men were the breadwinners and wives stayed at home. It could be said that it is a matter of culture or environment as to whether this traditional view is followed today.

ⓔ The student shows different viewpoints on Muslim ideas of gender equality/inequality and supports the ideas with explanations and reference to the sacred writings.

Since people are different, the question asked is, should they be treated equally? Should you treat someone who has done great things the same as someone who has lived a mundane life? Should Imran Khan who founded a cancer research hospital in Pakistan, or Muhammad Ali or even Malcolm X, the latter two renowned for their struggles against racial inequality, receive the same treatment as an office worker? On the Day of Judgement the Qur'an teaches that Allah will weigh up the good and the bad deeds of each person: 'And to every soul will be paid in full of its deeds' (Surah 39:70) and they will go to heaven.

Although this might suggest that those who are altruistic will get good treatment on judgement day, it should be remembered that Allah is balancing out deeds and intentions and if the balance is tipped to the bad side, then the person will go to jahannam (hell). Every Muslim wishes to please Allah and therefore they will try to pursue the principle of treating people equally in order to do so.

ⓔ **The student questions whether people who perform acts of social benevolence should be treated in the same way as people who do not. They develop this idea by referring to and commenting on the Day of Judgement.**

The Qur'an teaches that everyone is created by Allah and thus everyone is equal: 'Of His Signs is the creation of the heavens and the earth, and the diversity of your tongues and colour.' It could be said that Allah creates everyone the same but they all have the potential to react to this world in different ways, in other words become different and unique individuals. And so it is by their actions and their faith, whether it is strong or weak, which defines them. It is too simplistic to say that everyone in the world should be treated in exactly the same way because this is impossible, but this does not mean that they should not have the freedom of choice and equal opportunities to pursue their potential.

ⓔ **The student reaches a balanced judgement that it is not practical to treat everyone equally all the time, but that does not preclude the fact that everyone should be entitled to the same opportunities within their lives.**

Question 1
Student B

(a) Muslims believe that sex is a gift from Allah and should only take place in marriage, not out.

ⓔ **The student has alluded to the view that pre-marital sex is wrong but has not stated this explicitly. Two marks are awarded: one for the statement that 'sex is Allah's gift' and the second for the idea that sex should only take place in marriage.**

(b) It is usual for a Muslim wife to be responsible for bringing up the children and making sure her husband is cared for and that the house is well maintained. The Hadith teaches that a man should not marry someone for their good looks or wealth but because there is 'religious devotion' between them so that there can be a relationship of mutual love, faithfulness and cooperation. The role of the wife is important because she is the first point of call for the instilling of Muslim values into the children. The wife should also appear modestly because the Qur'an teaches that women 'should cast their outer garments over their persons'. A wife should also be faithful to her husband.

ⓔ **The student shows adequate but underdeveloped knowledge and understanding of the role of the wife in a Muslim family.**

(c) Although homosexuality occurs in Muslim society, many Muslims believe it is forbidden by their sacred writings. One Hadith teaches that 'when a man mounts another man, the throne of God shakes'. Thus the idea of a same-sex couple having a legalised union which allows them the same rights as a heterosexual couple is often not looked on with favour. Muslims believe sex is a gift from Allah which should only be between a man and a woman in order to have children, as told in the Qur'an, Surah 4. Some Muslims believe that civil partnerships undermine the sacredness of marriage, which has been taught in the Qur'an: 'He created for you mates from among yourselves, that ye may dwell in tranquillity with them.'

ⓔ **The student attempts to explain Muslim attitudes on civil partnerships but the analysis is implicit.**

(d) Although most people are different, they do have similarities and of course there are identical twins or triplets. However, does this mean that they should receive the same treatment throughout their lives? Is someone who is senile entitled to the same treatment as a baby? Their conditions may resemble each other, they need feeding, cleaning and protection, but surely there is a difference between the two extremes? Ideally, of course, people should have equal treatment or at least be entitled to the same equal opportunities. In the past, women were seen as 'stayers-at-home' while the men were the 'breadwinners'. In today's modern world, values have changed and traditions broken. Who knows what society's values will be in the 24th century?

(e) **The student attempts to demonstrate an understanding of the significance of the statement by using generic material.**

Muslims are against racial inequality. This is because they are a diverse society of cultures throughout the world. They see themselves as a Muslim first, regardless of their colour of skin or nationality. When Malcolm X went on the Hajj, he underwent a life-changing event which gave him a new outlook on integration. He met up with 'blonde-haired, blue-eyed men I could call my brothers'. So instead of excluding people from his teachings he had a message for all races. The Prophet Muhammad (pbuh) taught that everyone came from Adam and Eve and so therefore no one was better than anyone else. The first muezzin, chosen by Muhammad (pbuh), was an Ethiopian slave called Bilal. Yet though Muslims do not agree with racism, they themselves are often targets of racism because of the stereotypical view that they could be terrorists, or other misconceptions.

(e) **The student discusses the idea of racial inequality, supporting Muslim views with quotes and the example of Malcolm X.**

There are different Muslim attitudes to the view of equality between the genders. Some countries do not believe in their equality and in Saudi Arabia women were not allowed to drive until recently. In many other countries, Muslims believe that men and women are viewed the same by Allah but they have different roles due to their physical and emotional differences. Traditionally men would go out to work and women stay at home. Also they are often kept separate from the men at the mosque.

(e) **The student shows opposing Muslim views on the equality of women but they do not discuss or develop the ideas.**

Muslims are against poverty and social inequality. The third pillar of Islam is zakat, which is the obligatory gift of 2.5% of their earnings, which is distributed to the poor. This is taught in the Qur'an. Sadaqah is optional and additional charity.

(e) **The student uses the example of social inequality but does not relate it to the statement.**

Muslims are against inequality and will try by their actions to remedy the consequences of racism or poverty. However, because everyone is so different, it is too difficult to treat everyone the same.

(e) **The student makes a judgement but it is simplistic and the whole content of the response appears to be the student writing all they can think of on the topic of inequality rather than addressing and discussing the focus of the statement.**

Mark scheme

1   **(a)** Marks are awarded for a statement plus further development of that statement with either examples or references to sacred writings to support it. The student **might** refer to:
- pre-marital sex being wrong, some Muslims believe it is punishable
- marriage being the only place for sex, an act of worship, a gift from Allah

– social reasons why it is wrong: unwanted pregnancies, STDs
– Qur'an, Shari'ah law

Hints and tips

➤ This is a short question requiring knowledge only, so do not spend too much time on it.
➤ The question is asking for one belief, so make sure you focus on one and do not give several ideas.

(b) This response is marked by levels of response according to the student's knowledge and understanding of the question (AO1).

Knowledge and understanding (AO1)

Level	Description
1	A **weak** response with limited understanding (1–2 marks): the student may have outlined one or two ideas about the role of the wife in a Muslim family but in a simplistic way.
2	An **adequate** but **underdeveloped** response (3–4 marks): the student may have given and explained different ideas on the role of the wife in a Muslim family. These ideas will be outlined in a brief or descriptive way rather than showing the full depth of the student's understanding.
3	A **good** response (5–6 marks): the student **might** show knowledge and understanding of: – the idea of procreation and why it is important – religious devotion, companionship, obedience, fidelity, modesty – traditional and modern views – Qur'an, e.g. Surah 2:228, Hadith
4	

Hints and tips

➤ Although the command word is 'outline', the question is asking for both knowledge and understanding.

(c) This response is given **two** separate marks, both of which are determined by levels of response. Only **one** response is written but two different sets of **skills** are assessed by the examiner. The first mark is given for knowledge and understanding (AO1) and the second mark is awarded for the student's analysis and evaluation of the question (AO2). If the student simply writes down all they know about a specific topic, then the marks will be limited to the maximum marks for AO1. The examiner is assessing how the student uses their knowledge and understanding to relate to the specifics of the question/stimulus.

Knowledge and understanding AO1

Level	Description
1	**Some** demonstration of knowledge and understanding which is given 1 mark. This might include some information and understanding of the attitudes of Muslims towards civil partnerships.
2	**Adequate** but **underdeveloped** demonstration of knowledge and understanding which is given 2 marks. This **might** include: – a definition of the term civil partnership – scriptural reference to the view that homosexuality/lesbian relationships are seen as a sin – Qur'an, e.g. Surah 27:55, 30:21, Hadith, Muslim Council of Britain, Muslim Council of Scotland – the sacred institution and role of marriage

Analysis and evaluation AO2

Level	Description
1	A **weak** response – the student may have given only a single viewpoint or the response is simply a stated attitude of Muslims towards civil partnerships (1 mark).
2	A **limited** response – the student has perhaps given two or three Muslim attitudes towards civil partnerships, but these have not been developed by any comment and as such the analysis is limited. This might include a comparison or contrast of the sacredness of marriage with Islamic condemnation of same-sex relationships. There may be some inaccuracies or misunderstanding of the stances taken. **Or** the student may have attempted to comment and show judgement on one specific attitude (2 marks).
3	An **adequate** but **underdeveloped** response – the student has given different Muslim attitudes on civil partnerships but the ideas and comments are not developed enough to reach the highest level (3 marks).
4	A **good** understanding of the question. The student has responded with a variety of viewpoints on Muslim attitudes towards civil partnerships along with good analysis and evaluation (4 marks). The student **might** analyse and comment on: – the idea that civil partnerships are a step towards same-sex marriages – the fact that civil partnerships are a civil/social rule, not a religious one – different views held by Muslims, including the opinion that the Qur'an may not specifically prohibit civil partnerships and the views of some modern Muslims who may welcome civil partnerships; any other valid religious views

Hints and tips

➤ Read the question carefully and focus on the trigger/command word, which is 'explain'. This means you have to give reasons for a statement/idea – use the word 'because'.

➤ The question is asking about attitudes, which means you can give ideas for and against civil partnerships.

➤ Support your statements/ideas with reference to sources of wisdom and authority. The examiner will be assessing your ability to refer to sources of wisdom and authority.

➤ Remember to draw a conclusion from your explanations.

(d) This response is given **two** separate marks, both of which are determined by levels of response. Only **one** response is written but two different sets of **skills** are assessed by the examiner. The first mark is given for knowledge and understanding (AO1) and the second mark is awarded for the student's analysis and evaluation of the question (AO2). If the student simply writes down all they know about a specific topic, then the marks will be limited to the maximum marks for AO1. The examiner is assessing how the student uses their knowledge and understanding to relate to the specifics of the question/stimulus.

 OCR GCSE (9–1) Religious Studies Exam Question Practice

Knowledge and understanding AO1

Level	Description
1	A **limited/weak** demonstration of knowledge and understanding which is given 1 mark. This might include information and understanding about Muslim teachings on equality or inequality which are simplistic or just a list of ideas.
2	An **adequate** but **underdeveloped** demonstration of knowledge and understanding which is given 2 marks. This might include different ideas about inequality or equality supported with reference to sacred writings. These may have been contrasted with simplistic societal or generic ideas.
3	A **good** demonstration of knowledge and understanding which is given 3 marks. This might include different explanations of Muslim views on equality and inequality supported by reference to sacred while perhaps being contrasted with secular or generic ideas. The student **may** include: – explanations of teachings from the Qur'an, e.g. Surah 2:229, 30:22, 39:70, the Hadith and the example of the Prophet Muhammad – a definition of the various types of inequality/equality – a comparison of the differences between the roles of men and women – references to Muslim practices: the Hajj, zakat, salah

Analysis and evaluation AO2

Level	Description
1	A **weak** response – the student may have given only a single viewpoint or the response is simply a description of events rather than offering comments which demonstrate a judgement (1–3 marks). This might include a descriptive/simplistic account of one or two different Muslim views on the attitudes to inequality/equality. No attempt to offer a judgement/conclusion will have been made. In other words, the information is communicated in a basic way and there is no evidence of a **discussion** taking place.
2	A **limited** response – the student has perhaps given various ideas on Muslim views of different concepts of inequality/equality but these ideas have not been developed and there is little evidence of a conclusion. **Or** the student may have attempted to comment and show judgement on a specific Muslim idea contrasted with secular beliefs (4–6 marks). In other words, there is a line of reasoning/**discussion** which has some relevance to the stimulus.
3	An **adequate** but **underdeveloped** response – the student has perhaps given different views and has attempted to show some judgement/analysis on them but the ideas and comments are not developed enough to reach the highest level (7–9 marks). This might include various explanations of the different Muslim teachings on inequality/equality contrasted with secular/generic beliefs while linking them into the stimulus. However, they have not been discussed or analysed in sufficient depth to reach Level 4. A line of reasoning has been presented and **discussed** which is mostly relevant.
4	A **good** understanding of the question. The student has responded with a variety of viewpoints or different schools of thought, which are explained and analysed and a conclusion/judgement on the question has been made (10–12 marks). The student has offered a well-developed and sustained **discussion** which is coherent, relevant and well structured. For instance, the student **might** include: – the impossibility or possibility of everyone been treated the same all the time – comments on the contradictions within different cultures of the roles of men and women – comments and comparisons of different Muslim practices, e.g. the Hajj or zakat – comments and explanations and comparisons of the different types of equality/inequality

Hints and tips

➤ Read the stimulus carefully and identify its significance in your response, making sure you stick to the wording in the stimulus and do not divert into a concept that you would prefer to discuss.

➤ Remember that your response should be a **discussion** – try to present viewpoints for both sides as if you were having a conversation. Do not just list all the ideas for the stimulus in one paragraph and then all the ideas against in another paragraph.

➤ Refer to different beliefs and teachings and evaluate the importance of these differences.

➤ Try to refer back to what you studied in Part 1 of this course: beliefs and teachings and practices.

➤ Remember that you do not have to express a personal view – if you want to, you can, but make sure you justify your point of view with evidence and argument.

➤ Do not fall into the trap of saying 'An atheist does not believe in Allah and therefore would not agree with the religious point of view'. You are not adding to the argument/discussion at all.

Question 2

Student A

(a) Muslims are taught that life is a sacred gift from Allah and therefore contraception should not be used because Allah chooses when he will gift a child to a couple: 'He creates what He pleases.'

(e) **The first mark is given for the teaching of the sanctity of life, the second mark for the explanation that contraception should not be used, and the third mark goes to the development of Allah's choice supported by the Qur'an quote.**

(b) The Muslim family is at the heart of the Muslim community. Muslims believe Allah created the family to be the foundation of human society and ensure that the values and teachings on the virtues of love, kindness and compassion, which are taught in the Qur'an, are instilled in the children of the family. Therefore one of the purposes of marriage is to have children. This is important because every child is a gift of Allah and is born in fitrah, which means that they have the inner instinct of Islam and Allah. So one of the roles of the family is to ensure that the children grow up in the Islamic faith. The father will whisper the shahadah in the baby's ear when it is born. The mother has the responsibility for teaching haram (what is a wrong action) and halal (what is a right action). The family will celebrate festivals together and when the children are old enough they will observe Ramadan together. So the children are learning from the examples of their parents. The parents will discourage anti-social behaviour and ensure that their children grow up in a healthy, secure and encouraging environment. Another role of the family is to treat the elderly with dignity and respect. The Qur'an teaches 'act humbly to them in mercy'.

(e) **The student shows good knowledge and understanding of the role of the Muslim family and gives several ideas: teaching the faith, leading by example, treatment of the elderly.**

(c) The Qur'an teaches that both men and women are equal in the sight of Allah and that both genders are individually accountable for their actions. On judgement day, the men will be judged for what they have done and the women will be judged for what they have done: 'As for those who lead a righteous life, male or female, while believing, they enter Paradise…' However, it is also made clear that while men and women are equal, they are not the same – they have different purposes. It is obvious there are physical differences and so the Qur'an teaches that men are the guardians of their wives: 'Men are the protectors and maintainers of women, because Allah has given the one more (strength) than the other.' The Qur'an also teaches that men will have the last word within their household. Different cultures/societies treat the genders differently: in the Western world there appears to be the concept of gender equality, but in other countries such as Saudi Arabia there are occasions when it appears as if women are second-class citizens and gender discrimination happens.

Some Muslims might claim this is because it is justified in the Qur'an. Others say this is a cultural tradition in spite of the principle of equality that was promoted by the Prophet. The Qur'an asks men and women to show themselves in a state of modesty, but Muslim women are more noticeable than men for the use of veils. This has led to the idea that there is discrimination towards women. Nevertheless, Muslims believe that women have the right to pursue careers and should not be discriminated against in employment or education. The reality many Muslim women have faced discrimination from Muslim men might be due to tradition, which is challenged by many Muslims nowadays.

(e) **The student explains how Muslims treat people differently on the basis of gender. They show good knowledge and understanding that there should be no prejudice and discrimination and support these ideas with teachings from the Qur'an.**

(d) Like many religious believers, Muslims view marriage as a firm foundation for human society. Marriage provides a secure and loving environment in which to raise children and is a contract before Allah, Nikah, to marry for life. Therefore divorce is not looked upon kindly. However, it is recognised that sometimes marriages break down and unlike some of the other religions, the Qur'an gives instructions on how divorce should happen. Surah 2 details information about the 'iddah – the three-month waiting period in which the couple, with the help of their family and the Iman, will attempt to reconcile. They will live in the same house but no sex is allowed and the husband is financially responsible for the wife: 'When you divorce women, divorce them for their waiting period.' If after the three months reconciliation has failed and the wife is not pregnant, then divorce happens. Thus the teachings in the Qur'an would not support the statement that Muslims should never divorce. However, in that case why does the Hadith state that 'the most detestable lawful thing before Allah is divorce'? It is saying that divorce is lawful because of what is said in the Qur'an but it still does not please Allah. So it appears as though divorce can happen if it is an absolute necessity, but a Muslim would still be upsetting Allah.

(e) **The student indicates from the start of the response that they recognise the significance of the statement. Different sources of authority appear to contradict each other and so there is a question mark about whether Muslims should or should not divorce.**

Divorce breaks up the family and can cause bitterness between the couple. It causes emotional and mental stress for all the family, but especially for the children. Muslims are aware that at the last judgement they will be asked how they treated their children: 'Fear Allah and treat your children fairly.' So they consider their welfare before making the decision on whether to divorce or not. But sometimes divorce is the lesser of two evils in cases such as abusive behaviour and adultery. The Qur'an teaches husbands to live with their wives 'in kindness' and the Hadith teaches that a husband 'should not strike her in the face'. So a wife can free herself from abuse by returning her mahr. It seems unfair that the wife then has to worry if she will be judged harshly on judgement day but as Allah is compassionate he will see she had no choice. It is easier for a man to get a divorce because it is the husband who says the words 'I divorce you' three times during the 'iddah, however this has been banned in some countries. It also seems as though the Qur'an is male orientated and the rules are made for the man – 'when you divorce women' – but scholars dispute this and quote 'and women have rights similar to those of men', yet the ayat concludes 'men are a degree above them', which suggests that men are treated more sympathetically. So it could be argued that divorce is more emotionally and religiously difficult for the wife rather than the husband, but this does not mean to say that a Muslim should never divorce.

(e) **The student links divorce to the judgements of Allah and then contrasts a particular ayat in the Qur'an (Surah 2:228) to discuss whether it is more taxing for the wife than the husband. They conclude the response with analysis and a balanced judgement.**

Question 2
Student B

(a) The Conference on Islam and Family Planning teaches that contraception can be used if the mother's health is threatened.

ⓔ **The first mark is given for the teaching that contraception can be used and the second mark for one of the reasons it is allowable. Further development or explanation is needed for the third mark.**

(b) Although there is dispute between the Sunni Muslims and the Shi'a Muslims about how many children Muhammad (pbuh) had, it is accepted that he had a family and that he provides a good role model for all Muslim families. The husband and wives have different functions within the family unit, depending on the culture in which they are living, but both of them are responsible for bringing up their children in the Muslim faith. This is important because every Muslim believes every baby born on earth has the natural instinct of fitrah, which is awareness of Allah. So to ensure that the children do not become corrupted or led away from the true faith, the parents will teach them about Islam, go to the mosque together and celebrate festivals. They might even go on the Hajj together.

ⓔ **The student shows an adequate but underdeveloped knowledge and understanding of the role of the Muslim family. The ideas stated are correct but the student focuses only on the idea of educating children in the Muslim faith.**

(c) The Qur'an teaches that men and women are seen as being equal individuals in the eyes of Allah. This is reflected when Muslims go on the Hajj – whether they are male or female, they are all dressed in simple white garments to show equality. However, it is seen in the role of the family that the man is usually seen as the breadwinner while the wife brings up the children and stays at home. However, both are responsible for educating their children in the Muslim faith. The father recites the shahadah in the ear of each child as soon as they are born while the mother is responsible for teaching them the difference between right and wrong. The Hadith teaches that Muhammad (pbuh) taught that women should be shown respect when he said, 'Paradise lies at the feet of your mother.' So in some cases a Muslim would reject the idea that women should be treated differently and often less well on the basis of gender, at other times it seems as though women are not as important as men.

ⓔ **The student attempts to explain different Muslim ideas about prejudice and discrimination on the basis of gender, but it is disjointed: there is a lot about the different roles of men and women, with the last sentence trying to tie those ideas into the question.**

(d) Marriage for Muslims is a lawful union based on consent – if one of the couple has been forced into the marriage then it is declared to be invalid. Divorce is regulated in the Qur'an and Shari'ah law allows divorce. Thus it would appear as if the statement is wrong. However, just because divorce is legal in the eyes of the law and also religiously, it does not mean that divorce is a good thing. Otherwise if divorce is so easy then it undermines the whole idea of the Muslim family being the foundation for society and being a secure environment in which to raise children. A Muslim can divorce but it does not extend to the idea of 'must'.

ⓔ **The student attempts to demonstrate an understanding of the significance of the statement by referring to the legal and religious endorsement of divorce.**

A Muslim couple are allowed to marry and divorce, remarry and divorce again. This is taught in the Qur'an Surah 2:230. But after the third time they are not allowed to remarry unless the wife has married and divorced someone else in the meantime. This might seem strange to non-believers that a couple would want to divorce and remarry each other again and again. Normally most marriages end in bitterness, which is why a divorce is wanted, unless you are a celebrity and have 'conscious uncoupling' (Gwyneth Paltrow). It appears as though divorce could happen in a Muslim marriage for inconsequential things if they know they can remarry each other again and again.

(e) **The student discusses one of the rules of divorce but the link to the statement is implicit.**

Obviously there are times when a divorce is wanted, especially if one of the couple has committed adultery, because the Qur'an teaches that it is immoral and 'is evil as a way'. Either of the couple would feel let down and betrayed and find trust difficult after that. They might try to become reconciled during the 'iddah and turn to Allah for help because 'Allah will cause their reconciliation', but it would take an awful lot of courage to forgive someone for such a deed. Therefore, in some circumstances it is argued that divorce can happen and so the statement is wrong.

(e) **The student discusses the betrayal of adultery and comes to the judgement that divorce is sometimes inevitable and so the statement is wrong.**

Mark scheme

2 **(a)** Marks are awarded for a statement plus further development of that statement with either examples or references to sacred writings to support it. The student **might** refer to:
- contraception is not allowed: sanctity of life, Allah's choice, Qur'an 42:50–52, purpose of marriage to have children, family a fundamental unit of Islam
- contraception is allowed: in recent years the Conference on Islam and Family Planning agreed that it can be allowed if the mother's health is threatened, if there is a chance of the child being born disabled, or for financial reasons.

Hints and tips

➤ This is a short question requiring knowledge only, so do not spend too much time on it.
➤ The question is asking for one teaching, so make sure you focus on one and do not give several ideas.

(b) This response is marked by levels of response according to the student's knowledge and understanding of the question (AO1).

Knowledge and understanding AO1

Level	Description
1	A **weak** response with limited understanding (1–2 marks): the student may have outlined one or two ideas about the role of the Muslim family but in a simplistic way.
2	An **adequate** but **underdeveloped** response (3–4 marks): the student may have given and explained different ideas on the role of the Muslim family. These ideas will be outlined in a brief or descriptive way rather than showing the full depth of the student's understanding.
3	A **good** response (5–6 marks): the student **might** show knowledge and understanding of: – the reason for having children, provision of a healthy, secure and encouraging environment – fitrah, instilling of Muslim faith, father: shahadah, mother: haram and halal – Qur'an virtues: love, kindness and compassion – family playing an important role in the Muslim community – respect for the elderly – Qur'an, e.g. Surah 17:23–24, Surah 49:13, Hadith

Hints and tips

➤ Although the command word is 'outline', the question is asking for both knowledge and understanding.

➤ It is asking for beliefs, so make sure you give more than one idea about the role of the family.

(c) This response is given **two** separate marks, both of which are determined by levels of response. Only **one** response is written but two different sets of **skills** are assessed by the examiner. The first mark is given for knowledge and understanding (AO1) and the second mark is awarded for the student's analysis and evaluation of the question (AO2). If the student simply writes down all they know about a specific topic, then the marks will be limited to the maximum marks for AO1. The examiner is assessing how the student uses their knowledge and understanding to relate to the specifics of the question/stimulus.

Knowledge and understanding AO1

Level	Description
1	**Some** demonstration of knowledge and understanding which is given 1 mark. This might include some information and understanding of different ideas which Muslims have about treating people differently on the basis of gender.
2	**Adequate** but **underdeveloped** demonstration of knowledge and understanding which is given 2 marks. This might include several ideas which Muslims have about treating people differently on the basis of gender. The student **might** include: – Muslim ideas on men and women being equal in the sight of Allah and individually accountable for their actions, Surah 4:124 – men and women being physically different, so different purposes – men: Surah 2:229, Surah 4:35 – women: Surah 33:59 – Hadith: Sahih Al-Bukhari, Sunan An-Nasa'i

Analysis and evaluation AO2

Level	Description
1	A **weak** response – the student may have given only a single viewpoint or the response simply gives one idea which Muslims have about treating people differently on the basis of gender (1 mark). The idea is not developed or explained or supported with reference to sources of wisdom and authority.
2	A **limited** response – the student has perhaps given two or three simplistic ideas which Muslims have about treating people differently on the basis of gender, but these have not been developed by any comment and as such the analysis is limited. There may be some inaccuracies or misunderstanding of the stances taken. **Or** the student may have attempted to comment and show judgement on one specific idea (2 marks).
3	An **adequate** but **underdeveloped** response – the student has given different ideas which Muslims have about treating people differently on the basis of gender but the ideas and comments are not developed enough to reach the highest level (3 marks).
4	A **good** understanding of the question. The student has responded with a variety of viewpoints on the different ideas Muslims have about treating people differently on the basis of gender along with good analysis and evaluation (4 marks). The student **might** analyse and comment on: – the idea that culture/society has a definite impact rather than the teachings within the Qur'an – the fact that ignorance leads to prejudice and discrimination – that sometimes even religious teachings don't have an effect on an individual's ideas/thoughts and actions

Hints and tips

➤ Read the question carefully and focus on the trigger/command word, which is 'explain'. This means you have to give reasons for a statement/idea – use the word 'because'.

➤ Support your statements/ideas with reference to sources of wisdom and authority. The examiner will be assessing your ability to refer to sources of wisdom and authority.

➤ Remember to draw a conclusion from your explanations.

(d) This response is given **two** separate marks, both of which are determined by levels of response. Only **one** response is written but two different sets of **skills** are assessed by the examiner. The first mark is given for knowledge and understanding (AO1) and the second mark is awarded for the student's analysis and evaluation of the question (AO2). If the student simply writes down all they know about a specific topic, then the marks will be limited to the maximum marks for AO1. The examiner is assessing how the student uses their knowledge and understanding to relate to the specifics of the question/stimulus.

Knowledge and understanding AO1

Level	Description
1	A **limited/weak** demonstration of knowledge and understanding which is given 1 mark. This might include information and understanding about Muslim teachings on divorce which are simplistic or just a list of ideas.
2	An **adequate** but **underdeveloped** demonstration of knowledge and understanding which is given 2 marks. This might include different ideas about divorce supported with reference to sacred writings. These may have been contrasted with simplistic societal or generic ideas.
3	A **good** demonstration of knowledge and understanding which is given 3 marks. This might include different explanations of Muslim views on divorce supported by reference to sacred writings while perhaps being contrasted with secular or generic ideas. The student **might** include: – marriage – lawful union, contract before Allah, Nikah, to marry for life, family foundation for society – Qur'an and Shari'ah law allow divorce – rules: 'iddah three months, reconciliation, Surah 2:224–237 – last judgement – treatment of children – sources of wisdom: Surah 2:228, Surah 4:19, Surah 4:35, Surah 17:32, Surah 65:1, Hadith: Sahih al-Bukhari (2587), Abu Daud

Analysis and evaluation AO2

Level	Description
1	A **weak** response – the student may have given only a single viewpoint or the response is simply a description of events rather than offering comments which demonstrate a judgement (1–3 marks). This might include a descriptive/simplistic account of one or two different Muslim views on divorce. No attempt to offer a judgement/conclusion will have been made. In other words, the information is communicated in a basic way and there is no evidence of a **discussion** taking place.
2	A **limited** response – the student has perhaps given different ideas on Muslim views on divorce but these ideas have not been developed and there is little evidence of a conclusion. **Or** the student may have attempted to comment and show judgement on a specific Muslim idea contrasted with secular beliefs (4–6 marks). In other words, there is a line of reasoning/ **discussion** which has some relevance to the stimulus.
3	An **adequate** but **underdeveloped** response – the student has perhaps given different views and has attempted to show some judgement/analysis on them but the ideas and comments are not developed enough to reach the highest level (7–9 marks). This might include explanations of the different Muslim teachings on divorce contrasted with secular/generic beliefs while linking them into the stimulus. However, they have not been discussed or analysed in sufficient depth to reach Level 4. A line of reasoning has been presented and **discussed** which is mostly relevant.
4	A **good** understanding of the question. The student has responded with a variety of viewpoints or different schools of thought, which are explained and analysed and a conclusion/judgement on the question has been made (10–12 marks). The student has offered a well-developed and sustained **discussion** which is coherent, relevant and well structured. For instance, the student **might** include: – how culture/country might affect the decision of divorce – the emotional/mental/religious significance – an analysis and comparison of gender issues – an analysis and comparison of different teachings – divorce not liked by Allah but agreed to in the Qur'an and Shari'ah law

Hints and tips

➤ Read the stimulus carefully and identify its significance in your response, making sure you stick to the wording in the stimulus and do not divert into a concept that you would prefer to discuss.

➤ Remember that your response should be a **discussion** – try to present viewpoints for both sides as if you were having a conversation. Do not just list all the ideas for the stimulus in one paragraph and then all the ideas against in another paragraph.

➤ Refer to different beliefs and teachings and evaluate the importance of these differences.

➤ Try to refer back to what you studied in Part 1 of this course: beliefs and teachings and practices.

➤ Remember that you do not have to express a personal view – if you want to, you can, but make sure you justify your point of view with evidence and argument.

➤ Do not fall into the trap of saying 'An atheist does not believe in Allah and therefore would not agree with the religious point of view'. You are not adding to the argument/discussion at all.

Islam: the existence of God, gods and the ultimate reality

Question 3

Student A

(a) The Hadith teaches that Allah has 99 names which describe his nature. Three of them are:
1 The Forgiving
2 The Peace Maker
3 The All-Merciful

🅮 **The student gives three correct responses and so achieves 3 marks.**

(b) Although Muslims believe that Allah is transcendent and unknowable, there are 99 beautiful names which are an attempt to try and explain the nature of Allah. One of these names is 'The Doer of Good'. All of the 99 names are found in the Qur'an: 'Allah loves the doers of good.' Allah is prayed to as the All-Compassionate, the Protecting Friend and the Responder to Prayer, all of which are qualities of goodness. Muslims believe that Allah reveals his goodness through his creation and miracles. The revelation of the Qur'an to the Prophet Muhammad (pbuh) by the Angel Jibril is seen as a miracle and teaches humankind how to do good: 'We have appointed a law and a practice for every one of you' (Surat al-Ma'ida, 48). Allah is seen to be good because he does not force Muslims to obey him. Life is a test to see if they will obey his laws but humankind has free will to make their own choices. However, a Muslim knows that they will be judged on their decisions and actions at the Day of Judgement. Those whose good deeds outweigh their bad deeds will pass on to paradise (al-janna), which is a perfect world of pleasure with Allah, and those with too many bad deeds will go to hell (jahannam). Although even sinners, unless they have committed shirk, will eventually be allowed into paradise once they have been punished because Allah is merciful. Therefore Muslims have the fundamental belief that Allah is good through his actions and nature as stated in the opening verses of the Qur'an.

🅮 **The student shows good knowledge and understanding of the nature of Allah's goodness through the ideas of descriptions from the Qur'an, creation and miracles, the gift of free will and Allah's compassion.**

(c) There are many ways in which a Muslim can experience Allah. Perhaps the most important is through the reading of the Qur'an which Muslims believe to be the direct word of Allah. This is because the Qur'an was revealed over a period of 23 years to the Prophet Muhammad (pbuh) by the Angel Jibril. In the Qur'an Allah's nature is revealed through the 99 beautiful names, his commands for living a good life, and also his actions: 'God is the Creator of everything. He is the guardian over everything. Unto Him belong the keys of the heavens and the earth.' However, as well as the Qur'an there is the Hadith, which is a compilation of the practices, customs and traditions of Muhammad (pbuh). Muhammad (pbuh) was chosen by Allah to be his final prophet (Surah 33:40) and as such is a perfect role model for Muslims to follow. To a Muslim both are important ways, but perhaps because the Qur'an is the revealed message direct from Allah it could be said that the Qur'an is the most important. On the other hand, Sufis or Tasawwuf believe that knowledge of Allah and how to experience him should not just come from books but from teachers whose lineage can be traced back to the time of the Prophet. Sufis, who in their spiritual mystic sessions in their attempt to achieve ihsan (perfection of worship), surrender themselves to the love of Allah. The Hadith teaches 'ihsan is to worship Allah as if you see Him'. However, because Sufism is a form of mysticism it could be argued that only a few would choose this way to experience Allah.

ⓔ **The student explains some of the different ways in which a Muslim can experience Allah: through scripture (Qur'an and Hadith), through the Prophet Muhammad (pbuh) and through Sufism. The student makes comparisons between the different ways. They use sources of wisdom and authority to support their ideas.**

(d) The implication of the statement is that because Muslims believe Allah is good then it is somewhat unbelievable to think he would create a world in which there is so much suffering and evil. The Qur'an teaches that he 'created all things well'. But there are wars, natural disasters, poverty and human cruelty every day, so how can these things exist if the world is good? Muslims believe the world was designed by Allah for a purpose, but this then begs the question, if you accept that the world was a designed creation, what does it say about Allah's purpose for the world? Does it mean that Allah wanted humans to suffer?

ⓔ **The student understands the significance of the statement and points out the questions surrounding the problem of evil for a Muslim.**

However, although Muslims call Allah the Most Merciful and All-Loving, it does not mean to say that Allah cannot be the Judge or the Avenger. The two seemingly opposing sides of Allah are not separate. He is both compassionate and the avenger, the guide to repentance and the righteous teacher all at the same time. The world was designed in such a way as to bring out the goodness in humankind. This is because life is a test from Allah. All human beings, created by Allah, are born without sin (fitrah), but it is through their own free will, which is Allah's gracious gift to them, that they sin and will eventually be judged by Allah. Although this might appear as if Allah is being cruel, it is true to say that this is similar to a parent raising a child, the child must be allowed to make his or her own mistakes in order to learn from them. If someone does not experience evil and suffering, then how are they to know the difference between good and evil?

ⓔ **The student uses both the nature of Allah and the free will argument to counteract the criticisms made that Allah is not good if he created a world that contains evil and suffering.**

Some Muslims might say that evil and suffering occur because of the presence of Shaytan or Iblis. After Allah had created Adam from clay he ordered any angels and Jinn to bow down to his new creation. The Jinn are creatures made from a smokeless fire who were given the gift of free will.

Shaytan, one of the Jinn, refused and so Allah cursed him until the Day of Judgement: 'Then go thou forth hence, thou are accursed.' As a means of revenge Shaytan said that he would tempt humans for ever to choose the wrong rather than the right way. So Muslims see evil and suffering not as part of the design by Allah but as a result of Shaytan managing to tempt humankind to use their free will wrongly. However, the problem with this idea is that Allah was responsible for the creation of Shaytan and since Allah is omniscient, he must have known that Shaytan would refuse to bow down and what the consequences would be. So can it be argued that Allah's design of the world was faulty? Muslims might refer back to the free will gift and say that although Allah uses Shaytan to test the faith and obedience of a Muslim, Allah has put restraints on Shaytan: 'but he will not hurt them anything, except by the leave of Allah' (Surah 58). So perhaps although Allah knew of the outcome of the creation of Shaytan, it was for the good purpose of his testing of humans. If a human fails and sins, Allah has said that he will forgive them if they sincerely repent. He has shown he will do this through his forgiveness of Adam and Eve.

ⓔ The student develops the free will argument further by explaining the role of Shaytan in temptation. The student evaluates this concept.

People long for an ideal life where there is no evil and suffering but a Muslim remembers that their next life in paradise, if they pass Allah's test, will be just that. If everyone was guaranteed an automatic pass to paradise then people would complain about the unfairness of a bad person getting the same treatment as a good person. Allah's will is beyond human understanding, he is unknowable, indescribable and transcendent, so it can be argued that although people may claim Allah could not have designed the world because of the evil present, it is not up to humankind to try and second guess his purpose.

ⓔ The student returns to the problem of whether or not a good Allah could have designed a world where evil exists and comes to a balanced judgement, citing that Allah is beyond human understanding.

Question 3
Student B

(a) Allah is:
1 The Judge
2 The Just
3 The Teacher

ⓔ The student's first two responses are correct but the third one should be the 'Righteous Teacher' and so only 2 marks are awarded.

(b) The belief in Allah's goodness is a major part of the beliefs of a Muslim. They know they have to follow his example: 'Hold to forgiveness, command what is right, but turn away from the ignorant.' There are 99 names which attempt to describe the nature of Allah. Tradition holds that only the camels know the 100th name. Compassion, mercy, forgiveness are all qualities of goodness. Allah is the creator of all and every human being is born without sin (fitrah) but it is through their own free will that they sin and will eventually be judged by Allah. They know that if they choose to do good and be kind then Allah will reciprocate:

'Those who are kind and considerate to Allah's creatures, Allah bestows His kindness and affection on them' (Abu Dawud, Tirmidhi).

(e) **The student shows adequate knowledge and understanding of why Muslims believe Allah is good. There are plenty of ideas, but they are not developed to demonstrate how they relate to the question.**

(c) Muslims can experience Allah through a variety of ways, such as reading the Qur'an in which Allah revealed himself and his wishes, following inspirational role models, such as Muhammad (pbuh), the conscience, practices such as prayer and pilgrimage, and Allah performing miracles or answering prayers. Salat, prayer, is the second pillar of Islam. It should be performed five times a day and there are certain rituals which take place before prayer begins, such as wudhu. Prayer is for the benefit of the devotee because they are praying as if they are in the direct presence of Allah. The Qur'an instructs a Muslim to 'perform the prayer of My remembrance'. One of Allah's names is the Responder to Prayer and as such he may reveal himself to a person by answering their prayers. When a Muslim goes on the Hajj, the fifth pillar, they does so in order to get closer to Allah. All the practices undergone on the Hajj are performed according to the Qur'an: 'and proclaim among men the pilgrimage.'

(e) **The student gives various ideas on how a Muslim may experience Allah and some details on prayer and pilgrimage. However, they make no attempt to compare the different ways, they are just presented as a list. The student refers to sources of wisdom and authority to support their ideas within the response.**

(d) If the world was designed and not the result of chance, then there must be a designer. Because only a powerful entity could design and create the world, and for a Muslim this means that Allah is that designer. The Qur'an teaches: 'Surely your Lord is Allah, who created the heavens and the earth in six days.' Of course there are counter-arguments to this because many scientists see the world as being created by the Big Bang, which was a random event and there was no designer.

(e) **The student focuses on the first part of the statement only and does not show why this is relevant to the second part of the statement.**

When one looks at the world there are many natural disasters, such as earthquakes, floods and hurricanes. The Boxing Day tsunami in 2004 resulted in the deaths of 230,000 people in 14 countries. This led to people asking why does a good Allah allow such a thing to happen? Throughout the Qur'an there are stories of when Allah has punished people for rejecting the truth of his word. In Noah's flood the Qur'an says: 'We opened the gates of heaven with water pouring down, and We caused the earth to burst forth with springs, so the two waters met for a purpose, which had been pre-determined.' This then leads to the question, can Allah who is good also be a punisher? And should Allah be allowed to be so cruel as a punisher?

(e) **The student is now responding to the second part of the statement and is addressing the problem of evil, but this needs to be developed and analysed to ensure that it links in with the idea of Allah creating a good world.**

Many Muslims see evil and suffering as the consequence of a person falling into temptation by Iblis, like Adam and Eve who were banished from paradise for eating the forbidden fruit. Yet Adam and Eve were prepared to acknowledge their sin and so Allah forgave them: 'Thereafter his Lord chose him and turned again unto him, and He guided him.' Muslims see life as a test of Allah. They know that he is merciful and that he will forgive them if they truly repent. Islam means submission to Allah's will.

When a person states they are a Muslim, they begin with the shahadah, the first pillar, which sums up their belief that 'there is no god but Allah'. By letting tawhid (the oneness of Allah) grow in their hearts, it controls and shapes their lives and they trust in Allah and submit to his will and try to do good actions. Muslims are not forced to follow his wishes because they have Allah's gift of free will. Everything that happens is predetermined by Allah. He has decided what is best for his creation. So knowing that he is good and compassionate and merciful, a Muslim will strive to lead a good life so that they can be in paradise at akhirah, the Day of Judgement. They recognise that Allah's creation is good because it allows them to develop into good people and they can show this through the avoidance of temptation.

(e) **The student is now beginning to link the contradictory idea of a designed, good world containing evil and suffering.**

So saying that this world of suffering and evil does not point to a designed, good world by Allah is a wrong statement. If Allah is the guiding force of the Muslims, then they must have the belief that he designed this world for a specific purpose, which can be good if humans are good. A Muslim would say that if Allah did not create it, then no one else could have because only Allah has the power.

(e) **In the last part of this response, the student attempts to show some evaluation and come to a judgement.**

Mark scheme

3 (a) 1 mark is awarded for each correct response up to a maximum of three. The student **might** refer to:
   - The All-Merciful
   - The Peace Maker
   - The Forgiving
   - The Judge
   - The Just
   - The Righteous Teacher
   - The All-Compassionate
   - The Knower of All
   - or any other of the 99 names

Hints and tips

➤ This is a short question requiring knowledge only, so do not spend too much time on it.

(b) This response is marked by levels of response according to the student's knowledge and understanding of the question (AO1).

Knowledge and understanding AO1

Level	Description
1	A **weak** response with limited understanding (1–2 marks): the student may have described one or two ideas about the Muslim belief that Allah is good but in a simplistic way.
2	An **adequate** but **underdeveloped** response (3–4 marks): the student may have given and explained different ideas as to why a Muslim believes Allah is good. These ideas will be outlined in a brief or descriptive way rather than showing the full depth of the student's understanding.
3	A **good** response (5–6 marks): the student **might** show knowledge and understanding of: – the nature of Allah, the 99 names: Most Merciful, All-Compassionate, the Doer of Good, or any other valid names – Allah's actions: creation, revelation of the Qur'an, miracles, gift of free will – yawmuddin, the Day of Judgement – Qur'an, Hadith, Abu Dawud, Tirmidhi

Hints and tips

➤ The command phrase is 'describe why', so the question is asking for knowledge and a demonstration of **why** the beliefs are held. Therefore, your statements as to why Muslims believe Allah is good should be explained.

(c) This response is given **two** separate marks, both of which are determined by levels of response. Only **one** response is written but two different sets of **skills** are assessed by the examiner. The first mark is given for knowledge and understanding (AO1) and the second mark is awarded for the student's analysis and evaluation of the question (AO2). If the student simply writes down all they know about a specific topic, then the marks will be limited to the maximum marks for AO1. The examiner is assessing how the student uses their knowledge and understanding to relate to the specifics of the question/stimulus.

Knowledge and understanding AO1

Level	Description
1	**Some** demonstration of knowledge and understanding which is given 1 mark. This might include some ways in which a Muslim might experience Allah.
2	**Adequate** but **underdeveloped** demonstration of knowledge and understanding which is given 2 marks. The student **might** include: – explanations of meeting inspirational people – scriptural references, the Qur'an as the direct word of Allah – Allah's action in the world: miracles, answering prayers, conscience – various practices of a Muslim: the Five Pillars – mysticism, Sufism, visions

Analysis and evaluation AO2

Level	Description
1	A **weak** response – the student may have given only a single viewpoint on how a Muslim may experience Allah or has given a list of ideas but the ideas are not developed or explained or supported with reference to sources of sacred writings. There is no real attempt at comparison and analysis (1 mark).
2	A **limited** response – the student has perhaps given two or three simplistic ways of how a Muslim might experience Allah, but these have not been developed by any comment and as such the analysis is limited. This might include a comparison or contrast of the different ways and/or beliefs about how Allah may be experienced. There may be some inaccuracies or misunderstanding of the stances taken. **Or** the student may have attempted to comment and show judgement on **one** specific way (2 marks).
3	An **adequate** but **underdeveloped** response – the student has given different Muslim ways of experiencing Allah and has tried to compare/evaluate them but the comments are not developed enough to reach the highest level (3 marks).
4	A **good** understanding of the question. The student has responded with a variety of viewpoints on different ways a Muslim might experience Allah which are explained, compared and contrasted and a balanced judgement has been reached. The student **might** include: – a direct comparison between prayer (or other act of worship) and knowledge of Allah from the Qur'an – whether or not miracles could be proved – a judgement that there is no perfect way, it is a matter for each individual which way suits them best

Hints and tips

➤ Read the question carefully and focus on the trigger/command word, which is to 'compare'.
➤ Support your statements/ideas with reference to sources of wisdom and authority. The examiner will be assessing your ability to refer to sources of wisdom and authority.
➤ Remember to draw a conclusion from your explanations.

(d) This response is given **two** separate marks, both of which are determined by levels of response. Only **one** response is written but two different sets of **skills** are assessed by the examiner. The first mark is given for knowledge and understanding (AO1) and the second mark is awarded for the student's analysis and evaluation of the question (AO2). If the student simply writes down all they know about a specific topic, then the marks will be limited to the maximum marks for AO1. The examiner is assessing how the student uses their knowledge and understanding to relate to the specifics of the question/stimulus.

Knowledge and understanding AO1

Level	Description
1	A **limited/weak** demonstration of knowledge and understanding which is given 1 mark. This might include information and understanding about Muslim ideas on the problem of evil in Allah's design which are simplistic, or just a list of ideas.
2	An **adequate** but **underdeveloped** demonstration of knowledge and understanding which is given 2 marks. This might include different ideas about the problem of evil supported with reference to sacred writings. These may have been contrasted with simplistic generic ideas.
3	A **good** demonstration of knowledge and understanding which is given 3 marks. This might include different explanations of Muslim ideas on the problem of evil linked to the design argument supported by reference to sacred writings while perhaps being contrasted with generic ideas. The student **might** include: – different approaches to the problem of evil, such as Shaytan/Iblis, the free will argument, Allah's nature – transcendent and unknowable – specific examples of evil and suffering, such as natural and moral evil – Islam beliefs and practices: the Five Pillars, tawhid, fitrah, Islam meaning submission to Allah's will – references to Muslim sacred writings, e.g. Qur'an: Surah 7, 15:34, 20:120, 32:7, 54:11, 58:10

Analysis and evaluation AO2

Level	Description
1	A **weak** response – the student may have given only a single viewpoint or the response is simply a description of events rather than offering comments which demonstrate a judgement (1–3 marks). This might include a descriptive/simplistic account of one or two different Muslim ideas on the problem of evil. These may or may not be linked to the idea that Allah created a good world. No attempt to offer a judgement/conclusion will have been made. In other words, the information is communicated in a basic way and there is no evidence of a **discussion** taking place.
2	A **limited** response – the student has perhaps given different views on Muslim ideas of how the problem of evil can be answered in relation to Allah's good creation but these views have not been developed and there is little evidence of a conclusion. **Or** the student may have attempted to comment and show judgement on a specific Muslim idea contrasted with generic beliefs (4–6 marks). In other words, there is a line of reasoning/**discussion** which has some relevance to the stimulus.
3	An **adequate** but **underdeveloped** response – the student has perhaps given different views and has attempted to show some judgement/analysis on them but the ideas and comments are not developed enough to reach the highest level (7–9 marks). This might include comments with a judgement on the different ideas of how the problem of evil can be answered in relation to Allah's good creation which could be contrasted with generic or other religious beliefs while linking them to the stimulus. However, they have not been discussed or analysed in sufficient depth to reach Level 4. A line of reasoning has been presented and **discussed** which is mostly relevant.
4	A **good** understanding of the question. The student has responded with a variety of viewpoints or different schools of thought, which are explained and analysed and a conclusion/judgement on the question has been made (10–12 marks). The student has offered a well-developed and sustained **discussion** which is coherent, relevant and well structured. The student **might** include: – comments on the incompatibility of a designed good world with the problem of evil – comments on the different responses to the problem of evil – whether they are successful or not – comments on the unfairness of some of the responses – a balanced conclusion

Hints and tips

➤ Read the stimulus carefully and identify its significance in your response, making sure you stick to the wording in the stimulus and do not divert into a concept that you would prefer to discuss.

➤ Remember that your response should be a **discussion** – try to present viewpoints for both sides as if you were having a conversation. Do not just list all the ideas for the stimulus in one paragraph and then all the ideas against in another paragraph.

➤ The stimulus in this particular question is quite long, so make sure you address it as a whole and do not focus on the separate parts.

➤ Refer to different beliefs and teachings and evaluate the importance of these differences.

➤ Try to refer back to what you studied in Part 1 of this course: beliefs and teachings and practices.

➤ Remember that you do not have to express a personal view – if you want to, you can, but make sure you justify your point of view with evidence and argument.

➤ Do not fall into the trap of saying 'An atheist does not believe in Allah and therefore would not agree with the religious point of view'. You are not adding to the argument/discussion at all.

Question 4

Student A

(a) Muslims believe that fitrah is the idea that every child throughout the world is born with an inner feeling or instinct which leads them to right action of submission to Allah.

ⓔ **The first mark is given for the idea of 'every child', the second mark for the explanation of fitrah, 'inner instinct', and the development of what the instinct is about receives the third mark.**

(b) Muslims believe that Allah is eternal and beyond time and space. As a result, a Muslim is his servant, they must be completely obedient to him with no questions asked. If anything good or bad happens to them they will say 'Inshallah', which means God willing. This is acknowledgement of his authority and divine nature. Any act of worship, be it prayer, fasting or going on the Hajj, is an expression of a Muslim's status as a servant to Allah's will. The word 'Islam' means submission. A Muslim's purpose is to fulfil the wishes of Allah and behave well and treat each other fairly and correctly. The Qur'an teaches that Allah created both humans and the Jinn 'to worship him'. Allah cannot be seen or imagined in human terms or thought of like a human friend. The whole idea is to be completely obedient to him. However, Sufis believe they can have a personal experience with God as taught in the Qur'an: 'We are closer to him than his jugular vein.' Through their active meditation such as the whirling dervishes, they attempt to connect with Allah. So Muslims believe that their relationship with Allah is one of a servant to a master. They know that in order to receive Allah's love they have to show how much love they have for Allah. A Muslim is completely dependent upon Allah.

ⓔ **The student shows good knowledge and understanding of a Muslim's relationship with Allah. They describe various concepts, such as 'submission', 'dependency' and the status as a servant.**

(c) The conscience is said to be that inner voice within a person which directs them to making the right choice between good and bad actions. Some believe that the conscience is the direct voice of God, or that it is a feeling of guilt, due to how you have been brought up. Whatever belief you have about where the conscience comes from it is seen as an important tool in aiding decision making. Muslims believe that the conscience is important because it is an extra guide to help them in making decisions on things that are neither halal nor haram. Since they will be judged on the Day of Judgement they want to make sure that they are judged favourably and thus Allah's gift of the conscience is important. However, the conscience is not to be seen as a substitute for the Qur'an or Sunnah because the Qur'an is the direct revealed word of Allah. Muhammad (pbuh) taught about the importance of the conscience when he said, 'When a thing disturbs your heart give it up' (Hadith). Allah gave humans the gift of free will whereas the angels were created for the single purpose of worshipping him (Surah 16). So the conscience is important because it is another tool from Allah to help man live in complete obedience of him. They have the Qur'an, Sunnah and Shari'ah law to live by, but sometimes a person needs that extra nudge in the right direction. Muhammad (pbuh) told the story of the woman who had a kitten but would not feed it. She was sent to hell. But Allah pardoned the prostitute who gave a thirsty dog some water from a well. She had listened to her conscience and so her sins were forgiven. Sometimes when we do not listen to our conscience, or we allow ourselves to hold mistaken beliefs, we can make mistakes, but our higher conscience is the innate tendency towards good and as a result the conscience could be seen as one of the most important gifts Allah has bestowed on humankind.

(e) **The student shows good knowledge and understanding of the nature and purpose of the conscience, deliberating on its origins and explaining why it is important.**

(d) The Qur'an teaches that the world was created by Allah in six days: 'Allah who created the heavens and earth in six days and then established himself above the throne.' The Qur'an also teaches that Allah sustains the world: 'His Kursi extends over the heavens and the earth, and their preservation tires Him not.' So it might appear as if Allah is responsible for looking after the world. Yet Allah appointed Adam and his descendants to be khalifahs: 'We appointed you viceroys…to see how you behave.' This was supported by Muhammad (pbuh): 'The earth is green and beautiful, and Allah has appointed you his stewards over it' (Hadith). Therefore it can be argued that it is the obligation of humans to look after the world for Allah so that they are judged favourably on judgement day.

(e) **The student understands the significance of the statement and points out that although the Qur'an teaches that Allah did create the world and sustains it, he also appointed humans to be khalifahs.**

Muslims believe in tawhid – the 'oneness' of Allah, that he is indivisible and omnipotent. Tawhid is reflected in the unity of humankind and nature, therefore it is important for a Muslim to consider the benefits and wellbeing of everyone in the world and realise that it is the responsibility of humans to make sure the world is not spoiled and halt the destructive ways in which humankind has treated the earth in the past. The Qur'an remarkably taught about the 'corruption (which) doth appear on land and sea' as if describing the impact of pollution and acid rain. The Qur'an also taught that there should be no 'altering the creation of Allah' and therefore humans who ruin the environment will be answerable on the Day of Judgement. Since Muslims consider themselves to be Allah's agent, they will need to decide on how best to counteract the damage already caused. Therefore it can be argued that it is not Allah's responsibility to deal with the world's problems, not just environmental but also human suffering: men and women have caused them and so they should try to clean their own mess up. In truth, it is not just a Muslim's responsibility but the whole of humankind.

(e) **The student does not fall into the trap of giving a lengthy description on the problems facing the world but instead discusses how it should be humankind's responsibility to do something – not just a Muslim's responsibility.**

A Muslim knows that Allah made natural laws such as cause and effect and so the majority of suffering is a reaction to a specific action. Allah could intervene but there are times when he hopes humankind will do something in accordance with his wishes of being kind to others. Life is a test for Muslims, of their faith and submission, their intentions and deeds are being recorded by their two angels. It could be argued that it is Allah's responsibility to ensure the world is looked after and put to rights since he knew that humans would make a mess of it, but he was giving humans the chance to act properly and live in peace and harmony. Thus it is up to Muslims, and all the rest of humankind, to seize the opportunity and ensure that the world is returned to how it was when it was first created.

(e) The student indicates that Allah could take responsibility but if he did then that would not allow Muslims and the rest of humankind to show Allah what they are capable of.

Question 4
Student B

(a) Muslims believe that everyone is born a Muslim because they have fitrah, which is an impulse towards the true religion.

(e) The first mark is given for the idea that 'everyone is born a Muslim' and the explanation of fitrah gains the second mark. Further development such as support of the Hadith would have achieved the third mark.

(b) Tawhid, the oneness of Allah, is taught in the Qur'an. It signifies the belief that Muslims should always trust in Allah and make sure that they spend the whole of their lives doing as he wants. Muslims are not equal to Allah, they are in submission to him, which means they should never disobey his wishes. They know that life on earth is only temporary and is a test, so any hardships they experience are all part of Allah's plan to prepare them for judgement day. The shahadah is an expression of this relationship with Allah; Muslims state that Allah is the one and only God and they also accept that Muhammad (pbuh) is his messenger.

(e) The student shows adequate knowledge and understanding of the relationship between a Muslim and Allah. However, it is just a list of different ideas and the response would be improved by having a linking thread, such as 'submission', running through it.

(c) Most people have a conscience which helps them in making moral decisions. If we have a conscience it suggests we also have free will, which is important because it means we have the choice to either follow our conscience or not and thus any good action carried out would be a moral one. However, Muslims also believe in predestination and that Allah has already decided on what will happen. The Qur'an teaches that Allah knows 'what his (man's) soul whispers to him'. So does this mean that the conscience is not important because if Allah already knows, what is the point of it? Also, sometimes a person thinks they are following what is right according to their conscience but it may have a wrong outcome – so does this make the conscience important? The Universal Declaration of Human Rights declares that everyone is entitled to freedom of thought, conscience and religion. So it would seem as though both secular and religious ideas about the conscience mean that it is an important tool.

(e) The student has misread the question and gives different attitudes towards the conscience rather than explaining why Muslims believe it to be important. If the student had been able to compare whether the conscience is important or unimportant, this would then be credited. However, the link to free will is a valid point.

(d) The Qur'an teaches that 'Allah sends down rain from the sky', showing that Allah does show responsibility for the world he created. However, at the same time Muslims believe he also gave some responsibility to humans when he appointed them as khalifahs. So it could be argued that it is both Allah and the Muslim community who are responsible for the world.

(e) **The student attempts to address the implications of the statement but limits the response to the Muslim faith.**

Muhammad (pbuh) taught 'whoever plants a tree and diligently looks after it…is rewarded' (Hadith). This shows that part of a Muslim's submission to Allah is worshipping him through environmental actions, not just through prayer, fasting and going on a pilgrimage. It is a matter of doing good deeds. Being a vice-regent however is not just looking after the environment and stopping pollution but also ensuring that the rest of the community, the ummah, is treated fairly. This is why Muslims have the duty of zakat (the third pillar) and also sadaqah. During the festival of Eid-Ul-Adha, which celebrates the time when Abraham, in submission to Allah, would have sacrificed his son, Isma'il, Muslims who can afford it will sacrifice a sheep or goat and then divide it between family, friends and the poor. So Muslims all around the world are obedient in their responsibility of khalifah.

(e) **The student gives details of the purpose of a khalifah, demonstrating that it is not just about environmental concerns but also about humanity. As such the student is implicitly indicating that it is not Allah's responsibility to look after the world.**

So it can be argued that Allah's purpose of giving Muslims the responsibility of being a khalifah was to see what they would do with that responsibility.

(e) **The student comes to an abrupt end and the conclusion does not add anything to the rest of the response.**

Mark scheme

4   (a) Marks are awarded for a statement plus further development of that statement with either examples or references to sources of wisdom and authority to support it. The student **might** refer to:
   – inner instinct about the right action and submission to Allah
   – Hadith: each child is born in a state of fitrah
   – reversion: Hadith, 'I created my servants in the right region but the devils made them go astray'

Hints and tips

➤ This is a short question requiring knowledge only, so do not spend too much time on it.

➤ Make sure you are clear – you are asked to make a statement and then you can either develop it or explain it and support it with a specific example or a quote.

   (b) This response is marked by levels of response according to the student's knowledge and understanding of the question (AO1).

Knowledge and understanding AO1

Level	Description
1	A **weak** response with limited understanding (1–2 marks): the student may have described one or two ideas about the Muslim beliefs about their relationship with Allah but in a simplistic way.
2	An **adequate** but **underdeveloped** response (3–4 marks): the student may have given and explained different ideas about the Muslim beliefs about their relationship with Allah. These ideas will be outlined in a brief or descriptive way rather than showing the full depth of the student's understanding.
3	A **good** response (5–6 marks): the student **might** show knowledge and understanding of: – the purpose of human creation (Surah 51:56) – tawhid, shahadah, judgement day – obedience, submission, not equals – Sufis (Surah 50:16) – khalifah (Surah 2:28–29)

Hints and tips

➤ The command word is 'describe'; however, you are also expected to show knowledge and understanding.

➤ Try to develop a thread running through the response rather than just listing lots of ideas.

(c) This response is given **two** separate marks, both of which are determined by levels of response. Only **one** response is written but two different sets of **skills** are assessed by the examiner. The first mark is given for knowledge and understanding (AO1) and the second mark is awarded for the student's analysis and evaluation of the question (AO2). If the student simply writes down all they know about a specific topic, then the marks will be limited to the maximum marks for AO1. The examiner is assessing how the student uses their knowledge and understanding to relate to the specifics of the question/stimulus.

Knowledge and understanding AO1

Level	Description
1	**Some** demonstration of knowledge and understanding which is given 1 mark. This might include some Muslim beliefs about the importance of the conscience.
2	**Adequate** but **underdeveloped** demonstration of knowledge and understanding which is given 2 marks. The student **might** include: – a definition of the conscience – religious and secular – having a conscience implies free will – thus good actions are moral – conscience is not a substitute for the Qur'an or Sunnah – sources of authority: Qur'an: Surah 16:49–50, Surah 50:16, Hadith

Analysis and evaluation AO2

Level	Description
1	A **weak** response – the student may have given only a single viewpoint on some Muslim beliefs about the importance of the conscience or given a list of ideas but the ideas are not developed or explained or supported with reference to sources of sacred writings. There is no real attempt at comparison and analysis (1 mark).
2	A **limited** response – the student has perhaps given two or three simplistic ideas about some Muslim beliefs about the importance of the conscience, but these have not been developed by any comment and as such the analysis is limited. There may be some inaccuracies or misunderstanding of the stances taken. **Or** the student may have attempted to comment and show judgement on one specific way (2 marks).
3	An **adequate** but **underdeveloped** response – the student has given different Muslim beliefs about the importance of the conscience and has tried to compare/evaluate them but the comments are not developed enough to reach the highest level (3 marks).
4	A **good** understanding of the question. The student has responded with a variety of viewpoints on different Muslim beliefs about the importance of the conscience which are explained, compared and contrasted and a balanced judgement has been reached. The student **might** include: – analysis on the degree of importance – possible comparison of secular views of the conscience which might imply that Allah's gift of the conscience is important – analysis of what might happen if there was not such a thing as the conscience

Hints and tips

➤ Read the question carefully and focus on the trigger/command word, which is to 'explain'. This means you have to give reasons for a statement/idea – use the word 'because'.

➤ The question is asking for 'beliefs on the importance', so make sure you address this point.

➤ Support your statements/ideas with reference to sources of wisdom and authority. The examiner will be assessing your ability to refer to these.

➤ Remember to draw a conclusion from your explanations.

(d) This response is given **two** separate marks, both of which are determined by levels of response. Only **one** response is written but two different sets of **skills** are assessed by the examiner. The first mark is given for knowledge and understanding (AO1) and the second mark is awarded for the student's analysis and evaluation of the question (AO2). If the student simply writes down all they know about a specific topic, then the marks will be limited to the maximum marks for AO1. The examiner is assessing how the student uses their knowledge and understanding to relate to the specifics of the question/stimulus.

Knowledge and understanding AO1

Level	Description
1	A **limited/weak** demonstration of knowledge and understanding which is given 1 mark. This might include information and understanding about whether or not it is Allah's responsibility to look after the world, which are simplistic or just a list of ideas.
2	An **adequate** but **underdeveloped** demonstration of knowledge and understanding which is given 2 marks. This might include different ideas about whether or not it is Allah's responsibility to look after the world, supported with reference to sacred writings. These may have been contrasted with simplistic generic ideas.
3	A **good** demonstration of knowledge and understanding which is given 3 marks. This might include different explanations of Muslim ideas about whether or not it is Allah's responsibility to look after the world, supported by reference to sacred writings while perhaps being contrasted with generic ideas. The student **may** include: – definition of khalifah – Allah makes natural laws, Allah sustains, Allah creates – tawhid reflected in unity of humankind and nature – purpose of humankind, judgement day – Qur'an: 2:255, Surah 7:54, Surah 7:95–96, Surah 7:128, Surah 10:14, Surah 13:3–4, Surah 30:30, Surah 30:41, Surah 54:10–13, Hadith

Analysis and evaluation AO2

Level	Description
1	A **weak** response – the student may have given only a single viewpoint or the response is simply a description of events rather than offering comments which demonstrate a judgement (1–3 marks). This might include a descriptive/simplistic account of one or two different Muslim ideas about whether or not it is Allah's responsibility to look after the world. No attempt to offer a judgement/conclusion will have been made. In other words, the information is communicated in a basic way and there is no evidence of a **discussion** taking place.
2	A **limited** response – the student has perhaps given different comments on Muslim views about whether or not it is Allah's responsibility to look after the world, but these ideas have not been developed and there is little evidence of a conclusion. **Or** the student may have attempted to comment and show judgement on a specific Muslim idea contrasted with generic beliefs (4–6 marks). In other words, there is a line of reasoning/**discussion** which has some relevance to the stimulus.
3	An **adequate** but **underdeveloped** response – the student has perhaps given different views and has attempted to show some judgement/analysis on them but the ideas and comments are not developed enough to reach the highest level (7–9 marks). This might include different comments with a judgement on the different ideas about whether or not it is Allah's responsibility to look after the world, which could be contrasted with generic or other religious beliefs while linking them into the stimulus. However, they have not been discussed or analysed in sufficient depth in order to reach Level 4. A line of reasoning has been presented and **discussed** which is mostly relevant.
4	A **good** understanding of the question. The student has responded with a variety of viewpoints or different schools of thought, which are explained and analysed and a conclusion/judgement on the question has been made (10–12 marks). The student has offered a well-developed and sustained **discussion** which is coherent, relevant and well structured. The student **might** include comments and analysis on: – humankind's inability to be responsible for the world – that it is just not a Muslim responsibility – that it is Allah's responsibility (predestination) or that it is a joint problem

Hints and tips

➤ Read the stimulus carefully and identify its significance in your response, making sure you stick to the wording in the stimulus and do not divert into a concept that you would prefer to discuss.

➤ Do not fall into the trap of writing a response on environmental concerns/issues – this is not what the question is asking. It is asking about who should be responsible, Allah or humankind?

➤ Remember that your response should be a **discussion** – try to present viewpoints for both sides as if you were having a conversation. Do not just list all the ideas for the stimulus in one paragraph and then all the ideas against in another paragraph.

➤ The stimulus in this particular question is quite long so make sure you address it as a whole and do not focus on the separate parts.

➤ Refer to different beliefs and teachings and evaluate the importance of these differences.

➤ Try to refer back to what you studied in Part 1 of this course: beliefs and teachings and practices.

➤ Remember that you do not have to express a personal view – if you want to, you can, but make sure you justify your point of view with evidence and argument.

➤ Do not fall into the trap of saying 'An atheist does not believe in Allah and therefore would not agree with the religious point of view'. You are not adding to the argument/discussion at all.

Islam: religion, peace and conflict

Question 5

Student A

(a) Muslims believe that the fight against evil and in defence of Islam is known as a holy war, harb al-muqadis. The Qur'an teaches about holy war: 'Fight against those who fight against you in the way of Allah...' and states that self-defence is a just cause.

ⓔ The student has explained the purpose of holy war (first mark); this is further developed by a quote from the Qur'an (second mark) and the idea that self-defence is a just cause for a holy war (third mark).

(b) The word Islam comes from the word Salaam which means peace. Islam is a religion which encourages peace and peace-making. The Hadith teaches that 'faith is a restraint against all violence, let no Mu'min (a person with faith) commit violence'. The Qur'an teaches that one should be at peace even with one's enemy: 'It may be Allah will yet establish between you and those of them with whom you are at enmity, love.' A Muslim might work for peace because they feel concern for a part of the world where Muslims are involved in conflict, or are suffering as refugees. Their concern might be heightened as a result of the concept of ummah, that they are part of a worldwide community of believers and have a duty to help one another. When the Prophet led the Madinah community, he insisted that it was a city of peace and people of different tribes and religions were required to protect each other. Some people might think the concept of jihad means that Muslims do not work for peace, but this concept has often been misunderstood or misrepresented. There are two forms of jihad in Islam: the greater jihad is the personal inner struggle of an individual Muslim to abide by Allah's rules and to avoid evil. The Hadith teaches: 'the person who struggles so that Allah's word is supreme is the one serving Allah's cause'. The lesser jihad is the more physical struggle against injustices in the world but any fight must be done without hatred or vengeance. Once the wrong has been corrected there must be peace and reconciliation. Muslims see jihad as a way to peace.

The aim is to create a society where they can worship Allah in peace without others' beliefs or politics being forced upon them. By working for peace Muslims are building bridges and promoting the positive aspects of Islam.

(e) **The student has shown good knowledge and understanding of why a Muslim may work for peace, linking the ideas of the sacred writings to what is occurring in the world today.**

(c) A Muslim might go to war to protect the country they live in and whose rules they obey and benefit from. Muslim soldiers in the British armed forces therefore might see it as their duty to go to war as part of their vocation to help the country, just as Muslims in any field of work see what they do as important in helping Allah's created world. Muslims might also go to war if it is a holy war, harb al-muqadis, because this would be to defend the religion of Islam as instructed in the Qur'an: 'Fight against those who fight against you in the way of Allah...' A military war is also permitted – this is seen as the lesser jihad, a physical struggle against injustice. There are many rules in the Qur'an to ensure that the war is just and it is being fought in self-defence: 'Leave is given to those who fight because they were wronged'. So Muslims believe they should obey what is written in the Qur'an because it is the true revealed word of Allah. Muslims are not allowed to be the aggressors, they have to be attacked first. A Muslim should only fight in a just war and there are many rules of engagement to be followed. The war should be a last resort. It should be fought only to bring about good and peace, and the war must stop as soon as the enemy asks for peace. The Qur'an teaches: 'if they incline to peace, do thou incline to it, and put thy trust in Allah'. The war must be called by a legitimate ruler and the Muslim must have permission from their parents, if alive, to join the effort. A Muslim might go to war to follow the example of the Prophet Muhammad (pbuh) who led his followers into the Battle of Badr in order to protect the people of Medina. The Qur'an, Surah 3, tells how Allah helped the army and sent three thousand angels to reinforce the troops. So there are many teachings in Islamic sacred writings which promote the idea of war, however a Muslim will only do so if there is no other option and will fight for the purpose of peace.

(e) **The student has explained some of the different reasons why a Muslim may go to war, supported by teachings from the Qur'an. Implicit evaluation is present in the conclusion.**

(d) Justice is a central theme in the Qur'an, both as religious justice and social justice: 'We have sent down on thee the Book making clear everything, and as a guidance and a mercy...' The Qur'an considers justice to be a supreme virtue and so it can be seen therefore as an obligation for all Muslims. Some state that it is next in priority to tawhid (the oneness of God) and the truth of the prophethood of Muhammad (pbuh). However the word 'Islam' can mean either submission to Allah or peace. Muslims work and pray for peace, both inner peace and peace throughout the world. So therefore it would also seem that peace is important. But can you have justice without peace, or peace without justice? Surely it is difficult to separate one from the other.

(e) **The student has opened the response by recognising the significance of the statement and suggesting that perhaps it is difficult to have one virtue without the other.**

The ummah, the worldwide community of Muslims, is a symbol of justice in practice. The Hadith teaches 'Among those we have created there is a community who guide by the Truth and act justly according to it.' They have the responsibility to care for each other. Zakat, the third pillar of Islam, is the purification of wealth when every Muslim, if they are able, contributes 2.5% of their annual income to charity. This is a compulsory obligation. The Hadith teaches that if someone does not pay zakat then on the Day of Judgement, the wealth will become like a poisonous snake which will encircle and bite the non-giver. As well as laying down the obligations of zakat, the Qur'an also urges believers to fight to help those who are being oppressed. Men, women and children who, being oppressed, say 'Our Lord, bring us forth from this city whose people are evildoers'. However fighting or war is against the notion of peace. A definition of peace is an absence of war. War brings killing, maiming, destruction, refugees and all types of suffering which are not coherent with the thought of peace. So it appears as if the two virtues are incompatible. Is it then feasible to say that one is more important than the other?

e **The student has shown how sacred writings encourage justice and also the idea of fighting for justice. However this raises the dilemma of war being an absence of peace. The student has shown that they are addressing the significance of the statement by posing the question 'is one more important than the other?'.**

Shi'a Muslims might place particular emphasis on justice due to the events at Kerbala. They believe that Hussein had the rightful cause, but he could have pursued peace by accepting the leadership of what became Sunni Islam. Peace would have been the easiest option, but Hussein chose to fight to uphold what Shi'a Muslims regard as the legitimate leadership of the family of the Prophet. In the modern world, many Shi'a Muslims opposed Saddam Hussein as they believed his oppression was unjust, and they did not submit despite terrible suffering.

If someone is being persecuted for their religious or political beliefs, or if there is racial inequality or unfair treatment of women, surely this indicates that there is a lack of peace. Yet should they turn to violence in order to get justice? Malcolm X stated that 'our objective is complete freedom, justice and equality, by any means necessary'. He was prepared to use violence to ensure that justice was won, thus showing that for him justice is more important than peace. Can peace exist in an unjust society? If a person is living in absolute poverty do they experience peace? Their country might not be at war but surely the struggle to survive and watching children die of preventable diseases could not be described as a peaceful world.

e **The student has argued that in an unjust society peace cannot exist and therefore it appears necessary to fight for justice which makes justice most important.**

For some Muslims who live in areas of unrest, peace would seem to be more important. Many refugees are risking their lives and those of their children to escape from war and to find a new life of peace in a just country. Does this indicate that they recognise that peace and justice should be in harmony and that neither peace nor justice is more important than the other? Both are ideals and it could be that they can only be found together in paradise: 'Therein they shall hear no idle talk, no cause of sin, only the saying "Peace, Peace".'

e **The student has argued that through fighting to correct injustice, peace might not occur and therefore it is too difficult to say that one is more important than the other.**

Question 5
Student B

(a) Muslims can take part in a holy war if it is to defend Islam. This is because Muhammad (pbuh) led his followers into battle at the Battle of Badr.

e **The explanation of when a Muslim is allowed to take part in a holy war receives the first mark. The second mark is awarded for the implicit explanation that Muhammad (pbuh) was defending Islam. Further development or support from the Qur'an or Hadith would have received the third mark.**

(b) The ummah teaches that Muslims should work together for peace. The Qur'an teaches that: 'if two parties of the believers fight, put things right between them'. The Muslim Peace Fellowship was founded in 1994. In 2003, many Muslims joined the Stop the War Coalition march in London against the prospect of a war in Iraq. In November 2015, hundreds of Muslims took to social media condemning the Paris killings. These are examples of Muslims making their views known that violence is not the answer and as such they are working for peace. They do so because they want to stand up and show that they believe the actions taken by some are wrong and they want to educate people in recognising that, to a majority of Muslims, Islam is not a violent religion but that the name Islam means peace.

ⓔ **The student has shown adequate knowledge and understanding in an explanation of why Muslims work for peace, but the ideas are listed and have not been explained in depth.**

(c) Although Islam is a religion of peace Muslims believe there are times when war is a necessary evil. They can fight a holy war. Muhammad (pbuh) led his armies into battle during the final years of his life. The Qur'an forbids a Muslim from attacking first but they are allowed to fight in self-defence. They can go to war if it is a holy war, in order to defend their religious freedom. They can also go to war if it is a just war. However there are many terms and conditions which have to be followed, such as innocent people not being involved and that enemies must be treated with justice. This is because the Hadith teaches that a Muslim should 'hate your enemy mildly, he may become your friend one day'. However in this day and age, war is more brutal especially with technological weapons, such as drones or nuclear bombs, so that it is difficult to follow such rules of conduct. Civilians do get involved. So it seems as if some of the teachings on war are outdated.

ⓔ **The student has given various ideas on why a Muslim might go to war. There has been an attempt at evaluation but the response has diverted from the specifics of the question.**

(d) Justice is a blanket term for many aspects of fair behaviour. It can refer to legal justice, social justice, economic justice, etc. The Qur'an teaches that 'you approach not the property of the orphan, save in the fairer manner' continuing that when the orphan comes of age that 'measurement and weight with justice' be given. The Qur'an also refers to the teaching that men can marry more than one wife but that they must all be treated equally and if this cannot happen then the man must marry only one wife (Surah 4). The Qur'an, the most holy book for Muslims, sets out how Allah expects them to live their lives in submission to his will so that justice will come about through acts of compassion. So it would seem as if justice is more important than peace.

ⓔ **The student has suggested that justice is more important than peace through references to the Qur'an.**

Peace is also important to Muslims because the word Islam comes from the word Salaam, which is a common greeting among Arabs and Muslims. Many Muslims state that Islam is the religion of peace and although the Prophet Muhammad (pbuh) did lead his followers into war, it was for a just cause and in accordance with the teachings of the Qur'an. He went into battle to obtain justice for his followers so that they would be allowed to worship with religious freedom and not be persecuted for their beliefs. So he was fighting for justice and peace. This suggests that peace and justice are both important.

ⓔ **The student has discussed the idea of peace and referred to the Prophet Muhammad fighting for both peace and justice.**

However sometimes fighting against injustice can go too far. Fighting itself can create greater injustices than those being fought against. For example, in conflicts around the world, Muslims have sometimes fought against what they see as injustice, but in so doing have carried out acts which result in loss of innocent life including women and children. A cycle of violence has led to areas of the world where peace never seems to be achieved. So fighting to correct an injustice does not always bring peace and in fact it can lead to far worse consequences. Therefore peace is probably more important.

(e) **The student has argued for peace being more important by referring to areas of the world where there is violence today.**

The problem is would a person want peace at any cost? Would they want to live in a country that is ruled unfairly with a small minority having all the wealth? Would they want to live in a country that persecuted people of a certain faith? If the only way they could get justice was to fight, this might lead to more injustice. Therefore it is too difficult to state which is more important.

(e) **The student has attempted to come to a balanced conclusion but it is quite simplistic and nothing new has been added to the preceding comments.**

Mark scheme

5 (a) Marks are awarded for three short statements. The student **might** refer to:
- a definition of a holy war, harb al-muqadis
- just causes of a holy war: self-defence, strengthening Islam, protection of the faith, protection against oppression, putting right a wrong
- when a holy war is not permitted: forcing converts, conquering land for economic gain, demonstration of power, settlement of arguments
- references to the Qur'an or Hadith

Hints and tips

➤ This is a short question requiring knowledge only, so do not spend too much time on it.

(b) This response is marked by levels of response according to the student's knowledge and understanding of the question (AO1).

Knowledge and understanding AO1

Level	Description
1	A **weak** response with limited understanding (1–2 marks). The student may have explained one or two ideas about why Muslims work for peace but in a simplistic way.
2	An **adequate** but **underdeveloped** response (3–4 marks). The student may have given and explained different ideas on why a Muslim works for peace. These ideas will be given in a brief or descriptive way rather than showing full depth of understanding.
3	A **good** response (5–6 marks). The student may have shown knowledge and understanding in detailed explanations of why Muslims work for peace. The student **might** refer to: – the term Islam meaning peace, the idea of the greater and lesser jihad, the ummah, stereotyping of Muslims as terrorists, building bridges – sacred writings: the Hadith; the Qur'an, e.g. Surah 49:9; 60:7; the example of Muhammad – current case studies of Muslims working for peace: peace march, Muslim Peace Fellowship – receiving reward on the Day of Judgement.

Hints and tips

➤ The command words are 'describe why', so you are expected to show knowledge and understanding. Therefore your statements about why a Muslim might work for peace should be explained.

(c) This response is given **two** separate marks, both of which are determined by levels of response. Only **one** response is written but two different sets of **skills** are assessed by the examiner. The first mark is given for knowledge and understanding (AO1) and the second mark is awarded for the student's analysis and evaluation of the question (AO2). If the student simply writes down all they know about a specific topic, then the marks will be limited to the maximum marks for AO1. The examiner is assessing how the student uses their knowledge and understanding to relate to the specifics of the question/stimulus.

Knowledge and understanding AO1

Level	Description
1	**Some** demonstration of knowledge and understanding which is given 1 mark. This might include some explanation of why a Muslim might go to war.
2	**Adequate** but **underdeveloped** demonstration of knowledge and understanding which is given 2 marks. The student **might** include various explanations on: – the Qur'an, e.g. Surah 2:190, 3:120, 22:39; and the Hadith teachings on war – conditions of a just war and holy war – the example of Muhammad, the Battle of Badr – generic ideas on when war might be necessary

Analysis and evaluation AO2

Level	Description
1	A **weak** response – the student may have only given a single comment on why a Muslim might go to war or may have given only a list of ideas, which are not developed, explained or supported with reference to sources of sacred writings. There is no real attempt at analysis (1 mark).
2	A **limited** response – the student has perhaps given two or three simplistic explanations as to why a Muslim might go to war, but these have not been developed and as such the analysis is limited. There may be some misunderstanding of the stances taken. **Or** the student may have attempted to comment in detail and show judgement on **one** specific idea (2 marks).
3	An **adequate** but **underdeveloped** response – the student has given different explanations as to why a Muslim might go to war and has tried to evaluate them, but the comments are not developed enough to reach the highest level (3 marks).
4	A **good** understanding of the question. The student has responded with a variety of ideas on why a Muslim might go to war, which are explained, compared and contrasted, and a balanced judgement has been reached. The student **might** include: – a comparison between Islam as a religion of peace and the Qur'an advocating war – a judgement that war is different from when the Qur'an was revealed – a judgement that war is never wanted but sometimes there is no option

Hints and tips

➤ Read the question carefully and focus on the trigger/command word which is 'explain'. This means you have to give reasons for a statement/idea – use the word 'because'.

➤ Support your statements/ideas with reference to sources of wisdom and authority. The examiner will be assessing your ability to do so.

➤ Remember to draw a conclusion from your explanations.

(d) This response is given **two** separate marks, both of which are determined by levels of response. Only **one** response is written but two different sets of **skills** are assessed by the examiner. The first mark is given for knowledge and understanding (AO1) and the second mark is awarded for the student's analysis and evaluation of the question (AO2). If the student simply writes down all they know about a specific topic then the marks will be limited to the maximum marks for AO1. The examiner is assessing how the student uses their knowledge and understanding to relate to the specifics of the question/stimulus.

Knowledge and understanding AO1

Level	Description
1	A **limited/weak** demonstration of knowledge and understanding which is given 1 mark. This might include information and understanding about Muslim ideas about peace and justice or just a list of ideas.
2	An **adequate** but **underdeveloped** demonstration of knowledge and understanding which is given 2 marks. This might include different ideas about Muslim teachings on peace and justice supported with reference to sacred writings. These may have been contrasted with simplistic, generic ideas.
3	A **good** demonstration of knowledge and understanding which is given 3 marks. This might include different explanations of Muslim teachings on peace and justice linked to specific case studies/examples supported by reference to sacred writings while perhaps being contrasted with generic ideas. The student **might** include: – different teachings from the Qur'an, e.g. Surah 4:3, 4:75, 6:152, 16:89, 56:25, and the Hadith on peace and justice – specific examples of peace and justice (or injustice) such as 9/11, Syria today, wars in Iraq and Afghanistan, inequality, racism and poverty – reference to the example of the Prophet Muhammad or Malcolm X

Analysis and evaluation AO2

Level	Description
1	A **weak** response – the student may have given only a single viewpoint or the response is simply a description of events rather than a demonstration of judgement (1–3 marks). This might include a descriptive/simplistic account of one or two different Muslim teachings on peace and justice. Some generic comments may be made. No attempt to offer a judgement/conclusion will have been made. In other words, the information is communicated in a basic way and there is no evidence of a **discussion** taking place.
2	A **limited** response – the student has perhaps given different ideas on Muslim teachings on peace and justice, but these ideas have not been developed and there is little evidence of a conclusion. **Or** the student may have attempted to comment and show judgement on a specific Muslim teaching contrasted with generic beliefs. In summary, there is a line of reasoning/ **discussion** which has some relevance to the stimulus.
3	An **adequate** but **underdeveloped** response – the student has perhaps given different views and has attempted to show some judgement/analysis on them, but the ideas and comments are not developed enough to reach the highest level (7-9 marks). This might include different comments with a judgement on the different teachings of peace and justice which could be contrasted with generic or other religious beliefs while linking them into the stimulus. However they have not been discussed or analysed in sufficient depth to reach level 4. A line of reasoning has been presented and **discussed** which is mostly relevant.
4	A **good** understanding of the question. The student has responded with a variety of viewpoints or different schools of thought, which are explained and analysed. A conclusion/judgement on the question has been made (10–12 marks). The student has offered a well-developed and sustained **discussion** which is coherent, relevant and well-structured. For instance, the student **might** include: – comments on the dilemma of fighting for peace or injustice – comments on either peace being more important and why, or justice being more important and why – comments on the impracticability of both being achieved – a balanced conclusion which may or may not refer to paradise or the idea that both are needed to exist together

Hints and tips

➤ Read the stimulus carefully and identity its significance in your response. Make sure you stick to the wording in the stimulus and do not divert into a concept that you would prefer to discuss.

➤ Remember that your response should be a **discussion** — try and present viewpoints for both sides as if you were having a conversation. Do not just list all the ideas for the stimulus in one paragraph and then all the ideas against in another.

➤ Refer to different beliefs and teachings and evaluate the importance of these differences.

➤ Try and refer back to what you studied in Part 1 of this course: beliefs and teachings and practices.

> Remember that you do not have to express a personal view – if you want to you can, but make sure you justify your point of view with evidence and argument.

> Please do not fall into the trap of saying: 'An atheist does not believe in Allah and therefore would not agree with the religious point of view.' You are not adding to the argument/discussion at all.

Question 6
Student A

(a) Reconciliation means repairing of friendly relationships which have been broken after an argument or disagreement by offering forgiveness and finding a way forward.

ℯ The first mark is given for the meaning, which is 'restoration of friendly relationships', the second mark is given for the reason why relationships need repairing, and the third mark is for the development of how reconciliation might be done.

(b) There are many teachings in the Qur'an about forgiveness. Muslims know that Allah is merciful and forgiving and it is believed that even those who have led bad lives will be able to go to paradise but only after they have been punished and have shown that they have truly repented. This is because the Hadith teaches, 'were your sins to reach the clouds in the sky and were you to ask forgiveness of me, I shall forgive you'. However, if Muslims want to go to paradise they must show mercy or forgiveness to each other. The Qur'an teaches that 'whoever pardons and makes reconciliation – his reward is from Allah'. Forgiveness is very important in preparation for the Hajj (the fifth pillar) and also during it. Before even starting the pilgrimage, Muslims must make peace with all those they have fallen out with and ask for forgiveness from them and from Allah. During the Hajj on the Day of Arafat when they are at Mount Mercy, they will ask Allah for forgiveness. However, there are times when a Muslim believes that forgiveness is not possible. If the sin of shirk is committed, putting something or someone above Allah, which is the opposite of tawhid, they believe that this is unforgivable. The Qur'an teaches 'do not associate with Allah. Indeed, association is a great injustice'.

ℯ The student shows good knowledge and understanding of different Muslim attitudes about forgiveness. They show that Allah is all-forgiving and merciful and that Muslims should try to copy this attitude in their lives. The student describes the importance of forgiveness during the Hajj and shows the opposing attitude that sometimes forgiveness is not possible.

(c) The Hadith teaches 'do you know what is better than charity, fasting and prayer? It is keeping peace and good relations between people, as quarrels and bad feelings destroy humankind'. This teaching is stressing the value of not resorting to violence. Gandhi is famous for saying 'an eye for an eye and the whole world will be blind'. This shows that once violence begins, sometimes as a means of retribution, then violence escalates. The Hadith is also teaching this and is saying that the three pillars of zakah, sawm and salah are outranked by peace – in other words, the teaching is condemning violence. However, there are times when a Muslim may resort to violence, especially if they feel that Islam is being insulted or wronged. The Qur'an teaches that Muslims can 'fight in the cause of God those who fight you'. Muhammad (pbuh) fought several battles, including the Battle of Badr, which was to protect the Muslims in Al-Madinah, in the name of Allah. Yet violence does not necessarily mean going to war, it can be used in defence or protection. But a Muslim must be careful not to go too far because the Qur'an teaches 'if anyone killed a person – it would be as if he killed the whole people'. This teaching returns to the teaching of the Hadith which shows the destructive nature of violence. The Hadith teaches to 'hate your enemy mildly, he may become your friend one day'. It could be said that violence breeds violence and therefore should only be used as a last resort because it is much better to try and calm things down before lashing out and ending with regrets.

@ **The student explains some of the different Muslim attitudes towards violence, supported by teachings from the Qur'an and Hadith. The student makes it clear that violence is different from war, although of course wars involve violence. They show analysis throughout the response.**

(d) Islam is a religion which promotes peace and justice, but it is not considered to be a pacifist religion. An absolute pacifist is a person who refuses to adopt violence or fight under any circumstances. Pacifism is an ideal, but does it work? Muhammad (pbuh) tried non-violent methods before the Hijra travel but then began to turn to violence. Malcolm X first promoted violent means in his struggles against racism and equality in America but after his pilgrimage (the Hajj) he changed his views. However, he was killed by violence. So does that show that although you can admire someone for being a pacifist (it must take a lot of courage), it does not always work. In answer to the statement, it could be argued that a Muslim might believe in peace making but that sometimes there are occasions when it is necessary to use violence or fight. These people are called conditional pacifists.

@ **The student opens the discussion by recognising the significance of the statement and suggesting that it is not necessary for a Muslim to be an absolute pacifist but they could be a conditional one.**

The Qur'an teaches that Muslims are given permission to fight if 'they have been wronged'. They are allowed to fight 'in the cause of God', which is a holy war (harb al-muqadis). Muhammad (pbuh) fought at the Battle of Badr to protect the Muslims in Al-Madinah. When a Muslim is fighting an unbeliever they are commanded to 'strike their necks until, when you have inflicted slaughter upon them'. This ayat also promotes the idea that those who are killed during fighting for Allah will be rewarded: 'Never will He waste their deeds.' This has led to the idea that martyrs will go straight to paradise. These teachings perhaps are the reasons why non-believers stereotype Islam as a violent religion which spreads its beliefs through the sword. But there are individuals and groups within Islam which promote pacifism but usually do not reject violence completely, they often tolerate violence if it is for defence. However, belief in conditional pacifism is not accepted by many Muslims. Sufis believe in extending their love for Allah to include love for their fellow men. It is part of their spiritual struggle – the greater jihad. Some Sufis interpret Islamic teachings on conflict to refer to spiritual and not physical conflict, so maintain pacifism within the material world. But other Sufis do not reject war. So it can be argued that it is difficult for a Muslim to be an absolute pacifist. Yet the Qur'an (47.4) teaches a Muslim to be at peace with his enemy and to develop love and, if the so-called enemy does not seek to hurt Muslims, Allah commands Muslims to be nice to them 'from being righteous towards them and acting justly toward them'. So it appears some of the verses of the holy Qur'an can have different interpretations or can be misinterpreted by scholars who are trying to make a point for or against pacifism.

@ **The student discusses the different teachings in the Qur'an on going to war and contrasts them with some of the minor sects of Islam who are conditional pacifists.**

So in conclusion, the statement says that a Muslim cannot be a pacifist, but there is no teaching in the Qur'an which states that you are not allowed to be a pacifist. Recently, the Muslim Council of Britain took out an advert which condemned the Paris attacks, and in India in 2015, 70,000 Muslim clerics issued a fatwa on ISIS. This shows that they are against barbaric attacks of violence and want to live in harmony. I truly believe that although I would like to be a pacifist because that is such a courageous principle to hold, it is too difficult to do so. If someone were to attack a member of my family, I could not simply stand by and do nothing. So like a lot of Muslims, I think I am a conditional pacifist because that is better than demanding violence all the time.

ⓔ **The student concludes with a personal response. Although this is not required it can be used, but only if it is supported with good reasoning. The personal response suggests that conditional pacifism is better than nothing – the lesser of two evils.**

Question 6
Student B

(a) Reconciliation is the hope of returning to a state of friendship after matters have broken up through a falling out.

ⓔ **The first mark is given for the idea of 'returning to a state of friendship' and the second mark for the development of showing the need for reconciliation. Further development or even a supporting quote from the Qur'an is needed for the third mark.**

(b) The Qur'an teaches that 'a kind word with forgiveness is better than charity', which shows how important the act of forgiveness is for a Muslim. Muslims try and follow the example of Muhammad (pbuh) who showed forgiveness to those who had killed and mutilated the body of his Uncle Hamzah. It can be very hard to forgive but since Allah will forgive people who turn to him and ask for his forgiveness because they are sorry for the sins they have committed (Surah 2), then Muslims should try to forgive others themselves. However, some Muslims would argue that working against Islam and denying Muslim principles is unforgivable.

ⓔ **The student shows adequate knowledge and understanding in an explanation of different Muslim attitudes on forgiveness but the ideas are listed and they are not developed in depth.**

(c) Quite often non-believers of Islam see Islam as a violent faith, but this is because of media coverage of recent events in war zones and certain parts of the world. This is a wrong impression, however, because the word Islam comes from an Arabic word meaning peace and submission. So in reality, Muslims should not resort to violence. The Qur'an teaches that 'paradise is for…those who curb their anger and forgive their fellow men'. Violence which could begin with a shove or slap can quickly end up in something far worse and Muslims are told not to 'kill a soul which Allah has made sacred'. Therefore, by resorting to violence, they may end up doing something terrible and as a result may fail to go to paradise on judgement day.

ⓔ **The student shows some knowledge and understanding of Muslim attitudes towards violence but in a simplistic way. They use two teachings and make an attempt at evaluation. However, this response needs to be developed in much greater depth through more detailed explanations and the use of further teachings.**

(d) Pacifism means that someone will never turn to violence, no matter what has happened. The statement is saying that a Muslim cannot be a pacifist/cannot use violence – well, this might seem true when you look at the religion of Islam and realise that it does not teach pacifism. In other words, it does not command people to be a pacifist. Instead it promotes peace, because the word Islam comes from an Arabic word meaning peace and submission to Allah. However, the Qur'an appears to command war as well when it tells Muslims that 'permission has been given to those who are being fought, because they were wronged'. This is telling Muslims that they can go to war in self-defence. So since there seems to be no teaching which says you cannot use violence, perhaps the statement is correct.

e The student explains what the term pacifism means and tries to show that they can see the implications of the statement but the clarity of the argument is a little confused.

The Qur'an does teach that killing a person is bad because it is the same as killing 'the whole people'. In other words, it is showing that murder is a very bad crime. But a soldier who goes to war is not seen as a murderer because they are doing their duty and if the Qur'an teaches that it is all right to go to war to defend Islam, 'fight in the cause of God those who fight you', then it would seem as though pacifism is not the stance a Muslim should take.

e The student uses teachings from the Qur'an to show that although murdering a person is wrong, it is all right to go to war and not be a pacifist.

Although Islam believes in forgiveness and reconciliation and works for peace, Muslims realise that sometimes violence must be used as the lesser of two evils. It cannot be said that everyone does not like violence because there are some sick people who do, but when a Muslim turns to violence it is usually for good reasons. So in answer to the statement, it could be that a Muslim wants to be a pacifist but because of the world we live in, often violence has to be used to ensure a practical outcome.

e This is a nice conclusion showing a balanced judgement but it could have been developed to show a deeper understanding of the problems of being a pacifist.

Mark scheme

6 (a) Marks are awarded for a statement plus further development of that statement with either examples or references to sacred writings to support it. The student **might**:
   - offer a definition of the term reconciliation: restoration of friendly relationships
   - suggest a reason for the need for reconciliation
   - explain how reconciliation might occur
   - refer to the Qur'an: Surah 3:134, Surah 42:40

Hints and tips

➤ This is a short question requiring knowledge only, so do not spend too much time on it.

(b) This response is marked by levels of response according to the student's knowledge and understanding of the question (AO1).

Knowledge and understanding AO1

Level	Description
1	A **weak** response with limited understanding (1–2 marks): the student may have explained one or two ideas of different Muslim attitudes on forgiveness but in a simplistic way.
2	An **adequate** but **underdeveloped** response (3–4 marks): the student may have given and explained different Muslim attitudes on forgiveness. These ideas will be outlined in a brief or descriptive way rather than showing the full depth of the student's understanding.
3	A **good** response (5–6 marks): the student may have shown knowledge and understanding in detailed explanations of different Muslim attitudes on forgiveness. The student **might** refer to: – Allah: all-merciful, forgiving and compassionate – the Day of Judgement, tawhid, shirk, Hajj, example of Muhammad (pbuh) – Qur'an: Surah 2:222, Surah 2:263, Surah 31:13, Surah 42:40 – Hadith: Al-Tirmidhi (An-Nawas's Forty Hadith 42)

Hints and tips

➤ The command word is 'describe', however you are also expected to show knowledge and understanding.

➤ This question is asking about attitudes, so make sure you are able to show opposing views.

(c) This response is given **two** separate marks, both of which are determined by levels of response. Only **one** response is written but two different sets of **skills** are assessed by the examiner. The first mark is given for knowledge and understanding (AO1) and the second mark is awarded for the student's analysis and evaluation of the question. If the student simply writes down all they know about a specific topic, then the marks will be limited to the maximum marks for AO1. The examiner is assessing how the student uses their knowledge and understanding to relate to the specifics of the question/stimulus.

Knowledge and understanding AO1

Level	Description
1	**Some** demonstration of knowledge and understanding which is given 1 mark. This might include some ideas on Muslim attitudes to violence.
2	**Adequate** but **underdeveloped** demonstration of knowledge and understanding which is given 2 marks. The student **might** include: – meaning of Islam: peace and submission – teachings: Qur'an Surah 2:190, Surah 3:134, Surah 5:32, Surah 6:51, Hadith – the example of Muhammad, the Battle of Badr – shirk, tawhid, Day of Judgement – generic examples on the use of violence, Gandhi

Analysis and evaluation AO2

Level	Description
1	A **weak** response – the student may have given only a single comment on one Muslim attitude to violence or may have given only a list of ideas but the ideas are not developed or explained or supported with reference to sources of sacred writings. There is no real attempt at analysis (1 mark).
2	A **limited** response – the student has perhaps given two or three simplistic comments on the explanations about Muslim attitudes to violence but these have not been developed by any comment and as such the analysis is limited. There may be some inaccuracies or misunderstanding of the stances taken. **Or** the student may have attempted to comment in detail and show judgement on one specific explanation (2 marks).
3	An **adequate** but **underdeveloped** response – the student has given different explanations about Muslim attitudes to violence and has tried to evaluate them but the comments are not developed enough to reach the highest level (3 marks).
4	A **good** understanding of the question. The student has responded with a variety of ideas on the explanations about Muslim attitudes to violence which are explained, compared and contrasted and a balanced judgement has been reached (4 marks). The student **might** include: – analysis on the result of violence: destructive nature, useful sometimes – comparison of different teachings in the Qur'an on violence and peace – analysis of the difficulties of not using violence

Hints and tips

➤ Read the question carefully and focus on the trigger/command word, which is 'explain'. This means you have to give reasons for a statement/idea – use the word 'because'.

➤ The question is asking about attitudes, which means you can give ideas for and against violence.

➤ Support your statements/ideas with reference to sources of wisdom and authority. The examiner will be assessing your ability to refer to sources of wisdom and authority.

➤ Remember to draw a conclusion from your explanations.

(d) This response is given **two** separate marks, both of which are determined by levels of response. Only **one** response is written but two different sets of **skills** are assessed by the examiner. The first mark is given for knowledge and understanding (AO1) and the second mark is awarded for the student's analysis and evaluation of the question. If the student simply writes down all they know about a specific topic, then the marks will be limited to the maximum marks for AO1. The examiner is assessing how the student uses their knowledge and understanding to relate to the specifics of the question/stimulus.

Knowledge and understanding AO1

Level	Description
1	A **limited/weak** demonstration of knowledge and understanding which is given 1 mark. This might include information and understanding about Muslim ideas on whether they can be a pacifist or not which are simplistic or just a list of ideas.
2	An **adequate** but **underdeveloped** demonstration of knowledge and understanding which is given 2 marks. This might include different views about Muslim ideas on whether they can be a pacifist or not supported with reference to sacred writings. These may have been contrasted with simplistic generic ideas.
3	A **good** demonstration of knowledge and understanding which is given 3 marks. This might include different explanations of Muslim ideas on whether they can be a pacifist or not linked to specific case studies/examples supported by reference to sacred writings while perhaps being contrasted with generic ideas. The student **might** include: – a definition of pacifism, types of pacifism: absolute or conditional – different teachings from the Qur'an, e.g. Surah 2:190, Surah 5:32, Surah 6:51, Surah 22:39, Surah 47:4, Surah 60:8–9 and the Hadith on peace and justice – specific examples of pacifist stances: the Prophet Muhammad or Malcolm X, Gandhi or Martin Luther King, ideas from various groups, Sufis – Muslim Council of Britain: condemnation of the Paris attacks, India: 70,000 Muslim clerics, fatwa against ISIS

Analysis and evaluation AO2

Level	Description
1	A **weak** response – the student may have given only a single viewpoint or the response is simply a description of events rather than offering comments which demonstrate a judgement (1–3 marks). This might include a descriptive/simplistic account of one or two different Muslim ideas on whether they can be a pacifist or not. Some generic comments may be made. No attempt to offer a judgement/conclusion will have been made. In other words, the information is communicated in a basic way and there is no evidence of a **discussion** taking place.
2	A **limited** response – the student has perhaps given different comments on Muslim ideas on whether they can be a pacifist or not but these ideas have not been developed and there is little evidence of a conclusion. **Or** the student may have attempted to comment and show judgement on a specific Muslim teaching contrasted with generic beliefs (4–6 marks). In other words, there is a line of reasoning/**discussion** which has some relevance to the stimulus.
3	An **adequate** but **underdeveloped** response – the student has perhaps given different views and has attempted to show some judgement/analysis on them but the ideas and comments are not developed enough to reach the highest level (7–9 marks). This might include different comments with a judgement on the different Muslim ideas on whether they can be a pacifist or not which could be contrasted with generic or other religious beliefs while linking them into the stimulus. However, they have not been discussed or analysed in sufficient depth in order to reach Level 4. A line of reasoning has been presented and **discussed** which is mostly relevant.
4	A **good** understanding of the question. The student has responded with a variety of viewpoints or different schools of thought, which are explained and analysed and a conclusion/judgement on the question has been made (10–12 marks). The student has offered a well-developed and sustained **discussion** which is coherent, relevant and well structured. The student **might** include comments and analysis on: – the difficulties of pacifism – does it ever work? – the stereotypical view of Islam as a warring nation – the view that pacifism is not taught within Islam, it is a religion which advocates peace but is not pacifist

Hints and tips

➤ Read the stimulus carefully and identify its significance in your response, making sure you stick to the wording in the stimulus and do not divert into a concept that you would prefer to discuss.

➤ Remember that your response should be a **discussion** – try to present viewpoints for both sides as if you were having a conversation. Do not just list all the ideas for the stimulus in one paragraph and then all the ideas against in another paragraph.

➤ Refer to different beliefs and teachings and evaluate the importance of these differences.

➤ Try to refer back to what you studied in Part 1 of this course: beliefs and teachings and practices.

➤ Remember that you do not have to express a personal view – if you want to, you can, but make sure you justify your point of view with evidence and argument.

➤ Do not fall into the trap of saying 'An atheist does not believe in Allah and therefore would not agree with the religious point of view'. You are not adding to the argument/discussion at all.

Islam: dialogue between religions and non-religious beliefs and attitudes

Question 7

Student A

(a) Proselytisation is the process of converting someone from one religion to another. Since Muslims believe that everyone is born a Muslim with the idea of Allah (fitrah), whether they know it or not, it is not a matter of a Muslim converting from a different faith but of that person reverting to the true religion of Islam.

🅔 **The student has defined proselytisation (first mark). The explanation linking it to Muslim beliefs and the idea of fitrah gains the second mark, with the development of it being a reversion not a conversion gaining the third mark.**

(b) Great Britain is a multicultural society, which is home to many different religions, although Christianity is the main religion. There are different Muslim attitudes to inclusivism, which is the acceptance of other religious beliefs as being partially true. However, the Qur'an teaches that 'surely those who disbelieve, and die disbelieving, there shall not be accepted from any one of them', which would indicate to a Muslim that those who understand and reject belief are not worthy of jannah (heaven). This attitude suggests that Islam is the exclusive way to follow. Yet the Qur'an appears to teach inclusivism when it states that Jews, Christians and Sabaeans who believe in Allah and the last judgement and who do good actions will be rewarded (Surah 2). This indicates that Allah will allow them into jannah. This idea of inclusivism will promote harmony, as will the Muslim belief that everyone is born a Muslim, with the concept of fitrah. The Hadith teaches that the Prophet Muhammad (pbuh) taught that 'no babe is born but upon fitrah'. This indicates that there is a subconscious recognition of Islam as the true religion. Sufis teach that there are as many paths to God as there are souls on earth, which appears to be in support of inclusivism. In Britain, some Muslims prefer to send their children to Christian faith schools and enter interfaith dialogue sessions with Christians and others, suggesting a degree of tolerance and mutual respect for Christians.

🅔 **The student recognises the divergent religious beliefs in the UK and links some of the different attitudes of Muslims about inclusivism to promoting harmony within society. The student supports their ideas with teachings from the Qur'an and the Hadith.**

(c) Genetic manipulation is the alteration or addition of genes to an organism in order to cure diseases. There are many different Muslim ideas about when the soul enters the embryo/foetus, ranging from the moment of conception to 120 days. Sunni Muslims believe the soul enters 120 days after conception because of the teachings from Sahih Bukhari (Hadith): 'Then the soul is breathed into the body.' So they may support genetic manipulation of embryos in the very early stages because that would be a kind thing to do which would please Allah, because it would ensure that the foetus or baby does not suffer in the future. 'Allah loves those who do good deeds.' Also in support of genetic manipulation, in 2003, the Muslim World League agreed to the use of spare embryos from IVF procedures if they were used to help develop medicine and treatments. So they must have recognised that scientific advancements are useful in helping to prevent suffering.

However, the Muslims who believe the soul is present from conception would be against any form of genetic manipulation, especially if any spare embryos were destroyed even before the UK legal period of 14 days. Although the Qur'an (the holy word of Allah) was revealed to the Prophet Muhammad (pbuh) over 1,400 years ago, some Muslims believe that the Qur'an condemned genetic manipulation. The Qur'an teaches that Satan planned to lead people astray and get them to 'alter Allah's creation'. Muslims would see altering Allah's creation as shirk because the scientists would be trying to act as Allah. So it could be fair to say that a Muslim's religious beliefs determine which attitude they take towards genetic manipulation.

(e) **The student demonstrates good knowledge and understanding of different Muslim attitudes to genetic manipulation. The response begins with reasons why some might agree to it in the early stages of pregnancy or agree to the use of spare embryos from IVF. But the second half of the response shows the different attitude that some Muslims are totally against it. The student uses teachings from the Qur'an and a statement from the Muslim World League to support their response. There is evidence of analysis throughout and a balanced judgement at the end of the response.**

(d) Humanists or secularists believe that faith schools should be abolished because these schools do not allow for an inclusive system where children can learn from each other about different faiths and culture. This would then help to stop discrimination and people being treated with privileges just because of their faith. Children who grow up alongside their peers who are all of the same faith may find it more difficult to operate as adults in more mixed environments, and so may find it more difficult to settle in further education or take up various careers. Tolerance of those of other faiths and cultures is a core British value. If a child is raised in a faith school, they may feel less committed to the value of tolerance if they know less about others.

The British government now requires the teaching of two separate religions in Religious Education in its efforts to promote tolerance. The head of the British Muslim faith schools has called for the teaching of Judaism as the second religion for Muslims in order to contribute to community cohesion, British values and inter-faith relations. Can this be achieved within faith schools? Concerns have been reported in the media about the radicalisation of young people in particular through misuse of social media and other sites. The question has been raised: would education in a more mixed and inclusive environment better protect Muslim children from falling into such dangers? Perhaps faith schools should not be allowed because of what could happen, but is this the true picture of a faith school?

(e) **The student opens the response by recognising the significance of the statement and suggesting that in spite of all the secular reasons against faith schools, they might not be painting the true picture.**

The Prophet Muhammad (pbuh) believed it was the sacred duty of every Muslim to seek knowledge, he said 'seek knowledge from the cradle to the grave'. The revelation of the Qur'an by the Angel Jibril underlines the importance of education. The first word Jibril said was 'Read'. The Hadith teaches that 'the Father if he educates his daughter well, will enter paradise'. Thus education is important. The imparting of the beliefs and practices of a Muslim can be taught in an inclusive school, but will they be taught to the depth which the nature of the religion requires? A Muslim might wish to have such teachings taught in an environment which does not allow for distractions or perhaps wrong teachings by someone who is not a Muslim. Thus for them faith schools are essential.

(e) **The student argues that for a Muslim, faith schools could be essential in the true education of their faith.**

There are over 2,000 madrasas, which are schools attached to mosques, in the UK. These schools provide two paths of learning. The first is for children to learn Arabic so that they can memorise the Qur'an and become a Hafiz. The sacred nature of the Qur'an is kept sacred by the fact it remains in its original language, Arabic, and so has not been distorted or corrupted over the years, which Muslims believe has happened to the sacred texts of other religions. The other path is a course lasting for many years which enables the scholar to be accepted in the community and is a pathway to becoming an Imam. So Muslim faith schools help those who wish to specialise in these paths. Some parents feel they do not have time to teach their children enough about the details of their faith at home, and children would not receive this in detail from a non-religious school, so they feel that faith schools should be retained to help deliver information about Islam. Against this, some Muslim parents report bad experiences, such as the suspected use of corporal punishment, sectarianism or even the existence of illegal faith schools, which undermine the case for faith schools in general. On the other hand, there are some Muslim faith schools which have been praised for good standards. In a society where parents are granted freedom of choice in the way their children are educated, many Muslims believe faith schools should be permitted for those parents who wish to send their children to them.

ⓔ The student demonstrates the important role of the madrasas and counters the criticisms that might be made.

It could be said that some faith schools do promote intolerance by focusing entirely on one religion as if a child is brought up in a community which is exclusivist to other cultures, this could lead to misconceptions and prejudice. Faith schools are not bound by the National Curriculum Religious Education requirements and therefore some Muslims might feel their children are not being educated properly if their religion is absent from the curriculum. In the past, parents were allowed to withdraw their children from lessons which they felt were going against their beliefs, but teachers are campaigning to have this stopped. However, inclusive schools or even faith schools which allow for the diversity of its intake can promote cohesion. There are many Church of England schools which include Muslim children because although a faith school, they have an inclusive acceptance policy. As the Qur'an teaches, 'To you your religion, and to me my religion', which is perhaps an endorsement of the Sufis' idea of many paths to God. Perhaps the question which should be asked is not whether faith schools should be abolished but what would happen if there were no faith schools? Would society be any more tolerant or different?

ⓔ The student develops the idea of faith schools being at odds with the multicultural aspect of the UK and as such being viewed as being divisive. But the student presents analysis and draws a balanced judgement.

Question 7
Student B

(a) A Muslim believes that proselytisation, converting someone to Islam, is not allowed to be done by force.

ⓔ The definition of proselytisation, conversion, receives the first mark and the second mark is given for the statement that it is wrong to convert someone through force. If this had been developed further with reference to teachings from the Qur'an (Surah 2: 256), it would have achieved the third mark.

(b) Inclusivism is acceptance of other religions but does not suggest that they have the truth. This is an important way of thinking in this country because while there are many different religions, Christianity is said to be the religion of the country. Muslims believe that Islam is the only true religion and that they have a duty to bring people back to the faith because all people are born with fitrah and they have been brought up in another faith by their parents, or society or just because of the place they live in. Yet the Qur'an teaches that 'those who have rejected the faith' shall be punished on the Day of Judgement.

This appears to promote exclusivism and it could be suggested that it does not take into account the teaching that Iblis said that he would tempt humans to disobey Allah for ever after Allah had cursed him for not bowing down to Adam. Muhammad (pbuh), in his last sermon, warned people to beware of Iblis because his purpose was to 'divert you from the worship of Allah'. Muslims believe that Islam is the one true faith because Muhammad (pbuh) was the last prophet and received the final revelation from Allah in the Qur'an which speaks of how the people of the book, Jews and Christians, who also had Allah's truth revealed to them, were turned away and took on false beliefs. Muslims accept inclusivism because everyone is born a Muslim.

(e) **The student gives various ideas on Muslim attitudes to inclusivism but unfortunately the focus is more on exclusivism, although the student attempts to bring the discourse back to the question at the end.**

(c) Some Muslims believe that embryos left over from IVF can be used for research but they will not allow the creation of embryos. The Hadith teaches that the Prophet Muhammad (pbuh) said that 'the seeking of knowledge is compulsory for every Muslim'. Some Muslims believe that using genetic manipulation to prevent disease is part of their purpose as khalifahs. Muslims believe in the sanctity of life that Allah has created everything – 'Allah is the Creator of everything' (Surah 13) – and that the soul is present from conception: 'And slay not the soul' (Surah 17).

(e) **The student shows adequate knowledge and understanding in an explanation of different attitudes Muslims have towards genetic manipulation, but although the ideas are supported by references to sources of wisdom and authority, they read as a list. These ideas need to be developed in order to explain them in depth. There also needs to be evidence of a balanced judgement.**

(d) It is believed that some faith schools are divisive and encourage intolerance by not allowing children to encounter different ideas and beliefs. Newspaper reports comment that children in some faith schools grow up learning no English and thus they are isolated from the rest of society and view it with suspicion. However, Muslims believe that their faith schools are different in that they are for the purpose of studying their sacred scriptures in detail which they would not have the opportunity to do in an inclusive school.

(e) **The student opens the response showing the two opposing views on faith schools.**

Muslims believe that Allah created everyone so there is no reason why people should be divisive. 'O humankind, We have created you…that you may know one another.' So surely this is a good reason why faith schools should not be allowed unless they are prepared to teach comparative religions and not just focus on one faith. Yet with the time constraints placed on the National Curriculum and the emphasis on continual testing, the teaching of different beliefs and practices is often ignored or pushed to one side.

(e) **The student argues that the Qur'an teaches that Allah created everyone for the purposes of community (getting to know each other) and this precludes faith schools. But the student then counter-argues with the view that inclusive schools do not have the opportunity to teach in depth.**

Yet Muslims believe that their faith is the one true one and do not want their children to become corrupted by someone either not teaching their faith properly or by the allure of other faiths. The Qur'an teaches that Iblis was responsible for tempting the people of the book away from the true word of Allah. It is his purpose in life which he vowed to do after Allah had cursed him for not bowing down to Adam. They think that faith schools, which do not have to teach more than one faith, are the correct environment for a child to study in depth the beliefs and values taught in the Qur'an. They would learn to speak Arabic which is the original language the Qur'an was written in because Muslims believe that when the Qur'an is translated in other languages misinterpretations happen. If you check on the web the meaning of a certain ayat once it gets translated into English, there are many different interpretations. So it can be asked if there is anything wrong in a Muslim wanting their children to be taught in depth the true meaning of their religion. If you are in the same room where everyone has the same beliefs, it stops arguments from happening. So faith schools are a good idea.

ⓔ **The student argues for the usefulness of faith schools.**

In conclusion, because there are different views about the importance of faith schools (often they get a bad name in the press), it is perhaps the decision of the government of the country in which the Muslim resides.

ⓔ **The student makes an attempt to reach a balanced judgement but it needs to be discussed in more depth in order to relate to the significance of the statement.**

Mark scheme

7 (a) Marks are awarded for a statement plus further development of that statement with either examples or references to sacred writings to support it. The student **might** refer to:
  - a definition of proselytisation
  - an explanation of reversion, not conversion
  - the Qur'an teaching that conversion cannot be done by force (Surah 2: 256)
  - Islam being the one true religion

Hints and tips

➤ This is a short question requiring knowledge only, so do not spend too much time on it.

(b) This response is marked by levels of response according to the student's knowledge and understanding of the question (AO1). The examiner will also determine whether the student has responded to the instructions in the question about the diversity of religious traditions in Great Britain.

Knowledge and understanding AO1

Level	Description
1	A **weak** response with limited understanding (1–2 marks): the student may have described one or two ideas about Muslim attitudes to inclusivism but in a simplistic way.
2	An **adequate** but **underdeveloped** response (3–4 marks): the student may have given different ideas on different Muslim attitudes to inclusivism. These ideas will be outlined in a brief or descriptive way rather than showing the full depth of the understanding of the student.
3	A **good** response (5–6 marks): the student may have shown knowledge and understanding in detailed descriptions of different Muslim attitudes to inclusivism. The student **might** refer to: – Qur'an and Hadith teachings on inclusivism such as Surah 2, and the Sufis – all paths to God – the concept of fitrah and that Allah creates everyone – the people of the book – definitions of inclusivism and perhaps exclusivism – an explanation of why Muslims consider Islam to be the one true religion. – an indication that the religious traditions in Great Britain are diverse and thus it is important perhaps to have an attitude which embraces inclusivism

Hints and tips

➤ The command word is 'describe', which is asking you to set out the main characteristics. So the main characteristics of inclusivisiom' would be a definition of what it is and its general aims.

➤ Give a detailed description of various Muslim attitudes towards inclusivism, and perhaps support these attitudes with teachings from the Qur'an or the Hadith.

➤ You could also contrast these Muslim attitudes with other beliefs to show you fully understand the views held.

➤ Remember that the instructions with the question ask you to consider that 'religious traditions in Great Britain are diverse, but mainly Christian', so you must make reference to this in your response.

(c) This response is given **two** separate marks, both of which are determined by levels of response. Only **one** response is written but two different sets of **skills** are assessed by the examiner. The first mark is given for knowledge and understanding (AO1) and the second mark is awarded for the student's analysis and evaluation of the question (AO2). If the student simply writes down all they know about a specific topic, then the marks will be limited to the maximum marks for AO1. The examiner is assessing how the student uses their knowledge and understanding to relate to the specifics of the question/stimulus.

Knowledge and understanding AO1

Level	Description
1	**Some** demonstration of knowledge and understanding which is given 1 mark. This might include some explanations of Muslim attitudes towards genetic manipulation.
2	**Adequate** but **underdeveloped** demonstration of knowledge and understanding which is given 2 marks. The student **might** include: – Muslim teachings on the creation of life and the sanctity of life – references to the Qur'an (Sanctity of Life: Surah: 2:195, 4:119, 5:32, 13, 17) and the Hadith (Sahih Bukhari Volume 4, Book 55, No. 549, Ibn Majah 224) – 2003 Muslim World League declaration – the purpose of khalifahs – definition of genetic manipulation (but not too detailed)

Analysis and evaluation AO2

Level	Description
1	A **weak** response – the student may have given only a single comment on why a Muslim might support or not support genetic manipulation or the student may have given only a list of ideas but the ideas are not developed or explained or supported with reference to sources of sacred writings. There is no real attempt at a balanced judgement (1 mark).
2	A **limited** response – the student has perhaps given two or three simplistic comments about the explanations as to why a Muslim might support or not support genetic manipulation but these have not been developed by any comment and as such the analysis is limited. There may be some inaccuracies or misunderstanding of the stances taken. **Or** the student may have attempted to comment in detail and show judgement on one specific explanation (2 marks).
3	An **adequate** but **underdeveloped** response – the student has given various explanations as to why a Muslim holds different attitudes to genetic manipulation and has tried to evaluate them but the comments are not developed enough to reach the highest level (3 marks).
4	A **good** understanding of the question. The student has responded with a variety of ideas on why a Muslim might support or not support genetic manipulation which are explained, compared and contrasted and a balanced judgement has been reached. The student **might** include: – analysis and comparison between different Muslim beliefs on when the soul enters the body: conception, 40 days, 120 days, when there is movement from the foetus – comments/judgement on whether a Muslim believes that the scientific advancements of genetic manipulation are a step too far or that they are a good benefit to the world

Hints and tips

➤ Read the question carefully and focus on the trigger/command word, which is 'compare'. This means you have to explain the similarities or differences between two or more attitudes.

➤ Include some comments/analysis on the explanations.

➤ Remember to draw a conclusion/judgement from your response.

➤ Remember that this question is asking you to support your ideas with sources of wisdom or authority.

(d) This response is given **two** separate marks, both of which are determined by levels of response. Only **one** response is written but two different sets of **skills** are assessed by the examiner. The first mark is given for knowledge and understanding (AO1) and the second mark is awarded for the student's analysis and evaluation of the question (AO2). If the student simply writes down all they know about a specific topic, then the marks will be limited to the maximum marks for AO1. The examiner is assessing how the student uses their knowledge and understanding to relate to the specifics of the question/stimulus.

Knowledge and understanding AO1

Level	Description
1	A **limited/weak** demonstration of knowledge and understanding which is given 1 mark. This might include information and understanding about Muslim ideas on faith schools which are simplistic or just a list of ideas.
2	An **adequate** but **underdeveloped** demonstration of knowledge and understanding which is given 2 marks. This might include different ideas about Muslim views on faith and inclusive schools. These may have been contrasted with simplistic generic ideas.
3	A **good** demonstration of knowledge and understanding which is given 3 marks. This might include different explanations of Muslim ideas on faith and inclusive schools linked to specific case studies/examples, supported by reference to wisdom of authority while perhaps being contrasted with generic ideas. The student **might** include: – statement from the head of the British Muslim faith schools – specific examples of faith schools – their good and bad points, madrasas, hafiz – reference to teachings in the Qur'an and Hadith – the revelation of the Qur'an and its importance – British law on faith schools – knowledge is an obligation

Analysis and evaluation AO2

Level	Description
1	A **weak** response – the student may have given only a single viewpoint or the response is simply a description of events rather than offering comments which demonstrate a judgement (1–3 marks). This might include a descriptive/simplistic account of one or two different Muslim ideas on faith schools. Some generic comments may be made. No attempt to offer a judgement/conclusion will have been made. In other words, the information is communicated in a basic way and there is no evidence of a **discussion** taking place.
2	A **limited** response – the student has perhaps given different comments on Muslim ideas on faith schools perhaps contrasted with inclusive schools but these ideas have not been developed and there is little evidence of a conclusion. **Or** the student may have attempted to comment and show judgement on a specific Muslim view in depth contrasted with generic beliefs (4–6 marks). In other words, there is a line of reasoning/**discussion** which has some relevance to the stimulus.
3	An **adequate** but **underdeveloped** response – the student has perhaps given different views and has attempted to show some judgement/analysis on them but the ideas and comments are not developed enough to reach the highest level (7–9 marks). This might include comments with a judgement on the different Muslim ideas on faith schools which could be contrasted with generic or other religious beliefs while linking them into the stimulus. However, they have not been discussed or analysed in sufficient depth in order to reach Level 4. A line of reasoning has been presented and **discussed** which is mostly relevant.
4	A **good** understanding of the question. The student has responded with a variety of viewpoints or different schools of thought, which are explained and analysed and a conclusion/judgement on the question has been made (10–12 marks). The student has offered a well-developed and sustained **discussion** which is coherent, relevant and well structured. The student **might** include: – comments on the differences between faith schools and inclusive schools – which of them promotes the best educational environment – comments on the purpose of faith schools and their desirability while commenting on media misconceptions or otherwise – humanist or secular criticisms – a balanced conclusion

 OCR GCSE (9–1) Religious Studies Exam Question Practice

Hints and tips

➤ Read the stimulus carefully and identify its significance in your response, making sure you stick to the wording in the stimulus and do not divert into a concept that you would prefer to discuss.

➤ Remember that your response should be a **discussion** – try to present viewpoints for both sides as if you were having a conversation. Do not just list all the ideas for the stimulus in one paragraph and then all the ideas against in another paragraph.

➤ Refer to different beliefs and teachings and evaluate the importance of these differences.

➤ Try to refer back to what you studied in Part 1 of this course: beliefs and teachings and practices.

➤ Compare and contrast the religious views with secular views.

➤ Remember that you do not have to express a personal view – if you want to, you can, but make sure you justify your point of view with evidence and argument.

➤ Do not fall into the trap of saying 'An atheist does not believe in Allah and therefore would not agree with the religious point of view'. You are not adding to the argument/discussion at all.

Question 8

Student A

(a) Humanism started to make its mark when people began to challenge religious thought as far back as the 15th century with such people as Erasmus. The challenges focused on the idea that knowledge came from experience and so moral judgements should be based on reason rather than reliance on a transcendent deity.

e **The student focuses on the specifics of the question and the first mark is given for 'people (e.g. Erasmus) challenging religious thought', the second mark for knowledge from experience/empirical knowledge, and the third mark for 'reason rather than reliance'.**

(b) Pluralism is the idea that where there are lots of different religious beliefs in a society, all the members of each faith should try and co-exist peacefully and try and accept that all the religious beliefs should be considered to be equally true and valid. In the UK, although the religious tradition is mainly Christian, Muslims will try and follow the idea of pluralism by contributing to inter-faith dialogue, representing their faith on occasions such as Armistice Day at the Cenotaph, or taking part in local SACREs. However, Muslims believe that their faith is the one true faith because of the shahadah. This clashes with the Christian claim that Jesus is 'the way, the truth and the life'. Muslims would argue against this by saying that the Qur'an teaches 'If anyone desires a religion other than Islam, never will it be accepted of him'. Some Muslims put much time and effort into preaching about Islam in an effort to convert others to their faith. So there appears to be a direct clash of thought between Christians and Muslims. On the other hand, a minority of Muslims, particularly some Sufis, see different religions as different expressions of spirituality which are all valid. They support pluralism. Many Muslims are reportedly more tolerant of Judaism and Christianity because they are monotheists and are 'in the book'. Muslim men are permitted to marry women of Jewish and Christian background, but then the children are expected to be brought up as Muslims. So this again shows that Muslims find it difficult to accept pluralism where each faith is an equal way to God. Yet Muhammad (pbuh) taught 'to you shall be your religion and to me shall be my religion', which indicates that tolerance, which is what pluralism promotes, is allowed. So it could be said that most Muslims will go along with the example of their prophet.

e **The student recognises the divergent religious faiths in the UK and links some of the Muslim views on pluralism to the instruction in the question. Muslim belief that Islam is the one true religion is contrasted with Christian belief. The student supports their ideas with teachings from the Qur'an and the Hadith.**

(c) Many people think of arranged marriages as forced marriages. However, this is not accurate. Muslim marriage is a religious duty, 'He created for you mates', and is viewed as a contract through the consent of both the husband and the wife. However, this is not to say that sometimes emotional blackmail cannot be brought into the situation and either the husband or the wife feels that it is their duty to obey their parents and to agree to the marriage. This is because disobedience to parents is the sixth greatest sin, 'abstain from angering the parents', because if they do they will not be allowed into paradise. Since traditionally Muslims do not go out on dates or socialise with members of the opposite sex, they are usually willing to allow their parents to choose their prospective partner because they know their parents will do their best to get the best suitable partner for them. One Hadith teaches that when 'a man and a woman are alone together, there is a third presence – shaytan'. In other words, dating can lead to sexual intercourse which is only allowed in marriage. Also, some Muslims have the idea that arranged marriages are more stable and there is less divorce, as the marriage is supported by social pressure from the wider family who were involved in arranging it in the first place. The Hadith teaches that a man should 'choose the one with faith' for a successful marriage. Mutual belief and respect for faith seems to be a good foundation on which to build a marriage so the parents of the prospective husband will ensure that the girl they chose will be a strict Muslim. However, many Muslims who live in the West may decide to choose their own partner and not go with an arranged marriage because of the values of the culture and society in which they live. Some see arranged marriages as more of a cultural tradition and gain strength from Islam in rejecting partners they do not agree with. It is also possible that they may decide to involve their family in honouring the tradition as well as selecting a partner themselves.

ⓔ **The student shows good knowledge and understanding of different Muslim attitudes to arranged marriages. The ideas are supported with reference to sources of wisdom and authority and each idea is firmly linked to the keyword in the question: 'attitudes'. Analysis is shown throughout.**

(d) Many people these days think that it is wrong to allow people to suffer as they are dying and so believe that euthanasia, sometimes called 'mercy killing', should be allowed. Sometimes people who have a terminal illness which means they will die in pain appeal to the courts but are usually denied their request for someone to help them die when the time is right – this is called assisted suicide. However, Muslims are against euthanasia because the Qur'an teaches: 'Do not take life, which Allah made sacred.' This means for a Muslim that every life belongs to Allah and as such is special to him. This is called the sanctity of life: 'To Allah we belong and to Him we will return.' However, the statement is asking whether it is 'always' wrong for euthanasia to happen. So is the teaching in the Qur'an applicable to all occasions?

ⓔ **The student opens the response by recognising the significance of the statement and asking whether the Muslim belief in euthanasia being wrong is applicable to all occasions.**

Muslims believe that life is a test from Allah so that a Muslim can be judged on judgement day to see how well they have lived by the teachings in the Qur'an. The sufferings they have to go through are a test of their iman (faith). They believe that nothing which happens, however dreadful, is a good enough excuse for euthanasia. Muhammad (pbuh) taught that anyone who kills himself will go to hell (Hadith). Instead they should turn to du'a and ask Allah to help them through the pain: 'Seek the help of Allah.' However, although it would be wrong to have a DNR (do not resuscitate) order, the Islamic Code of Medical Ethics has stated that doctors should not struggle to keep people alive if they are in a 'vegetative state'. So a doctor would be allowed to switch off a life support machine because it is something mechanical which is keeping the person alive – doing the breathing for him.

Yet if the doctor were to also give a drug which might hasten death, then that would be wrong. So there is a contrast here between Christian thinking which allows the double effect – the giving of a lot of pain relief which in fact slows the breathing down and as a result hastens death.

ⓔ The student shows that Muslims can turn in prayer to Allah to relieve suffering and that a life support machine can be switched off, but any other intervention is not allowed. This thought is contrasted with the Christian idea of the 'double effect'.

Although Muslims are specifically against euthanasia, it must be very difficult for them to watch a loved one die in pain. The Qur'an teaches 'bear with patient constancy whatever befalls you'. Yet words or teachings do not help if one is struggling to breathe and every bone within your body is in agony. So possibly for some Muslims they might consider going against the Muslim teachings and helping someone who is going to die anyway. They know they will have to face Allah's judgement for this but he also judges intention. So perhaps it might be worth it even if you have to go to hell to be punished because if you truly repent, Allah will forgive you in the end because he is the most merciful. Euthanasia might be wrong but there are times when it could be considered to be the lesser of two evils.

ⓔ The student suggests in the balanced conclusion that although euthanasia is forbidden, there might be occasions when a relative takes a chance on Allah's mercy because the pain of watching a loved one suffer is too hard to bear.

Question 8
Student B

(a) Humanism challenges religious thinking that the truth comes from God and focuses on concern for the welfare of all humanity. They see a human has only one chance at life so they need to make it as meaningful as possible.

ⓔ Unfortunately the student has misread the question and although the response contains valid information about humanistic thinking, it does not say anything about its beginnings. If perhaps the tense of the verb 'challenges' had been changed to 'challenged', the response might have received some credit because the past tense implicitly refers to the beginnings.

(b) It is doubtful if Muslims view pluralism with much pleasure since they believe that Islam is the one true religion: there is no god but Allah and Muhammad (pbuh) is his prophet. Muslims believe that everyone is born a Muslim anyway, every child has fitrah, which is the natural instinct of Allah. So a Muslim might try and get people of different faiths to renounce their beliefs and revert to Islam. Muslims use different tactics to influence others to accept Islam: some by setting a good example and caring for people; others by preaching and inviting others to take on Islam as their religion. Muslim scholars agree that 'There is no compulsion in religion' (Qur'an 2:256) and compulsion to convert is forbidden, even though there are cases where this has happened in spite of the Qur'anic teaching.

ⓔ The student shows an implicit understanding of what pluralism is but just focuses on the idea of fitrah and reversion. They do relate their response to the diversity of religions in the UK but they need to develop how Muslims co-exist in harmony with people who practise other religions or no religions.

(c) Arranged marriages are where the parents decide on who you should marry. Dependent upon the culture, the couple might not even meet until the day of the wedding. This seems strange to people in Western society who are used to going out on dates and having fun with the opposite members of the sex. But Shari'ah law says sexual intercourse is only for married couples, so to avoid the temptation of sex, it is wrong for Muslims to go out on dates. Therefore the only way in which to find a husband or wife is by asking your parents to find one for you. People usually believe their parents know what's best for them anyway and so will trust them to find a suitable partner. However, the media often reports young women in particular being forced into marriage because the parents think they should marry a cousin in order for him to come and live in the UK but this is wrong because the Qur'an teaches that 'it is not lawful' to marry someone who has been forced into the marriage. Some say arranged marriages have benefits that you work hard at making the marriage work while if you marry someone you think you love, you might find that after some time you change your mind.

e **The student shows adequate knowledge and understanding of Muslim attitudes towards arranged marriages but much of the response is not supported by sources of wisdom and authority which the question demands. It tends to read as a generic overview rather than a specific Muslim response.**

(d) There are different types of euthanasia but usually a question like this refers to active euthanasia, which is when someone kills someone who is dying in pain or helps them to die (which is called assisted suicide). Islamic teachings are firmly against the killing of anyone unless for legal reasons, such as capital punishment. So therefore the statement is correct: euthanasia for a Muslim is always wrong.

e **The student opens the response by agreeing with the statement but the agreement is not supported by an argument or reference to specific teachings.**

In the Hadith collection of Sahih Bukhari, Muhammad (pbuh) tells the story of a man who was wounded and who then made it worse so that he could die. Muhammad (pbuh) said that Allah had said, 'My slave turned to bring death upon himself so I have forbidden him (to enter) paradise'. This is because all life belongs to Allah because he creates all life. 'He creates what he pleases.' Muslims see life as a test because the Qur'an teaches, 'We will surely test you with something…', and as a result any suffering they undergo is from Allah to see if they will turn to Iblis. If they fail the test, they will be sent to hell on judgement day to be punished. Muslims also believe that 'no one can die except by Allah's leave'. So with all the teachings from the Qur'an and the Hadith it is always wrong for a Muslim to commit euthanasia.

e **This is an occasion when there appears to be only a one-sided argument for the statement – Muslims are totally against euthanasia – and thus it might seem hard to argue otherwise. However, the command word is 'always', so a discussion can be made concerning that word. The Islamic Code of Medical Ethics could be used in support of turning off life support machines. Or another religion could be used to show that Muslims might agree with euthanasia on compassionate grands, or even a secular view stating that patients should not be kept alive because of medical costs. Then the student could return to the viewpoint by stating that a Muslim would not accept this. There has to be some idea of a balanced discussion showing as many different views as possible. A one-sided argument either agreeing or disagreeing with the statement will not receive many marks.**

Mark scheme

8 (a) Marks are awarded for a statement plus further development of that statement with either examples or references to sacred writings to support it. The student **might** refer to:
- its beginnings in the 15th century – Erasmus
- possible development: cosmological revolution having an impact: Copernicus and Galileo
- experience/empirical knowledge, reason not reliance on a transcendent deity

Hints and tips

➤ This is a short question requiring knowledge only, so do not spend too much time on it.

➤ The command word 'rise' is asking for a description of how humanism began, so do not be fooled in writing about what humanism is.

➤ This question does not ask for a Muslim attitude or belief – it only requires knowledge on how humanism began, so there is no need to try to put some Muslim views into the response.

(b) This response is marked by levels of response according to the student's knowledge and understanding of the question (AO1). The examiner will also determine whether the student has responded to the instructions in the question about the diversity of religious traditions in Great Britain.

Knowledge and understanding AO1

Level	Description
1	A **weak** response with limited understanding (1–2 marks): the student may have described one or two ideas about Muslim views on pluralism but in a simplistic way.
2	An **adequate** but **underdeveloped** response (3–4 marks): the student may have given simplistic different ideas on different Muslim views on pluralism. These ideas will be outlined in a brief or descriptive way rather than showing the full depth of the student's understanding.
3	A **good** response (5–6 marks): the student may have shown knowledge and understanding in detailed descriptions of different Muslim views on pluralism. The student **might** refer to: – a definition of pluralism (social and religious – not specified in the question), the aims – examples of how Muslims respond to the aims of pluralism – possible contrast between Muslim beliefs and another religion/s – shahadah, fitrah, reversion, persuasion, – Qur'an: Surah 2:256, Surah 3:83, Surah 3:84, Surah 109: 1–6

Hints and tips

➤ The command word is 'describe', which is asking you to set out the main characteristics. So the main characteristics of 'pluralism' would be a definition of what it is and its general aims.

➤ Give a detailed description of various Muslim views on pluralism, and perhaps support these views with teachings from the Qur'an or the Hadith.

➤ You could also contrast these Muslim ideas with other beliefs to show you have full understanding of the views held.

➤ Remember that the instructions with the question ask you to consider that 'religious traditions in Great Britain are diverse, but mainly Christian', so you must make reference to this in your response.

(c) This response is given **two** separate marks, both of which are determined by levels of response. Only **one** response is written but two different sets of **skills** are assessed by the examiner. The first mark is given for knowledge and understanding (AO1) and the second mark is awarded for the student's analysis and evaluation of the question (AO2). If the student simply writes down all they know about a specific topic, then the marks will be limited to the maximum marks for AO1. The examiner is assessing how the student uses their knowledge and understanding to relate to the specifics of the question/stimulus.

Knowledge and understanding AO1

Level	Description
1	**Some** demonstration of knowledge and understanding which is given 1 mark. This might include some specific or generic views of Muslim attitudes towards arranged marriages.
2	**Adequate** but **underdeveloped** demonstration of knowledge and understanding which is given 2 marks. This might include various Muslim attitudes towards arranged marriages. The student **might** include: – an explanation of the term 'arranged marriages' with possible contrast to 'forced marriages' – reasons why Muslims favour arranged marriages: avoidance of sexual temptation, parents know best, less chance of divorce – reasons why some modern Muslims might not want an arranged marriage: culture clashes, prefer to use their own free will – references to the Qur'an, Surah: 24:19, Surah 30:20–21, Hadith, Wasa'il ul-Shia, Shari'ah law – possible generic comments – but main focus should be on Muslim attitudes

Analysis and evaluation AO2

Level	Description
1	A **weak** response – the student may have given only a single comment on why a Muslim might support or not support arranged marriages or the student may have given only a list of ideas but the ideas are not developed or explained or supported with reference to sources of sacred writings. There is no real attempt at a balanced judgement (1 mark).
2	A **limited** response – the student has perhaps given two or three simplistic comments about the explanations as to why a Muslim might support or not support arranged marriages but these have not been developed by any comment and as such the analysis is limited. There may be some inaccuracies or misunderstanding of the stances taken. **Or** the student may have attempted to comment in detail and show judgement on one specific explanation (2 marks).
3	An **adequate** but **underdeveloped** response – the student has given various explanations as to why a Muslim holds different attitudes on arranged marriages and has tried to evaluate them but the comments are not developed enough to reach the highest level (3 marks).
4	A **good** understanding of the question. The student has responded with a variety of ideas on why a Muslim might support or not support arranged marriages which are explained, compared and contrasted and a balanced judgement has been reached. The student **might** include: – analysis and comparison between different Muslim attitudes dependent on where they live/ culture or society (East versus West) – analysis and comment on whether arranged marriages last better than those done for 'love' – analysis and comment on how an arranged marriage can sometimes become a forced one due to the idea that it is wrong to disobey parents

Hints and tips

➤ Read the question carefully and focus on the trigger/command words. This question is asking for attitudes so make sure you give different views on arranged marriages.

➤ Include some comments/analysis on the explanations.

➤ Remember to draw a conclusion/judgement from your response.

➤ Remember that this question is asking you to support your ideas with references to sources of wisdom or authority.

(d) This response is given **two** separate marks, both of which are determined by levels of response. Only **one** response is written but two different sets of **skills** are assessed by the examiner. The first mark is given for knowledge and understanding (AO1) and the second mark is awarded for the student's analysis and evaluation of the question (AO2). If the student simply writes down all they know about a specific topic, then the marks will be limited to the maximum marks for AO1. The examiner is assessing how the student uses their knowledge and understanding to relate to the specifics of the question/stimulus.

Knowledge and understanding AO1

Level	Description
1	A **limited/weak** demonstration of knowledge and understanding which is given 1 mark. This might include information and understanding about Muslim beliefs on euthanasia which are simplistic or just a list of ideas.
2	An **adequate** but **underdeveloped** demonstration of knowledge and understanding which is given 2 marks. This might include different ideas about Muslim beliefs on euthanasia. These may have been contrasted with simplistic, generic ideas.
3	A **good** demonstration of knowledge and understanding which is given 3 marks. This might include different explanations of Muslim beliefs on euthanasia linked to specific case studies/examples supported by reference to sacred writings while perhaps being contrasted with generic ideas. The student **might** include: – a simple definition of euthanasia (do not go into this at great length) – the statement from the Islamic Code of Medical Ethics – specific case studies, e.g. Tony Bland, Daniel James, Tony Nicklinson – Qur'an: Surah 2:155, Surah 2:153–156, Surah 3:145, Surah 16:61, Surah 17:33, Surah 31:17, Hadith, Sahih Bukhari 4.56.669 – comparison with other religions, e.g. Christianity 'double effect' or Hinduism 'karma'

Analysis and evaluation AO2

Level	Description
1	A **weak** response – the student may have given only a single viewpoint or the response is simply a description of events rather than offering comments which demonstrate a judgement (1–3 marks). This might include a descriptive/simplistic account of one or two different Muslim beliefs on euthanasia. Some generic comments may be made. No attempt to offer a judgement/conclusion will have been made. In other words, the information is communicated in a basic way and there is no evidence of a **discussion** taking place.
2	A **limited** response – the student has perhaps given different comments on Muslim beliefs on euthanasia but these ideas have not been developed and there is little evidence of a conclusion. **Or** the student may have attempted to comment and show judgement on a specific Muslim view in depth contrasted with generic beliefs (4–6 marks). In other words, there is a line of reasoning/**discussion** which has some relevance to the stimulus.
3	An **adequate** but **under-developed** response – the student has perhaps given different views and has attempted to show some judgement/analysis on them but the ideas and comments are not developed enough to reach the highest level (7–9 marks). This might include different comments with a judgement on the different Muslim beliefs on euthanasia which could be contrasted with generic or other religious beliefs while linking them into the stimulus. However, they have not been discussed or analysed in sufficient depth in order to reach Level 4. A line of reasoning has been presented and **discussed** which is mostly relevant.
4	A **good** understanding of the question. The student has responded with a variety of viewpoints or different schools of thought, which are explained and analysed and a conclusion/judgement on the question has been made (10–12 marks). The student has offered a well-developed and sustained **discussion** which is coherent, relevant and well structured. The student **might** include comments and analysis on: — the emotional problems which euthanasia causes — the difficulties Muslims face when presented with such a dilemma due to the rigid teachings in the Qur'an — secular ideas on euthanasia compared with Islamic teachings — secular ideas of monetary costs of keeping people alive

Hints and tips

➤ Read the stimulus carefully and identify its significance in your response, making sure you stick to the wording in the stimulus and do not divert into a concept that you would prefer to discuss.

➤ Remember that your response should be a **discussion** – try to present viewpoints for both sides as if you were having a conversation. Do not just list all the ideas for the stimulus in one paragraph and then all the ideas against in another paragraph.

➤ Refer to different beliefs and teachings and evaluate the importance of these differences.

➤ Try to refer back to what you studied in Part 1 of this course: beliefs and teachings and practices.

➤ Compare and contrast the religious views with secular views.

➤ Remember that you do not have to express a personal view – if you want to, you can, but make sure you justify your point of view with evidence and argument.

➤ Do not fall into the trap of saying 'An atheist does not believe in Allah and therefore would not agree with the religious point of view'. You are not adding to the argument/discussion at all.